Praise for *Seeking Social Democracy*

"The substance and unique format of this wonderful book bring profound historical lessons and a wisdom and understanding of our political conundrum, culminating in a realization that we have the power to change our world.

"'To champion a socialist vision in a capitalist world is, in a sense, a strangely paradoxical act of faith,' could only have been said by the legendary Ed Broadbent, who demonstrates over and over what we are fighting for and why. I couldn't stop reading this profoundly brilliant book that threads political and economic history, personal experience, and an unwavering commitment to genuine equality that, in his words, 'rejects the idea that there's a necessary trade-off between principle and the pursuit of power.'

"The insights in this unique, deeply personal writing will have you turning page after page, wanting more. It affirmed my beliefs about what we are fighting for and why."

— LIBBY DAVIES, MP for Vancouver East 1997–2015 and author of *Outside In*

"Ed Broadbent and his colleagues have produced a welcome if uncommon book for our troubled times: a hopeful conversation across three generations about what it will take to build a future where we might live in harmony with one another and with nature. It is also a book about the leadership we need to get there: honest, humble, respectful, and with a passionate commitment to democracy, equality, and human rights — the kind of leadership Ed Broadbent exemplifies."

— ALEX HIMELFARB, Former Clerk of the Privy Council and Chair of the Canadian Centre for Policy Alternatives, National

"Seeking Social Democracy is an excellent read and a major contribution to social democratic theory and practice. Ed Broadbent somehow manages to be simultaneously a tough partisan and a genial intellectual of high principle: politically pugnacious and a deep thinker who also respects conservative and liberal ideas and principles."

— ANDREW JACKSON, economist and author of Fire and the Ashes

"We should all be grateful that Ed Broadbent has chosen to provide his reflections on his career and his advice for future generations of the Left. In the pages of this memoir, we can read, feel, and hear Ed's profound decency, thoughtfulness, humanity, and wisdom. Read this book and you will be inspired by someone who has dedicated his life to seeking to improve the lives of Canadians and citizens across the world."

— ED MILIBAND MP, Former Leader of the U.K. Labour Party

"Through conversations with leading progressive thinkers from different generations, this compelling book paints a vivid vision of social democracy on the canvas of the remarkable life and work of one of Canada's preeminent social democrats, Ed Broadbent."

— JAGMEET SINGH, Leader of the New Democratic Party of Canada

"This book tells the story of an exceptional politician: a social-democratic leader who is also a very insightful political theorist. Indeed, Ed Broadbent could have had a stellar academic career. The result is a rare account of political life, and its dilemmas, forged by both practical experience and deep theoretical reflection."

— CHARLES TAYLOR, Professor Emeritus of Philosophy, McGill University

"An interesting and instructive read about the history and contemporary reality of social progressivism in Canada, from one of its singular leaders."

— HON. JODY WILSON-RAYBOULD, PC, OBC, KC

**ED BROADBENT** WITH **FRANCES ABELE, JONATHAN SAS & LUKE SAVAGE**

# SEEKING SOCIAL DEMOCRACY

## Seven Decades in the Fight for Equality

Copyright © Ed Broadbent, Frances Abele, Jonathan Sas,
and Luke Savage, 2023

Published by ECW Press
665 Gerrard Street East
Toronto, Ontario, Canada M4M 1Y2
416-694-3348 / info@ecwpress.com

Editor for the Press: Jennifer Smith
Cover design: Jessica Albert
Front cover photo: Bernard Weil, *Toronto Star*
Back cover photo: Gail Harvey

Every effort has been made to record the source of all photographs,
but due to their age and the absence of identifying information, this
was not always possible.

LIBRARY AND ARCHIVES CANADA CATALOGUING
IN PUBLICATION

Title: Seeking social democracy : seven decades in the fight
for equality / Ed Broadbent, Frances Abele, Jonathan Sas,
and Luke Savage.

Names: Broadbent, Ed, 1936- author. | Abele, Frances,
author. | Sas, Jonathan, author. | Savage, Luke, author.

Description: Includes index.

Identifiers: Canadiana (print) 20230237371 | Canadiana
(ebook) 2023023738X

ISBN 978-1-77041-738-0 (hardcover)
ISBN 978-1-77852-215-4 (ePub)
ISBN 978-1-77852-217-8 (Kindle)
ISBN 978-1-77852-216-1 (PDF)

Subjects: LCSH: Broadbent, Ed, 1936- | LCSH: Socialism.
| LCSH: Equality. | LCSH: Canada—Politics and
government.

Classification: LCC HX73 .B76 2023 | DDC 335—dc23

This book is funded in part by the Government of Canada. *Ce livre est financé en partie par le gouvernement du Canada.*
We also acknowledge the support of the Government of Ontario through the Ontario Book Publishing Tax Credit, and
through Ontario Creates.

PRINTED AND BOUND IN CANADA

PRINTING: FRIESENS     5   4   3   2   1

# Table of Contents

# A Note from Ed Broadbent

This book is the product of four collaborators representing, from the 1950s on, three generations of thinking. They are Frances Abele (academic), Jonathan Sas (policy strategist), Luke Savage (writer), and me, the elderly retired politician.

The reader will immediately see how unorthodox this book is. It consists of ten chapters, each preceded by a short essay by me, followed by, most interestingly, a series of exchanges about politics, history, philosophy, economics, and policy between me and my three interlocutors. Their questions are rich, multifaceted inquiries about my ideas and my past, often addressing moments in Canada's history I have lived through.

I also want to acknowledge with deep appreciation the important role played directly in my public life by eight individuals, all of them friends: Anne Carroll, my longtime secretary (who became affectionately known as "the gatekeeper"); Bill Knight, my caucus colleague in the 1970s and later my chief of staff in the 1980s; Hilarie McMurray, a speechwriter who advised me on feminist issues; Diana Bronson, policy advisor and comrade in arms at Rights and Democracy; Terry Grier, deeply admired and respected as national campaign manager; George Nakitstas, insightful head of research on Parliament Hill and my political advisor in the 1980s; Andrew Jackson, a leading researcher with great integrity; and Nester Pidwerbecki, political colleague and first constituency manager colleague from my earliest days in Oshawa.

One of my favourite authors of all time is Oliver Sacks, the great British neurologist, physician, and writer who spent most of his life in the United States. When we first began our work on this book, I found myself thinking of a very interesting essay he wrote just before he died. For a number of years, Sacks had been using an anecdote in his talks to explain a key point — a personal story which swung on his having been in a particular city (let's say Chicago, because I don't actually remember where it was) on a particular date. He kept repeating this anecdote until his brother finally, in effect, told him to "quit lying." Sacks's brother pointed out that the story was not actually true at all, because on the date Sacks said it took place, he was in fact in New York at his brother's home rather than in Chicago.

Having been duly corrected, Sacks took to telling the story to make a point about the fallibility of memory: that you can tell the most intricate story believing that it's true, while ultimately getting the basic facts wrong. And I'm very aware of this anecdote right now in terms of what the reader is about to go through: I'm going to be asked a series of questions, the answers to which overwhelmingly depend on my memories of the past and on my own past thinking and behaviour. Every effort has been made to fact-check this book and its many details. Nonetheless, I would like to enter that, if I turn out to be misleading in a particular anecdote, I will invoke Oliver Sacks every time.

# Introduction by Luke Savage

This book is neither a traditional autobiography nor a purely theoretical reflection. At times, it may closely resemble one or the other, though very often it is both at once, and more.

Nearly a decade ago, when the project was first imagined and discussed, Ed Broadbent made clear that he was looking to write something concerned with political ideas in the broadest sense: that is, with wider questions of theory and practice as well as history, and with the values of the social democratic tradition to which he has devoted his life. My own earliest record consists of a few handwritten notes, penned by Ed in bullet form and affixed to an email sent to our mutual friend Michael Valpy in August 2013. "Common space versus markets," read one note, followed a few inches below by another reading, "local versus globalization." Some notes were abstract, among them intriguing provocations like "political ideas and their limits," "equality as a key democratic value," and "the usefulness of philosophy." Others, in contrast, were more direct — naming specific personalities that ranged from fellow politicians like Tommy Douglas, Pierre Elliott Trudeau, and Brian Mulroney to political theorists like the nineteenth-century English philosopher and member of Parliament John Stuart Mill.

While there are certainly many excellent political memoirs, it was evident that Ed envisioned something beyond a strict chronicle of his career. Structurally speaking, this somewhat sweeping remit presented a series of potentially daunting questions and challenges. If this was not to be a straightforward autobiography, how would it proceed? On the other hand, given Ed's public-facing role in so many important and formative debates, how could those kinds of details possibly be left out? And, assuming they were to be included, could theory, philosophy, and history work effectively in concert with the intimacy of anecdote and the immediacy of personal experience?

What the enterprise demanded was a narrative scaffold capable of sustaining these weighty and disparate contents — and, to this end, a near-perfect template obligingly presented itself. *Thinking the Twentieth Century*, a joint effort by Tony Judt (the brilliant, and now sadly late historian of postwar Europe) and his collaborator Timothy D. Snyder, was freshly published and looked to be a worthy candidate for emulation. Described by Snyder in its foreword as a pastiche of "history, biography, and ethical treatise," the book's unique format — a series of personal essays followed by dialogues between himself and Judt — enabled it to weave together all three without ever seeming forced or overly digressive. Alternating between different modes and registers, and sometimes partaking in several at the same time, the unorthodox structure of *Thinking the Twentieth Century* allowed its coauthors to traverse large swathes of history and thought while remaining grounded in the different eras of Judt's life.

In its own unique way, this book draws significant inspiration from their example. The major exception has to do with our lead author's direct involvement in many of the episodes and events discussed. Having been a professor at York University before his first run for Parliament in 1968, Ed speaks with authority about the abstract issues of concern to political theorists. Unlike most theorists or historians, however, he has also spent the bulk of his career as a politician and public figure engaged with much more immediate questions of policy, practice, and democratic persuasion. Throughout, he therefore takes on a dual role as both observer and participant, the perspective shifting from the imminent to the general and the descriptive to the prescriptive depending on the topic or time period at hand.

This book's somewhat unconventional format notwithstanding, it does in some ways still resemble a traditional political memoir. Biography provides its main impetus and, while the conversations in a given chapter might occasionally leap forward, backward, or even outside of its implicit temporal parameters, readers will find that themes, ideas, and history unfold in a mostly chronological way. Ed's life and career are, however, as much a terrain for discussion as they are a subject and narrative anchor. If biography and history form the skeletal structure of this book, then political and moral ideas are its ligaments and flesh.

I am a left-wing writer and journalist in my early thirties. Though I first met Ed Broadbent a little over ten years ago, I was, in another sense, already well-acquainted with him. Growing up in rural Ontario, I knew Ed as many Canadians do: namely, as the widely respected former leader of the New Democratic Party, and as the figure most singularly responsible for turning several members of my family into lifelong NDP voters.

While an undergraduate at the University of Toronto, I came to know his career more closely through my studies of, and involvement in, the political left. At the now tragically defunct Ten Editions bookstore on Spadina Road, I discovered his pamphlet *The Liberal Rip-Off: Trudeauism vs. the Politics of Equality* — an eightyish-page book addressing issues that ranged from taxation and corporate power to scientific research and inflation. Published in 1970 during Ed's first term as an MP and rarely remembered today, it was bracingly radical in outlook but also intellectually serious and practically minded — the approach seeming to bridge some invisible chasm separating abstract theory and felt conviction. Often torn, as I was at the time, between my emerging socialist identity and the more dispassionate ethos of academic political science, it was a formative and memorable discovery.

In my opinion, Ed Broadbent is one among only a small handful of parliamentarians, past or present, who could have produced something like *The Liberal Rip-Off*. Intellectuals, I think it would be fair to say, do not always make the best politicians and, taking the Canadian political spectrum as a whole, obvious exceptions like Pierre Trudeau or René Lévesque are arguably few and far between. As the Czech writer Eda Kriseová once observed, the intellectual turned politician is often "by nature self-critical" and thus "unable to campaign in his or her own favour." Possessing a critical attitude toward power, and also a general lack of confidence in it,[1] intellectuals rarely tend to find success in political life, if indeed they ever seek it out in the first place.

Insofar as Ed exhibits this kind of reflexive skepticism, it evidently did not limit his effectiveness throughout more than two decades in politics — or override his conviction that Canada's parliamentary left should aspire to wield power for itself rather than remaining content to exert it from a place of permanent opposition. Perhaps no one said it better than the great American socialist Michael Harrington, who wrote in his 1988 autobiography, *The Long-Distance Runner*:

> Ed Broadbent...[is] living proof that even in North America an intellectual can be a serious and effective politician — he regularly tops the Canadian polls as one of the most admired figures in the country. Indeed, when I spoke in Canada I often said, thinking of Ed and his comrades, that I came from the politically underdeveloped country to the south. In this case, Broadbent also demonstrated that ethical sensitivity and passion had a crucial play in our movement.[2]

If questions of theory, practice, and the role of ideas in politics run throughout the discussions in this book, their fulcrum is Ed's vision of social democracy. The meaning of virtually any political label is bound to be somewhat unstable and contested and, in this respect, social democracy is certainly no exception. At the beginning of the twentieth century, the likes of Vladimir Lenin, Eugene Debs, and Rosa Luxemburg could be heard calling themselves social democrats. By the turn of the millennium, on the other hand, so could Tony Blair. Readers belonging to my own generation (or those from outside of North America) may therefore associate the phrase with the accommodationist liberalism of some erstwhile left parties since the 1990s and prefer the label democratic socialism for that reason. For the purposes of this book, as has been the case throughout his life, Ed uses both social democracy and democratic socialism interchangeably to describe the essence of his convictions and the political vision that arises from them.

Something that I think will strike readers is the remarkable consistency of those convictions from the 1960s to the present day. Born in industrial Oshawa in 1936, just as the effects of the Great Depression were beginning to wane, Ed inherited the progressive disposition of a generation fortunate enough to come of age during a period of rising prosperity and increasingly restless democratic ambition. While at university, he adopted the essence of a political framework that embraced and celebrated traditional liberal rights while also viewing them as insufficient guarantors of human freedom.

The liberal, as Ed argued in a 1969 speech entitled *Socialist & Liberal Views on Man, Society and Politics*, believes that human beings are essentially selfish by nature and thus in a state of perpetual competition and conflict with others. The socialist, by contrast, is more likely to emphasize the human capacity for cooperation and see the coarser features of human behaviour as the product of specific historical or socioeconomic conditions. In the former view, life is like a race in which "individuals start out crossing the continent in winter, with each going their own way." The purpose of politics is therefore to set down and enforce the proverbial rules of the road and ensure that the competitors succeed (or fail) according to their respective levels of talent or effort. Socialists, as Ed came to see it, conceive of society in a different way:

> All people start off at the foot of the mountain, each bound to one another. As they proceed up the mountain, they do so as a group. None gets ahead of the other and each is dependent on their fellows while making their own contribution. Occasionally, the climbers will take a break and untie the rope which links them. During this interlude some will go off by themselves; some will fish; some will write poetry; and others will make love. However, once the journey is resumed, they will link themselves together again and proceed up the mountain. The mountaintop, like the end of the continental road race, does not exist. Some of

the mountaineers know this and some do not — but they
all believe it is the climbing together that really counts.[3]

What emerged from these foundations was a vision of social democracy
that distinguished itself from the atomistic liberalism of someone like
Pierre Trudeau while also eschewing the model of state socialism then
found throughout the Eastern Bloc.

Absolutely central to Ed was the issue of corporate power, which was
continuing to limit the exercise of genuine freedom and equality despite
the important gains that had been made under universal suffrage. From
amidst the chaos and unspeakable suffering of the first half of the twentieth century, Canadian farmers, workers, and reformers had successfully
organized to wrest a modern welfare state from their country's elite.
Though a marked improvement, the problem was that so much unchecked
power remained with large corporations who sometimes had, as Ed put it
in *The Liberal Rip-Off*, "a more immediate and profound effect on the lives
of Canadians than most decisions made by governments."[4] If ordinary
people had won for themselves the vote, pensions, public health insurance,
and the right to join a union, their daily existences — at work and outside
of it — were still being heavily shaped by market forces, while control of
most of the investment capital needed for public goods remained in the
hands of a small number of powerful private firms.

Democratic self-determination, in both an individual and a national
sense, therefore necessitated going beyond the liberal welfare state and its
rudimentary bundle of civil and political rights. The means to that end
was a political program that accepted the principle of public ownership
in some industries while also seeking to empower citizens and workers
through new forms of economic and industrial democracy. Though the
state would have a significant role to play as an economic steering mechanism, it was therefore no panacea. As Ed put it in his 1986 eulogy for
the recently assassinated Swedish prime minister Olof Palme, a true
democracy "must ensure that the same principles of liberty, equality, and
participation are found in both its political and economic institutions.
[Palme] was quite correct in seeing this, and not state ownership, as the
fundamental principle and basic goal of democratic socialism."

From the beginning of his public life to the present day, Ed's basic moral and ethical commitments have, as far as I can discern, remained largely unchanged. If there is a narrative arc to the story he tells in this book, it is driven more by the challenges inherent in advancing a transformative project against the much less pristine realities of political life in a complicated, plural, and rapidly changing society. When Ed first arrived in the House of Commons in the late 1960s, the welfare state and the Keynesian settlement were sufficiently accepted among liberals and conservatives that many on the left felt confident enough to push beyond them. During the 1970s, as the Canadian economy faced faltering growth and rising inflation, and as the institutions of federalism came under strain, both the terrain and focus of political debate drifted steadily in a more conservative direction — a trajectory which ultimately culminated in the rolling back of social democracy and the consolidation of corporate power under neoliberal globalization and free trade.

Other changes were much more positive. Both from within and outside the institutions of Canada's left, an assortment of activists and social movements pressed their demands for a broader and more inclusive society — winning new rights and recognition and compelling social democracy to broaden and clarify its project. From feminist activists mobilizing for reproductive justice and pay equity to Indigenous peoples resisting colonialism, these movements would make themselves strongly felt during the protracted debates that eventually produced Canada's 1982 constitution and its Charter of Rights.

Throughout this uniquely tumultuous period in Canadian history, Ed's creative stewardship of the NDP broke new electoral ground for his party and won him the respect of millions of Canadians. By the late 1980s, as one historian put it, the phrase "Honest Ed" had come to be synonymous not only with Toronto's most famous department store but also the country's most popular political leader.[5]

This book can be roughly divided into three acts.

Chapters One to Three span the years between Ed's birth in the mid-1930s to the end of his second term as the member of Parliament for Oshawa in 1974. Chapters Four to Eight span the entirety of Ed's leadership of the NDP from 1975 to 1989 and constitute the book's longest section. The third and final act in Chapters Nine and Ten spans the period following Ed's retirement from the NDP leadership in 1989 to roughly the present day. Throughout, Ed recounts and reflects on innumerable episodes big and small, many of which have never been put into print. His relationships with individual people, comrades and adversaries alike, texture the story along the way and are every bit as integral as philosophy and history.

This book also has an important story of its own. First imagined by Ed in 2013, it underwent several stops and starts before its coauthors came together to begin dedicated work in 2021. Ed's life was struck by tragedy when his wife, the brilliant Marxist theorist and historian Ellen Meiksins Wood, fell ill with cancer. Ellen, as it happened, had reached out to Jonathan Sas at the Broadbent Institute in 2015 and urged him to make sure that Ed's legacy and contributions to public life were captured and given their due. That year, I happened to begin working at the Institute and, being firmly on the left flank of its staff, Jonathan and I became fast friends. Following Ellen's passing at the beginning of 2016, Jonathan and our colleague Alejandra Bravo worked on publishing a series of essays from various contributors on social democracy as a kind of tribute to Ed's thought and legacy, but the more expansive book project never quite materialized.

Having been witness to the book's early stages, I was disappointed. Ed's remarkable career and thought, for one thing, had never received the fulsome treatment they so obviously deserved. In 1987, *Globe and Mail* journalist Judy Steed had written a detailed political biography of Ed but, among other things, it was now many years out of date. Nearly a decade later, Ed's friend Joseph Levitt of the University of Ottawa published an exquisitely researched study of his parliamentary career that was primarily focused on policy. Both were worthy and well-executed efforts but, alongside others who knew him, I badly wanted to see Ed himself write a book that spanned the full breadth of his life, career, and thought.

That occasion finally arrived when Ed was developing the Broadbent Principles at the end of 2020: a social democratic manifesto in miniature published by the organization that bears his name. Jonathan, who had since gone on to work in posts as a senior ministerial advisor in the government of British Columbia and as director of communications at the BC Federation of Labour, had not forgotten about Ellen's message and, at Alejandra's persistent urging, decided to raise Ed's original idea for the project once again. Ed was enthusiastic, and within a matter of weeks, our team was assembled. Frances Abele — a close friend of Ed's, former student of Ellen's, and a scholar nationally recognized for her work on Canadian political economy and Indigenous rights — joined as well. I was no longer working at the Institute and knew nothing of these machinations but soon learned of them with delight.

Over the next several weeks, the quartet discussed the book and settled on the idea of dialogues between Ed and the trio. We had a good rapport and decided that the perspectives of multiple interlocutors from different generations could add richness to the discussions as each member of the trio drew from their own particular areas of expertise. Much of the raw material for this book was compiled throughout 2021 and early 2022 in the form of structured and lengthy conversations (conducted over Zoom because of the pandemic) that were recorded and subsequently transcribed. This crucial task was taken up by Jonathan's brother Robin, who worked with tremendous care to give us readable versions of the dialogues — the sum total of which ran longer in transcribed form than *Crime and Punishment*, *Great Expectations*, or *Moby Dick*.

A further component was archival. Since the 1960s, Ed has given countless speeches in Parliament, at party events, and in public forums. He has also written prolifically since his earliest days as an academic, though much of this writing is only findable through privileged online databases while some now cannot be found via conventional means at all. For this reason, Frances made regular visits to Library and Archives Canada, where an extensive archive of Ed's materials is preserved. The results of these excavations proved nothing short of extraordinary: turning up a trove of old lectures, correspondence, speaking notes, and significant pieces of writing. These, too, are an important part of this book's process and story and add considerably to the richness of its discussions (a few particularly special items, many of them never published before, have been included in the Appendices).

This project has been a monumental labour, but at every stage it has been a deeply rewarding one. A major concern of my own writing is the feeling that our present political order lacks the dynamism and progressive ambition once promised to us by the democratic age. In this sense, I see the chapters that follow as a chronicle of Ed Broadbent's remarkable legacy as a leader and thinker, but also as something more: namely, a testament of the rich political and moral vision that throughout much of the twentieth century expressed itself under the names social democracy and democratic socialism. Every generation faces unique circumstances and must wage its own battles accordingly. But in our current era of ossified political imagination, inequality, and multinational capitalism, there is a wellspring of inspiration to be drawn from the examples of those who have looked to brighter horizons and struggled for an alternative.

We all want progress, as C.S. Lewis once wrote. But progress means getting nearer to the place you want to be and, if you've taken a wrong turn, then going forward doesn't get you any closer. If you find yourself on the wrong road, progress means doing an about-turn and walking back down the right one.

— LUKE SAVAGE, TORONTO, SEPTEMBER 2022

## CHAPTER ONE

# Thinking My Way to Social Democracy

*"If someone takes away your bread, he suppresses your freedom at the same time. But if someone takes away your [political] freedom, you may be sure that your bread is threatened, for it no longer depends on you and your struggle but on the whim of a master.*

*Poverty increases insofar as freedom retreats throughout the world, and vice versa. And if this cruel century has taught us anything at all, it has taught that the economic revolution must be free just as liberation must include the economic. The oppressed want to be liberated not only from their hunger but also from their masters. They are well aware that they will be effectively freed of hunger only when they hold their masters, all their masters, at bay."*

— ALBERT CAMUS, "Bread and Freedom" in
*Resistance, Rebellion, and Death*

No one, I suspect, arrives at their politics via a single route — and, in an important sense, one never exactly arrives at all. Political convictions are ultimately a journey rather than a final destination, and for those of us who stand for elected office or seek political leadership, there's inevitably a tangled interplay of personal experience, theoretical reflection, and practical education involved. When it comes to the evolution of my own politics, as it turned out, this was more or less the trajectory of influences.

I was born in 1936 in Oshawa, Ontario, a working-class town then coming into its own as an economic powerhouse thanks to the burgeoning automotive sector. The city's working-class character was reflected not only in the employment of so many at The Motors (which was how we all referred to General Motors) but also in worker militancy and a notable tradition of trade unionism. That tradition, still fighting for its legitimacy in industrial towns and cities throughout North America, would have an important influence in my earliest years. Company bosses had spent much of the Depression years laying off workers by the thousands. In 1936, General Motors posted the highest-ever profits in its history and proceeded to try to cut wages for the fifth successive time. Even for those fortunate enough to keep their jobs, annual pay was no more than $500–700 at the best of times, and workers' lives were constantly subject to the whims of management.

When I was barely a year old, thousands of them — including my uncle Aubrey, who was seventeen at the time — fought back in an historic strike for better pay and working conditions and official recognition of their union (United Auto Workers, Local 222). "3,700 Motor Workers Strike at Oshawa," read the *Toronto Star*'s headline on April 8, 1937, as Ontario premier Mitchell Hepburn threatened to send in a 400-strong militia dubbed Hepburn's Hussars to break the strike. The militia never arrived, but it had been instructed to shoot the strikers at the knees if ordered to fire. In the face of this opposition, and with broad community support, the workers held their ground and management was ultimately compelled to accept many of their demands.

While the company still officially refused to recognize the United Automobile Workers (UAW), it was a turning point for industrial unionism in Canada — and would define both my childhood and the city in which I came of age. Members of the Broadbent family have put in over 250 years of cumulative work at GM. Without union wages and stable employment, many of those years would have looked very different.

Six years after the strike, in the Ontario election of 1943, Hepburn's Liberal Party would drop to third place and the still-fledgling Co-operative

Commonwealth Federation (the predecessor to the NDP) would come within a few seats of forming a government. Though the CCF would also be thwarted in its attempt to form a federal government, Tommy Douglas would lead it to power in Saskatchewan in 1944 — marking the first election victory of a socialist party in North America. Though I was too young to recognize it at the time, these events formed part of an important continuum that would help bring the modern Canadian welfare state into being.

Politics was not yet on my mind when I visited Ottawa as a twelve-year-old paperboy. Having sold the most subscriptions to the *Oshawa Times*, I was rewarded with a trip to the capital and a stay at the Lord Elgin Hotel, where I celebrated by enjoying a few Lucky Strike cigarettes. With other young people, I benefitted from the work of adult volunteers who coached hockey and baseball and ran the local chapters of the Cubs and Scouts. It was not long, however, before I began to develop an interest in politics. In ninth grade, I got involved in the student council and helped draft the student constitution at Oshawa's Central Collegiate high school. The following year, I wrote an essay in which I argued that Dwight Eisenhower ought to stay in Europe rather than return to the U.S. and run for president (I favoured the progressive and witty Democratic governor of Illinois, Adlai Stevenson). In 1954, I travelled to Ottawa once again to participate in the Rotary Club Adventure in Citizenship program and was taken with other rotary-select students on a tour of the House of Commons and Supreme Court. During my four-day visit, I also shook hands with Prime Minister Louis St. Laurent and met my local MP Mike Starr — the popular Conservative cabinet minister who would eventually be my first political opponent in 1968.

No one in my family had gone to university, but in the affluent post-war climate it proved relatively easy to save throughout high school and, by the time I graduated, I had enough set aside to pay for my first year at U of T. Though just down the highway from Oshawa, Toronto seemed like another world, and I began my life there with great enthusiasm, enjoying the city every bit as much as my coursework. Enrolled at Trinity

College, I couldn't afford to live in residence and opted in my first year for the student co-op on Huron Street instead,* later settling at another one on Spadina.

Throughout my undergraduate years, I explored everything Toronto had to offer including outings to the Alhambra Cinema on Bloor Street, where I saw films by the Marx Brothers, Ingmar Bergman, and eventually those of the French New Wave; a performance by Sarah Vaughan at a bar downtown; a debate between my later friend and colleague David Lewis and William F. Buckley of *National Review* at Convocation Hall; Greek-American soprano Maria Callas singing Verdi and Puccini to a packed crowd at Maple Leaf Gardens. Many a Friday night was spent drinking beer with friends and discussing left politics at the Silver Dollar near the co-op or in the King Cole Room at the Park Plaza Hotel. (Among other things, these blissfully carefree evenings laid the foundation for my later belief that socialism and pleasure are not necessarily a contradiction in terms.)

Wanting to study how institutions worked, I had originally planned to major in political science. I changed course quickly after attending a few lectures on philosophy by the erudite and witty Professor Emil Fackenheim. Other memorable early classes included Professor Douglas Dryer's course on Kant, Professor Thomas Goudge on analytic philosophy, and one on ethics taught by Professor Bruno Morawetz. During my undergraduate years, I immersed myself in Plato, Aristotle, Kierkegaard, Kant, and Bertrand Russell, staying in the philosophy department to write my master's thesis on the nineteenth-century British legal theorist John Austin.

Despite my interest in philosophy, I decided to switch to political economy for my Ph.D. because I wanted to study with the great democratic theorist C.B. Macpherson. Changing departments meant that I had to take some makeup courses in political science, but it was worth it because it allowed me to work with Brough — whose own

---

* Webb House, as it was known, was named for Sidney and Beatrice Webb — the famous British socialists who had helped found the Labour Party, the *New Statesman* magazine, and the London School of Economics, where I studied as a graduate student.

scholarship was motivated by a desire to balance social needs with individual rights in the modern age. A creative fusion of the best currents from the liberal and socialist traditions, Macpherson's thought had a profound impact on me in my studies and beyond. As supervisor for my Ph.D., he was inspiring and personally supportive. On a glorious day I've never forgotten, Professor Macpherson said to me: "Would you like to spend a year at Oxford or the London School of Economics?" to which I replied "Are you kidding? Of course." After giving it some thought, I opted for the LSE, and the two of us discussed how I might use the year ahead to develop a thesis topic. Macpherson arranged for my Canada Council scholarship to be transferred across the Atlantic and, while in London, I enjoyed its great offerings of classical music and cinema — and belonged to its New Party club alongside Giles Endicott, Gerry Caplan, John Wilson, and a number of other Canadians who were living and studying in London.* I also immersed myself in the Reading Room of the British Museum where I pursued the work of the great English philosopher (and friend of John Austin's) John Stuart Mill.

It was there that I read *Principles of Political Economy*, Mill's essays on labour, *The Subjection of Women*, as well as the well-known political science texts *Representative Government* and *On Liberty*. But it was Mill's work on political economy — which viewed the economy as a system of social relations — that struck me the most. I found many of his arguments both morally and intellectually compelling and the language notably clear compared to what I'd read (very little) of Karl Marx, though they were both grappling with many of the same issues. Under Macpherson's supervision, I subsequently wrote my dissertation *The Good Society of John Stuart Mill*, which celebrated the democratic impulse at the core of Mill's thought while criticizing the inegalitarian capitalist aspects of his economic theory from the left. From its conclusion:

---

\* Between 1958 and 1961, as the CCF and the Canadian Labour Congress merged to create the New Democratic Party, what became the NDP was for an interim period known as "The New Party."

Although he saw that industrialism in the nineteenth-century had produced much that was distasteful to civilized life, at the same he fully realized that potentially it would enable the majority . . . for the first time in history to develop their capacities in a way previously available to a minority only . . . The first nation with a collectively owned economy has been dominated not by the majority but by a dictatorial elite. This elite has used its power in part to suppress the non-economic liberal freedoms required by the good society. At the same time, it is clear in principle that only a collectively owned economy can avoid exploitation, and thus make the good society realizable. It remains to be seen whether a nation, while rejecting Mill's normative economics, can retain his other social values, and so make the co-operative individualist life a reality.

Both my study of philosophy and the global context in which it took place informed my emerging analysis. My years as an undergraduate at U of T coincided with the Soviet Union's brutal suppression of the popular uprising in Hungary in 1956 and also the first stirrings of de-Stalinization in the USSR itself. At the same time, a whole generation of European intellectuals were moving away from communist thought, a development reflected in the 1949 essay collection *The God That Failed*, which had a formative impact on my own thinking. By the time I had finished my Ph.D. in the mid-1960s, I was firmly grounded on the democratic left and regarded myself a committed social democrat or democratic socialist (throughout this book, as has been the case throughout my life, I tend to use the terms interchangeably). Though I joined the NDP shortly after its founding, it would still be some years before party politics became my full-time vocation.

**Frances Abele:** In excavating the origins of your commitment to social democracy, perhaps it makes the most sense to begin at the beginning. You grew up in wartime and in the immediate post-war years in Oshawa. Despite it being a terrible war in which many were dying, the war years themselves were also a sustained period of high employment, relative working-class prosperity, and stable social institutions and relationships, including rising trade unions. Perhaps we can begin by discussing how those circumstances influenced your political thought and your turn to social democracy?

**Ed Broadbent:** Unquestionably. Growing up in that period and in that town against a backdrop of broadly shared prosperity played a huge role in shaping my political outlook well before it became something I could articulate in detail. Oshawa was working class, but by no means poor. The south end of the city where I grew up was the lower-income part of town — the doctors, lawyers, and other professionals lived in the north. But in the southern neighbourhood where I lived, the direct economic benefits of a strong union — in this case, the United Automobile Workers — were readily apparent, as was the deeper sense of community the union fostered (I still remember the big annual picnic on Lake Ontario in which they gave away cars on draws to lucky numbers). All of this gave me an important psychological foundation of optimism and a deep-seated belief that anything was possible. I've carried these with me throughout my life. This is quite different from the unequal and uncertain times that young people are experiencing today.

Thinking back, that optimistic outlook was something I developed very early. I delivered newspapers as a boy and later worked in the circulation department at the *Oshawa Times* and in a clothing store on Saturdays to save for university, but there was never any sense of deprivation or the feeling that this was some great struggle. I took it as being very natural and possible for someone like me — from an ordinary family where no one had a postsecondary education — to make an effort and get into the University of Toronto. This optimistic spirit and shared prosperity prevailed in many cities like Oshawa across Canada during the postwar years.

There was another side to this. Although I was headed to university, many of my fellow students dropped out before graduation. There were nine classes of grade 9 at Central Collegiate, but by the time I graduated, there were only enough students to fill one class of grade 13. The low graduation rate was in good measure due to the prosperity generated by General Motors. So many of my male friends could quit school on Friday, go to work at General Motors on Monday, and qualify for a loan to buy a new car a few weeks later. This generation of autoworkers would go on being well-paid until they retired. I learned from my friends who got to university from St. Catharines or Windsor or Oakville that they too witnessed the dropping off of many of their high school friends because of the availability of well-paid jobs in the automotive industry.

I later came to realize that while white working-class boys could readily get ahead in life, this was certainly not happening for girls or people of colour. While realizing this, I also gained an intuitive sense of the importance of the tremendous gains groups of workers could win for themselves if they banded together. In Oshawa, we didn't have the benefits of a car in every driveway because management at General Motors thought it would be nice to give them out to the workers. It was because workers at General Motors were conscious, organized, and in a position to withhold their labour and extract concessions if it became necessary, that is, to strike.

**Jonathan Sas:** You began your studies at U of T in 1955, at a time when there were formative struggles going on inside the left, among other things, in response to global events. The following year saw the beginnings of the Khrushchev Thaw* and with it a

---

* Coming to power in the Soviet Union in 1953, Nikita Khrushchev began to speak more frankly about the repressive climate that had prevailed under Stalin and presided over a period of de-Stalinization and domestic liberalization.

broader opening up inside the Soviet Union but also the violent repression of the revolution in Hungary. What was the intellectual climate like on campus, particularly as the repression unfolded, and how did the events of that period shape your emerging thinking?

**EB:** My first serious engagement with socialist literature began while I was an undergraduate at U of T, and much of what I read was of the social democratic and anti-communist variety. During the late 1940s and early 1950s, many Western European intellectuals in particular were reassessing their identification with communism, a turn captured in *The God That Failed*, which featured essays from former communists like André Gide, Arthur Koestler, and Ignazio Silone. With varying degrees of emphasis, their opposition turned on the matter of individual liberty and its restriction under the communism of the USSR. That was a major influence on my early thinking: the idea that individual autonomy and liberty would be suppressed in a society in which everything was owned by the state.

Another formative influence, as you've already mentioned, was Hungary. As I've said, I already possessed a skeptical orientation toward state socialism, but the Hungarian Revolution and the viciously cruel way it was put down had a real impact on me (and on plenty of others). Some students who had come to Toronto from Hungary lived at the student co-op where I was living in 1956. The descriptions they offered about what was going on in their homeland and why they were rebelling against it had a marked impact on my thinking. As we speak, I can see the face of one particular young guy I knew who had become viscerally anti-communist and observably glad to get out of his own country. But my sense is that, rather than representing something new in my thinking, what happened there simply confirmed my existing apprehensions about the Soviet model.

The ideas I was exposed to during my years as an undergraduate were important in the development of my thinking, though I hasten to add they didn't yet constitute a coherent conception of social democracy that I could have articulated lucidly. But there was already the kernel of ideology that was both anti-capitalist and critical of deterministic state socialism — and sympathetic to a welfare state that would provide its citizens with both individual liberty and a broad set of social and economic rights.*

**Luke Savage:** You've used the phrase "state socialism" a couple of times. What did you associate with that concept during your university days?

**EB:** In those days, there were people who genuinely believed there was a quasi-theological inevitability to communism; that it was simply coming. The intelligent option would be to either just join in and follow the movement or perhaps join in with a critical attitude and try to work from within. Versions of this were commonplace at the time. There were significant reformers within communism itself, like those who participated in the Hungarian uprising and later in Czechoslovakia with the Dubček government in 1968. I would describe them as left-wing social democrats. The Dubček communists wanted what they called "socialism with a human face," and what that really meant was getting the repressive aspects of the state off of people's backs, getting ordinary people affected by economic planning more directly involved in it, and enshrining a range of political and civil rights. Both the Hungarian and Dubček experiments were brutally stamped out, which only reinforced my own instinct not to be associated with the prevailing model of the Eastern Bloc.

---

\* A fulsome treatment of social and cultural rights can be found in Chapter Four: The Rights Revolution.

**FA:** I don't remember 1955 very clearly, but I recall that people tended to talk in terms of scientific socialism. In those days, many thought the question was a matter of positivist science: some communists thought socialism and communism were inevitable because of empirically identifiable conditions embedded in capitalism.

**EB:** Yes, exactly. And I just didn't believe in that kind of sequence of events or grand theory of history. On the contrary, human agency plays an absolutely critical role. Parties like the NDP have made a great difference in history by providing a democratic vehicle for progressive change.

**FA:** During the 1940s and 1950s, one of the problems was that people who belonged to or were aligned with communist parties in the West had some doubts about what was really going on behind what Churchill had called the Iron Curtain. To a certain extent, people could remain blind to the realities of Stalinism until events like the Khrushchev speech and the revelations that emerged following it.

**EB:** Khrushchev's Secret Speech was undoubtedly a significant moment, but in my recollection, that kind of thing was more of a confirmation for me than it was a shocking new disclosure. I, and many of my friends at the time, had always described ourselves as democratic socialists, and the *democratic* part of that implied a critical rejection of Stalinist state socialism. That speech and the suppression of the Hungarian Revolution, however, did have a marked impact on some of my friends and acquaintances here in Canada. We all have certain ideological blinkers, but after Hungary and once Khrushchev had said those things, it was no longer possible for leftist intellectuals who had been deeply committed before then to remain in the party. Within mere weeks of Khruschev's speech, 30,000 people in the United States had quit the CPUSA.[1] A man who was to become my best friend, Joe Levitt, and his wife, political economist Kari Polanyi Levitt, were among the many Canadians who could no longer in good faith remain supporters of the Communist Party. A number of developments, of course — both internal to the USSR and external to it — ultimately encouraged people to break away from the big "C" communist model well before Gorbachev began his reform efforts several decades later.

I was already aware of Scandinavia's burgeoning social welfare state back then, and many of us started to look to Scandinavia as an alternative to both the rip-and-run capitalism found throughout much of the West and the rigidly authoritarian communism associated with the Eastern Bloc. It was described by some as a Third Way, which combined strong social and economic rights with a market-based economy. (This was of course very different from the neoliberal Third Way that came later with Tony Blair.). My own thinking was certainly influenced by the Swedish example, but there were also strong influences closer to home. That included, in particular, the brand of liberal Marxism articulated by C.B. Macpherson. This was a model of socialism or social democracy that incorporated all of the traditional liberal freedoms while drawing on aspects of Marx's critique of capitalism and the inevitability of inequality that comes with it.

**LS:** It seems there were two complementary aspects to your thinking during these formative years: one being an aversion to the more deterministic and authoritarian currents of socialist thought associated with the Soviet Union, the other a critical attitude toward capitalism and the hierarchies it produces.

**EB:** Indeed. And both the threads you've identified came to be reflected in my work with Macpherson, who nourished both my developing concern for individual liberty and my critical attitude toward capitalism. Macpherson believed that the egalitarian parts of liberalism — its stated commitment to equality for all and the freedom of individuals to flourish — were undermined by its long-standing allegiance to capitalism and its promotion of a market society. I'm deeply grateful to Macpherson for the conceptual clarity he offered in showing how capitalism was, by definition, exploitative. My thinking emerged in opposition to that aspect of liberalism, though at the same time I was drawn to the idea of autonomous individuals free to develop their unique capacities and talents, which was a major preoccupation for John Stuart Mill and is something I embrace to this day. I would also argue that social democracy realizes that kind of individualism much more fully and richly than a classical liberal, or in present-day parlance, neoliberal model of the state.

**FA:** What exactly drew you to John Stuart Mill, particularly as opposed to Marx?

**EB:** I came to Mill as an undergraduate, before I read Marx. Interestingly enough, I came to Marx just when his early writing was first being published and made available in the West. I found Mill's work very interesting from an ethical point of view, in contrast to what seemed like the more rigid, deterministic kind of philosophy that many radical circles on campus were then enamoured with.

It was at the LSE, of course, that I really read Mill in depth. I also had the great pleasure of attending a seminar there conducted by the conservative Michael Oakeshott, who wrote brilliantly about the practice of politics.

**FA:** The central aspect of Marx's critique of political economy was that Mill and others failed to recognize that capitalism, as a system of social relations, inevitably produces inequality. Would you share that criticism?

**EB:** I think anyone with a reasonable degree of intelligence can take any writer and find contradictions in their work. To some extent, I did exactly that with Mill: I applied a classic Marxist, ethical, and sociological analysis — which I had absorbed in my work with Macpherson — to the structure of capitalism. I argued that capitalism not only creates a highly commercialized society with many undesirable aspects but also has inequality built in by design.

Mill was just as explicit about that as Marx. He too argued that workers under capitalism have no choice but to sell their labour power because they don't own the instruments of capital and the capitalists do. But Mill ultimately sought to justify that very ownership structure, which his own social analysis saw as so pernicious. So, yes, there was certainly a contradiction. But he tried to deal with it in various ways in a series of essays on socialism and principles of political economy and then, just before he died, in a work called *Socialism*. He liked the cooperative ethic of socialism much better than the acquisitive ethic of capitalism. On a pragmatic basis, Mill talked about the importance of competition, which he thought socialists were too quick to denigrate.

If you don't have competition, in Mill's view, you have a monopoly of power, whether in the state or in the economy. Competition is useful for breaking up concentrations of power. Comparing the managerial class in communist and capitalist societies, you're going to get a more competitive (and therefore more productive) managerial group in the latter. Mill would say that centralized power and an absence of competition in a socialist society creates a less productive managerial class. It's a view I encountered early in my reading of Mill and one I've, on the whole, retained.

THINKING MY WAY TO SOCIAL DEMOCRACY

**LS:** It strikes me that there's something of a unified theme running through your early critiques of state socialism and capitalism: namely a belief that a truly democratic society naturally entails a diffusion of power. There's a quote widely attributed to the Canadian-born liberal economist John Kenneth Galbraith that comes to mind here: "Under capitalism, man exploits man. Under communism, it's just the opposite." It's a facetious remark, but it feels germane to your own early analysis.

You were drawn to the socialist idea of equality and the socialist critique of class hierarchy but thought that the big "C" communist model was far too centralized. You were sympathetic to Mill's ideas about the need for a society structured so that individuals could flourish, but thought his retention of capitalist notions of property ownership and wage labour undermined that very aspiration. How did you try to synthesize these competing thrusts in Mill? And how would you say this effort informed your later thinking and work?

**EB:** The subtitle of my doctoral dissertation was *The Political Theory of Cooperative Individualism*, which was an obvious play on the title of Macpherson's best-known work, *The Political Theory of Possessive Individualism*. Developing ideas I'd found by way of both Macpherson and Mill, I argued that the goal of good government should be to foster the development of creative and cooperative human beings. Mill had broken with conventional utilitarianism. In conventional utilitarian theory, all objectives have equal weight. For Mill, this is not the case. Some objectives in life are qualitatively superior to others. Although I don't think I ever used the phrase during my political life, "cooperative individualism" broadly describes the kind of society and social ethic I favour.

There's a rich and textured notion of equality that can be drawn from this idea. If every human being has the equal right to develop his or her talents, I would argue that necessarily implies having equal access to the means to do so. This is where the classic liberal argument about "equality of opportunity" quite clearly falls short. You can't come close to realizing equality of opportunity, even as liberals themselves understand the concept, if you don't have substantial equality at the outset. From my academic studies and throughout my political life, I have viewed all my activity, broadly speaking, through this kind of lens: whether we're talking about economic and social rights, industrial democracy, or decommodification — the idea of making particular goods universal and removing them from the domain of market competition altogether.

To return to your question then, the insights I gained through my studies, and particularly my critical reading of Mill, became the intellectual foundation for the ideas I championed as an elected politician and party leader. The two most important characteristics of social democracy for me are a commitment to equality and a commitment to decommodification, with the two being mutually reinforcing. It's not either/or, it's both. I have always seen decommodification as an end in itself but also a means to other things.

It's an end in itself in that it helps promote a society in which there are fewer things to compete over. If you have, for example, decommodified childcare or pharmacare, then a working family doesn't have to worry about getting the income to pay for those things. This advances equality. But it also means that you have a less commercialized society. The more that becomes decommodified, the less you have a community that's simply a big cash register in which people must constantly be preoccupied with economic concerns. In another sense, then, it's also a means for individual self-development. If you provide many goods and services that are based on a notion of rights rather than the capacity to pay or buy into the market, you're effectively liberating people to make other decisions in their lives — to engage in recreation, volunteer work, hobbies, or anything else they chose — because they don't have to struggle to work for an income just to meet their basic human needs. So decommodification is a very important component of a healthy social democratic society for that reason. And it follows quite naturally as an idea from the notion of cooperative individualism.

**JS:** You have raised the contradictions in both state socialism and liberal capitalism for human flourishing and individual liberty. For some of its critics on the left, the contradictions of liberalism persist under social democracy. Would you not agree that the confines of the market economy and power of business interests constrain social democracy and prevent the deeper freedom and flourishing you've been talking about?

**EB:** I think contradictions do continue in social democracy, but I would argue that they continue in any feasible form of society. In any model of society, once you have the division of labour and hierarchy of organization, you're bound to have some degree of inequality and exploitation because there are always people in those structures who will have more power than others. In a totally publicly owned economy, for example, you would have bureaucrats or senior politicians in control of the state. Sociologically speaking, the people in those positions are going to have more power than the ordinary citizens in that society, even with some form of representative democracy. Some inequality is inevitable.

Once you have organization and structure, you also have a form of exploitation by those who are at the top of the system compared to those who are at the bottom. The real challenge is then to minimize the degree of exploitation and inequality by maximizing the power of those who are at the bottom or who are in the majority. It's for exactly that reason that I favour a social democratic model of society with a mixed economy. It has a greater chance of holding those with power accountable than the competing models offered by neoliberal capitalism on the one hand or state socialism on the other.

Another formative book in this regard was John Kenneth Galbraith's *The New Industrial State*, which articulated his concept of countervailing power. Galbraith talked, for example, about the importance of the trade union movement as a countervailing power to the owners of capital. In a social democratic state, strong unions are crucial for precisely this reason: they are alternative centres of power and, as such, can have a democratizing effect on both capital and the state. This argument made a lot of sense to me when I first encountered it and it still does. That was a major reason I became interested in questions of ownership, worker participation, and industrial democracy during my early years as an MP.

## CHAPTER TWO

# Ideology and Respect

*"The form of association, however, which if mankind continues to improve, must be expected in the end to predominate, is not that which can exist between a capitalist as chief, and work-people without a voice in the management, but the association of the labourers themselves on terms of equality, collectively owning the capital with which they carry on their operations, and working under managers elected and removable by themselves."*

— JOHN STUART MILL,
*Principles of Political Economy*

*"We, on both sides, wrongly imagine that empathy with the 'other' side brings an end to clear headed analysis when, in truth, it's on the other side of that bridge that the most important analysis can begin."*

— ARLIE RUSSELL HOCHSCHILD,
*Strangers in Their Own Land*

M y first foray into political activism was during the 1962 federal election in Toronto's Rosedale riding. Rosedale had some of the richest people in the country but also some of the poorest, including, in those days, the leafy mansion-lined streets of Rosedale as well as areas with large social housing blocks like Regent Park. Strange as it may seem, I was sent to canvas in the wealthier neighbourhood with NDP candidate Des Sparham, who proudly drove us through the affluent part of Rosedale with a megaphone on top of his car, proclaiming with some exuberance: "This is Desmond Sparham, your socialist candidate . . ." Needless to say, Des didn't quite make it into Parliament.

Three years later, I was invited to run in my home riding of Oshawa-Whitby. Both trade unionist and non-trade union members of the riding association thought I would be a good candidate, but I was still engaged in writing my thesis. I politely declined the offer and, throughout most of the tumultuous early 1960s, remained engrossed in my studies. In 1965, I began my new life as an assistant professor of political science at the recently established York University. For the next three years, I enjoyed teaching first-year students and offering a third-year course on political theory.

In 1968, however, life took a different course. That year saw the arrival of Pierre Elliott Trudeau as leader of the Liberal Party. Trudeau had won a surprise triumph over several better-known party figures at a convention deemed "the most chaotic, confusing, and emotionally draining convention in Canadian political history"[1] and called an election almost immediately. Though excitement about him was neither universal nor uniform across the country, the phenomenon of Trudeaumania was certainly real, particularly in middle-class and professional milieus like my own department at York. This concerned me for a number of reasons, among them that the conservatively inclined finance minister Mitchell Sharp had dropped out of the leadership race and offered Trudeau his endorsement. However seductive or resonant Trudeau's rhetoric might have been, the fact of Sharp's support suggested that, on economic matters at least, the long-standing view of many that the Liberals campaigned from the left then governed from the right would soon be borne out yet again. In the face of these developments, I felt a strong impulse to work publicly for the social democratic alternative I felt within my bones. From the very outset of my political life, I understood this task as a battle with the Liberals and, in many ways, as a battle with Trudeau himself.

A small delegation from the NDP association in Oshawa-Whitby approached me to be the candidate in the 1968 election. This time, I accepted. Oshawa, being my hometown, was the only place I had ever wanted to run. At a packed constituency meeting, I was nominated by UAW Local 222 president Abe Taylor. In good faith, though also in considerable naivety, I made an academic speech that devoted portions to Karl Marx and John Stuart Mill (who, as you can imagine, were not figures of much interest to the trade union delegates who had turned out for the meeting). Taylor, who subsequently became a friend but whom I had just met for the first time that night, later remarked that if he had heard my speech before nominating me, he would probably have nominated the other guy. It was only partly in jest.

Despite this awkward misstep, I won the nomination and went to work as a local candidate, occupied mostly with what I quickly learned was the main activity: going door-to-door and meeting as many people as I could throughout the constituency. I took to this work enthusiastically and still remember the 1968 constituency campaign as the most enjoyable of my life. It being my hometown, I'd already had plenty of non-political contact with many of those whose support I was now seeking — because I knew them from childhood, from Central Collegiate, or because we had played minor hockey together. During door-to-door encounters, I had the great pleasure of meeting old friends that I had not seen for years — talking politics, but also trading memories from our high school days. Canvassing was a new and challenging experience, but the people and surroundings made it all very enjoyable and that summer turned out to be a glorious one.

Though most of the responsibility for the campaign fell to local activists in Oshawa, a rotating cast of my students from York University numbering perhaps seven or eight would make the trek from Toronto almost every evening to help. Emblematic of the campaign was Marion Radelaar, a bright, vivacious left-wing student who would often go canvassing with a rubber worker in his 50s named Vic Ailing. Vic was a classic Old Labour Brit of an earlier generation. He found Marion captivating and she found him a seriously committed worker. They enjoyed debating and door-knocking together and would often conclude their day's work with a beer at the Queen's Hotel.

The riding had been held since 1952 by Conservative Mike Starr, a popular minister of labour during the Diefenbaker years, and had never been won by the NDP. From the outset, at any rate, the race thus felt like a longshot.* I certainly had no inkling it was merely the first of eight elections I would ultimately fight, or that these very memorable weeks in the summer of 1968 would mark the beginning of a long political life. (If I had lost this campaign, I would have returned to academic life — a very enjoyable alternative.) As the campaign drew closer to election day, however, I remember a growing sense of momentum and an increasingly positive reception at the door, boosting my optimism that we might actually break through. Thanks to the coalition of enthusiastic younger supporters, local labour bedrock, and a well-organized campaign office led by Vi Pilkey, we came out victorious. By a wafer-thin margin of just fifteen votes, I became the first New Democrat ever elected federally in Oshawa-Whitby.

The actual work of being an MP, much like that of being a local candidate, proved challenging but quickly grew on me. Though I hadn't anticipated this while I was running, much of the satisfaction in these early years would come from constituency work rather than my caucus responsibilities in Ottawa. As I soon learned in the House of Commons, speeches and other parliamentary business tended to have very low visibility unless they concerned especially contentious debates. Even cabinet ministers, in fact, often delivered their remarks surrounded by empty seats, so in retrospect it's decidedly unsurprising that my own maiden speech as a non-government backbencher (given on a Friday afternoon, no less) was given to a nearly empty House.** As I began speaking, I looked around me and welcomed the crowd: which numbered no more than five.

An effective performance might at best earn a positive response from other MPs. But, in the days before TV cameras had entered the House of Commons, its ultimate reach rarely went beyond Parliament Hill. Local work, by comparison, was an area in which I could see tangible results, and it quickly became a source of great personal satisfaction. Though my

---

\* Cliff Pilkey, later president of the Ontario Federation of Labour, had been elected MPP the previous year. My own campaign benefited greatly from the work done by Cliff and his team.

\*\* My maiden speech is included in the Appendices.

main residence was in Ottawa, I came back to the riding each weekend and, while I initially rented a place in Whitby, I soon let it go and stayed instead with my parents at our family home in Oshawa. By donating a portion of my salary, and with financial help from the UAW local, we established what became the first real constituency office in Canada. Up to that point, with the exception of a few MPs whose law practices doubled as local offices, the only way for most voters to have contact with their representatives had been by writing letters. (The venerable New Democratic MP Stanley Knowles, for example — like most MPs of his generation — devoted considerable time to penning detailed replies to constituent correspondence, but rarely returned to his constituency in Winnipeg while the House was sitting.*)

In contrast to the business of making speeches in the House, direct contact with the people of Oshawa during weekend meetings gave me the opportunity to do work that made a material impact for people, and it was visibly appreciated. The problems were close to home: people experiencing difficulties while trying to secure a Canadian Mortgage and Housing Corporation (CMHC) mortgage; a pension cheque that hadn't come through as expected; a delayed passport. Because civil servants tend to respond promptly to MP queries regardless of party, I was often in a position to provide useful help that directly affected the people I represented. Over time I grew to respect the great diversity of people in my hometown and derive great satisfaction from working to understand their problems. In this work, I was aided for most of my time as an MP by two exceptional people: Nestor Pidwerbecki and Beverly Johnson. They kept the office open and running during the week when I was in Ottawa. When I retired in 1990, Beverly would similarly step back from political life while Nestor would become a well-respected, long-serving councillor in Oshawa.

---

\* First elected in 1944 as an MP for the CCF, Stanley was one of the party's longest-serving members in the House, and I regularly sought his counsel. Not long after I first arrived in Parliament, I came to see him to ask a series of nagging questions about political life: Was there a place for professors in politics? Could I do my job well and still have time to think and write? Over tea in his office, he assured me that I could indeed make the time and suggested choosing a particular issue area to make into a speciality — just as he had done with pensions.

This constituency work, intrinsically rewarding as it was, also paid political dividends when Mike Starr challenged me for his old seat in the next election. The Conservative vote actually went up by nearly 8,000 in 1972 but, as it turned out, we were able to add an even greater number to my original result in 1968. I remain convinced that the immersive local work, which included regular contact with constituents and a quarterly newsletter I developed in collaboration with my staff, is what made the difference.


The late 1960s were at once a moment of tremendous energy and palpable frustration across Canada's left. Throughout the decade, the country's GDP had grown by giant steps and more Canadians than ever were experiencing the plenty of postwar capitalism. With affluence came optimism, and a general feeling that the country was open to progressive change, particularly among the young. Feminists called attention to the exploitative nature of traditional gender roles. A generation of students was being drawn into the anti-war movement sparked by America's deadly war in Vietnam and awakening to broader anti-colonial struggles. At the same time, new nationalisms were flourishing across the country. As the Quiet Revolution swept away the repressive legacy of the Duplessis regime in Quebec, a new generation of Québécois fought to control their own economic and social destiny under the slogan "Maîtres chez nous" ("masters in our own home") — abolishing repressive labour legislation and restrictions on civil liberties and challenging the dominance of both the old Anglo economic elite and the Catholic Church. In English Canada, meanwhile, many on the left — and some in liberal circles as well — were animated by a growing concern that the country was being inexorably pulled into a subordinate relationship with the American economy.

Founded in a spirit of great optimism at the decade's outset, the sixties had partly blunted the ambitious electoral aspirations of the NDP. Between its first federal election in 1962 and my own run in Oshawa six years later, the party's overall vote share had risen from just over 13 percent to just under 17: a good increase, but still well short of the numbers needed to form a government. As the sixties drew to a close, many young activists in particular were agitating for renewal and increasingly looking beyond the horizons of both consumer society and the liberal welfare state. Against the wider backdrop of nationalism, this zeitgeist rallied strongly behind demands for greater public ownership of the Canadian economy — and, by extension, for economic independence from the tidal forces of multinational capital represented by the United States.

Some of these ideas were incorporated in the Waffle Manifesto, a document produced by a group on the left of the NDP which included myself, economist Mel Watkins, and the political scientist James Laxer. Reflecting the radicalism and transformative spirit of the 1960s, the manifesto encompassed issues of corporate power, public ownership, Quebec sovereignty, and the need to deal with foreign control of the Canadian economy. It being my own area of interest, I contributed the section on industrial democracy. However, I decided to withhold my support from the final text because of its rhetoric. In my view, its language — rhetorically extreme and aimed at academics — would lead workers in Oshawa and beyond to reject even consideration of its substantive proposals. An alternative document containing much of the substance but framed in more hospitable language was adopted by a large majority at the 1969 federal convention with the full support of Tommy Douglas.

My own engagement with questions of industrial democracy was in many ways the natural outgrowth of the convictions I had brought with me into politics. On an intellectual level, I believed that the egalitarian ends sought by the best parts of the liberal tradition ultimately required socialist means to fulfill. More than anything, that meant going beyond the traditional welfare state and trying to realize a fuller and richer democratic life for ordinary citizens. That, in turn, entailed challenging the colossal power of the modern corporation and extending democratic principles into the area where most people spend the bulk of their waking lives: namely, the workplace.

By the late 1960s, industrial democracy was attracting widespread interest throughout North America and beyond, counting among its enthusiasts European socialists like newly elected Swedish prime minister Olof Palme, young intellectuals in Czechoslovakia, and assorted trade unionists from both the Western and Eastern blocs. As a parliamentary observer with the Canadian delegation at the United Nations in the early autumn of 1968, I had the opportunity to discuss the tragic invasion of Czechoslovakia with a Czech diplomat. One of the principal reasons for the invasion, he stressed, was Soviet opposition to the new economic reforms of the Dubček government, a central part of which was to give working people more direct control in industry.

**Jonathan Sas:** I want to pose a somewhat rudimentary question about your jump into politics just as your career in the academy was beginning. Why seek public office as opposed to other avenues like working in the trade union movement or remaining an academic?

**Ed Broadbent:** It was ultimately a straightforward matter of personal choice. I believe deeply in the obligation of citizens in a democratic society to participate in politics and would always encourage my students to get involved in one way or another. This doesn't mean, of course, that everyone is obligated to run for office. Obviously, there are many other ways someone who is politically engaged can get involved — two of which are the academy and the labour movement. Like many big decisions in life, much of it ultimately comes down to personal choice — and, in my case, I felt a strong desire to engage directly and to one day elect a social democratic government that could legislate real change in people's lives.

**Frances Abele:** You've said that you consider yourself a politician more than an academic, even though you began your career as the latter. When do you think a political streak developed that was independent of a more purely intellectual one? And what do you think are the most important distinctions between being a politician and being an academic?

**EB:** I've thought about the distinction between these two vocations quite a lot. I think an academic is concerned, in a somewhat exclusive way, with getting at deep intellectual truth and maintaining total intellectual consistency without letting other considerations interfere. For that reason, some people can have quite disagreeable personalities and still produce solid academic work. When it comes to our judgements about politicians or leaders, on the other hand, we're compelled to talk about personal character and to ask questions that are central to it: Can someone effectively motivate people to work for a cause, whatever it might be? Do they generate loyalty? Do they have empathy? Are they honest with the public? These are largely considerations you wouldn't have in relation to an academic, but they are absolutely central in judging a politician.

I started my adult life as an academic but decided after my election in 1968 to shift my emphasis toward these kinds of concerns. Was I acting in good faith and with integrity toward my constituents? Could I animate people and get them enthusiastic about our shared objectives? Did I have a constructive relationship with fellow politicians, particularly in my own party?

I found that the kinds of activities and the style of decision-making I pursued very quickly fit more into the mould one would expect of a politician as compared to an academic — with everything, good or bad, that might entail. I think I started to move away from what had been a more or less exclusive focus on making arguments that were not only correct but also intellectually airtight. Also, as an academic, I spoke in lengthy paragraphs that included semicolons and subordinate clauses and always qualified the thesis en route. As a politician, I quickly learned to state my meaning outright and put the conclusion first. (Gord Brigden, one of the best organizers in the history of the NDP, in hearing my early speeches, would stand at the back of the room pulling his hair out while I made my way through various subordinate clauses, semicolons, and qualified theses.) My ideological formation in university life did provide a necessary analytic framework for understanding political and economic structures, but it was similarly necessary to set aside some of the analytical language to be able to engage directly with the interests of non-academics.

**Luke Savage:** I'm keen to probe this theme of academic vs. politician a little further by asking about some of the big policy concepts you were pursuing during your first term as an MP and their relationship to your constituency work. You took a strong interest in the idea of industrial democracy, and I'm curious about the extent to which it was informed by developments that were happening locally. In your 1970 book, *The Liberal Rip-Off*, for example, you cited the closure of a plant in Oshawa operated by Duplate Ltd. How did a case like that play a role in your thinking?

**EB:** By way of the intellectual route that led me into politics, I already had my own abstract ideas about industrial democracy. I was also immersed in the reality of what was going on in my constituency, and the Duplate case in particular was something that strongly reinforced my belief in it. As I recall, there were about 300 workers directly affected by the management's decision to relocate their Oshawa plant to another part of the province — and when you included their family members and the impact on neighbouring companies, the number of people actually affected by the closure was around 1,200 in total. I don't remember exactly what lay behind the move, but it was deemed to be financially advantageous (which is to say profitable) for the company in some way. So here you had hundreds of workers, some of whom had invested thirty or forty years of their lives in Duplate, being profoundly affected by a decision they had played absolutely no part in — and a profitable company that packed up and moved just to make higher profits. Such a decision shows the complete absence of the respect that a company owes to its workers. Their human dignity was denied outright.

That was merely one case, but it helped make abstract notions like industrial democracy and worker participation a lot more concrete for me and, in the process, only strengthened my conviction that we had to cut into the so-called sacred rights of management. For example, if the Duplate workers themselves had been represented in the decision-making process or if they had wielded influence over the firm's investment priorities or other significant areas of company policy, they would quite clearly have rejected the company's move.

**LS:** Perhaps it's a sign of how radically politics have shifted since this time, but "industrial democracy" is not a term broadly known or discussed anymore. Could you talk a bit more directly about the concept of industrial democracy and what it actually means in practice?

**EB:** At the core of it all is the need to challenge the set of rights allocated to corporations and modify them with more democratic and participatory structures of decision-making. In a capitalist economy, management makes all kinds of choices that have a profound impact not only on workers employed by particular firms but on society as a whole. Who, for example, plans and executes the vast majority of investment decisions? Who determines which commodities are produced and at what price? Who tends to play the biggest role in directing scientific and technological research? Who is ultimately responsible for the lion's share of pollution? The answer is, of course, corporate managers who are predominantly accountable to small groups of shareholders rather than to workers or the public at large and for whom the main imperatives are generally profit and growth.

In our existing legal tradition, anything that hasn't been explicitly negotiated in a contract falls under the so-called "prerogatives of management," which in effect has meant the owners of capital. The philosophical case that follows from that is something we've discussed already: from a democratic standpoint, people cannot be fully free and self-determining in either an individual or a collective sense if so much responsibility rests with unaccountable private power. A society cannot be meaningfully democratic if people do not have a say in decisions that have such a serious effect on their day-to-day lives.

In thinking about industrial democracy, I was also influenced by John Kenneth Galbraith's writings on how modern economies actually operate. I came to think that what is generally called "the free market" is often a fiction — at least as far as the large firms that make the vast majority of important economic decisions are concerned. In the early 1970s, Galbraith's book *Economics and the Public Purpose* made a persuasive case that the market economy typically imagined by most economists and Chambers of Commerce is long dead. In its place, there are actually two parallel economies: what he called a "minor" one, consisting of small or medium-sized firms, which still bears some resemblance to the competitive, neoclassical free-market model; and a planning sector consisting of larger companies who wield power on an altogether different scale.

Representing Oshawa, I certainly thought the latter applied to General Motors and its various equivalents in other sectors who were not so much responding competitively to the market as they were shaping it. What Galbraith wrote remains true today, as we see with dominant companies like Amazon, Apple, and Google — to say nothing of the big media and communications companies who now have the power to direct, shape, and control huge swathes of public consciousness. Part of the solution is for the democratic state to take on a much stronger regulatory role. But, because I also don't want to replace overly centralized corporate power with overreaching state power, a big part of the solution for me has always lain with the trade union movement — an alternative form of power which actually consists of the people it represents.

**JS:** In 1969, you submitted a proposal to the NDP's federal council on industrial democracy which would have reformed Canadian labour law such that firms over a certain size would be unionized automatically. Seen from today's vantage point, after decades of assaults on unions and labour rights, the proposal is, pardon the pun, striking. Workers would also be able to bargain over management rights as well as wages and working conditions. How did that proposal come about and how was it received?

**EB:** It came simply from thinking abstractly, and the manner in which I went about proposing it showed my naivety as a politician at the time — because the reaction from trade union people was quite negative. I'll return to that in a moment, but I actually thought the idea of industrial democracy flowed quite naturally from the role of organized labour.

Since their inception, unions have already in one way or another been attacking the basic premise underlying management rights: that the simple fact of property or capital ownership conveys some exclusive authority for management to exercise far-reaching power over the lives of workers. So why not extend that critique to the many prerogatives management still retains and take the scope of union activity beyond representing workers in a purely defensive way? In my early writing on industrial democracy, I would cite a contract negotiated by the UAW that included important demands around plant conditions but also encompassed price levels and pollution controls. The specific details aren't hugely important. What mattered was the precedent set: that the union in those negotiations was representing its members not only as workers but also as *citizens* — and, by extension, was concerning itself with a wider range of *human* (as opposed to simply economic) needs.

Anyway, my proposal went nowhere. The political representative of the Canadian Labour Congress who dealt with the NDP caucus was appalled. People thought it would never happen for starters, and that no government would support it. There was also a view that trade unions should never be involved in the decision-making role of managers. Their role should be simply to fight to improve labour conditions and secure a greater share of the pie for workers. I think, for many in union leadership positions, there was a related anxiety that greater participation would undermine the unions' antagonistic relationship to capital. Some felt strongly that the initial struggle for union recognition was itself a prerequisite for getting a vigorously active trade union in the first place. Union drives for legal recognition are thus integral to labour's identity. Consequently, the automatic right to union membership, as I was proposing, would be counterproductive.

**FA:** There is, as you know, a long-standing left critique of worker participation which asserts that labour will be co-opted by sitting in the same room with management. There are also potential problems of internal democracy because the representatives of some unions might not represent the interests of all workers. We might think today, for example, of carbon-intensive industries where workers and management would actually have a shared stake in a company remaining profitable even if it's in the business of extracting oil that scientists are telling us needs to stay in the ground. It does seem like there are a lot of conflicting interests at play. What do you think about the potential danger that the labour movement would become vulnerable to co-option if workers themselves become more involved in the actual running of enterprises?

**EB:** There are inescapable tensions and conflicts in any structure. On a fundamental level, I don't think there's any greater danger of co-option with the structural changes I was proposing than there is now in the current political structure. In serious negotiations with a company, management can already invoke the need to raise prices or freeze wages in order to protect jobs or continue to pay workers, and bargaining teams sometimes reach collaborative agreements with management along precisely these lines. For that reason, something I advocated strongly for was workers being given full access to information about the financial realities at a company: that is, being privy to its books, its current planning around technological innovation or investment, and all the other things that are involved in running a complex enterprise. With that kind of information on hand, workers are in a much better position to debate and decide whether a particular company policy is in their interest or represents a risk worth taking. Access to all such information in the final analysis is due, as a matter of respect, to workers involved in an enterprise.

Of course, those decisions will sometimes be criticized by some of the workers involved. But that's an inevitable consequence of democracy and it's how the political domain outside the workplace already operates: parties do things, which are in turn criticized and subjected to scrutiny through open public debate, and voters have a chance to accept or reject them. Similarly, under more equitable and democratic models of industrial relations, there would be decisions that were popular and others that were not. Again, that's what democracy is all about, and I'd rather have workers at risk of getting "co-opted" if it means they get to participate in the decisions that affect them — as opposed to being excluded and just having to pick up the pieces after (as in the Duplate case).

In my old age, I've become more open to the idea that there might need to be variation across certain sectors and that the exact mechanisms we might want to put in place would be contingent on the types of work being performed and the specific unions involved.

On an intellectual level, I frankly never bought the co-option arguments or the other criticisms that were made. As citizens in a democracy, we don't have to fight to renew the right to vote: we passed laws that guarantee it and don't force citizens to relitigate the issue ahead of each election. In principle, why shouldn't we establish the right to join a trade union as soon as someone starts work? There are certainly other practical questions that come with that, like which union a newly created local affiliates with: does it join the Steelworkers or the Autoworkers or form an independent association of its own? There would obviously need to be some means of disaffiliating from one union and switching to another. But, to me, the automatic right to a trade union still makes sense.

**FA:** It occurs to me that the relationship between labour and the NDP is unique to social democratic parties and that there's nothing really analogous for the Liberals or Conservatives. They might have to worry about the banks and about Bay Street, but it's not the same kind of dynamic, is it? In the NDP there's a large and powerful constituency that's affiliated and very important to the party's identity.

**EB:** Yes, I think that's very much the case. The other parties do have particular interests to consider when formulating their policies or message, but they don't play the fraternal role that the trade union movement has historically played within the NDP. When it comes to the project of industrial democracy, or any move toward power-sharing arrangements in places of work, I think it will need to emerge from a strong and cooperative partnership between social democratic parties and trade unions. The latter's traditional role — advancing worker interests at the bargaining table and serving as a countervailing power to management — will probably remain as it is in the near future. Expanding it will require some combination of electing a social democratic government and an evolving mood of reform within the trade union movement itself.

In any case, the whole experience on the issue of industrial democracy ultimately taught me that I needed to engage people before advocating something for them as a matter of respect. It also caused me to think seriously about my role as an MP and also about the orientation of social democratic parties in relation to the union movement. The fact is, a social democratic government is going to have a very difficult time getting elected without the support and active involvement of the trade union movement. This could be achieved either through a formal alliance or simply as is normally the case today, via coordinated campaigns during and between elections. In any case, changes affecting workers must have their active support.

I came to think that maintaining the relationship between the NDP and the labour movement was a fundamental obligation. It's one thing to meet in private or debate these things at conferences and try to persuade people. But, as an elected social democratic politician, to go public without consultation of the union itself is a mistake. That's why David Lewis, for example, was polite but clear to me as a new member of caucus that, in his view, I was making a mistake on industrial democracy. It's also why, when I became leader, I brought a representative from the Canadian Labour Congress into caucus for meetings on a weekly basis and would reach out to particular unions before I discussed issues related to them or their industries in public. By and large, my working relationship with the trade union movement was very positive, save for the initial hiccup with the union proposal at the start of my political life.


**JS:** I'd like to interrupt the discussion on industrial democracy for a minute to ask about David Lewis, who was a significant figure in both the CCF and the NDP. What was your relationship with him like when you first arrived in Parliament?

**EB:** David became a great friend and mentor. He was an extraordinarily able person and was one of the most important figures in the creation of the NDP. Though I'd seen him debate William F. Buckley at Hart House while a student, I did not know him when I was first elected and, out of youthful arrogance, I think, some of us viewed him as belonging to an older leadership that had to be challenged. Of all the political decisions I've made in my life, one I seriously regret is running against David for the NDP leadership in 1971. He won on the fourth ballot over myself, James Laxer, John Paul Harney, and Frank Howard — and he absolutely deserved to. Soon after the leadership contest, I was elected caucus chair. As we worked together, I got to know David, and the more I got to know him, the more my admiration grew.

**LS:** We've been discussing industrial democracy and worker empowerment in somewhat abstract terms thus far. But there was also a wave of nationalism sweeping the country during the late 1960s and early 1970s that very much animated the Canadian left and became interwoven with its most radical ideas at the time. It's mostly been forgotten, but George Grant's book *Lament for a Nation: The Defeat of Canadian Nationalism* was hugely influential on the left — and, paradoxically, ended up articulating and inspiring the very national identity Grant was himself eulogizing. How would you characterize the influence of nationalism in those days and your own relationship to it?

**EB:** There was definitely a strong nationalist uptick across Canada, and not only on the left or within the NDP. There was a liberal version of it too, represented by business-friendly nationalists like Walter Gordon, who had chaired the Royal Commission on Canada's Economic Prospects in 1956–57.* Later, as minister of finance, Gordon commissioned a task force on foreign ownership chaired by Mel Watkins.

I suppose I felt the first stirrings of nationalist sentiment within myself as an undergraduate. And, as is the case with virtually all forms of nationalism, it partly defined itself against something. The big "something," of course, was the United States and its war in Vietnam, which I opposed on the grounds the U.S. was attempting to stop a legitimate struggle against colonialism by the people of Vietnam. As I just mentioned, there was also the very real question of foreign ownership of the Canadian economy, which overwhelmingly meant U.S. ownership and our ability to have control over our own social and economic future.

For that reason, there was a quite natural relationship between socialism and nationalism and there weren't at all the kinds of intellectual divisions that existed in European circles around those categories for understandable reasons. On the left, it was about control of our own destiny: we wanted to take national control of our industrial development. This would entail some public ownership — particularly in the resource sector and the petroleum industry. Resources were central to this push for economic and industrial democracy because so much of Canada's economy had become purely extractive, meaning that we were exporting raw materials to America to be refined and manufactured rather than doing so here.

The resource-dependent structure of the Canadian economy was inhibiting the building of a dynamic and modern industrial economy that we could direct toward common ends: a "staples trap" that made it difficult for Canada to shift away from natural resource dependence and made the Canadian state susceptible

---

* For a deeper discussion of foreign ownership, see Chapter Three. For a more in-depth discussion of nationalism see Chapter Eight.

to political capture by resource capital.* We were also confronting a proliferation of American branch plants, as Kari Polanyi Levitt described in her influential book *Silent Surrender*, and fears that Canada would drift further under the control of foreign multinationals.

**LS:** Something else that seems to have been part of the zeitgeist, which I think is almost entirely absent these days, was a critique of consumerism and the consumption economy. In the book you published during your first run for the NDP leadership in 1971, you refer to consumption as "a wasting sickness" and write that our economic system "inevitably promotes the development of dissatisfied, consumer-oriented human beings who are disconnected and atomized." This kind of thing followed from the wider critique of corporate power people like you were making. It's particularly striking because consumer society is now so axiomatic and ubiquitous that there isn't really a critique of it as such — even on the left.

**EB:** That's an interesting point. Something that informs my own version of social democracy is capitalism's built-in propensity to stir up a level of permanent discontent. It's always put in positive terms of choice: about buying this or that, taking a holiday somewhere, getting a new and better product, etc. But in order to stimulate market demand there is incessant pressure, even on wealthy or comfortable people, to be discontented with what they have and to always crave more. I think that's very damaging to society and to individuals as human beings.

---

* The dynamic of the staples trap, developed in his article *A Staple Theory of Economic Development*, was a key contribution of Mel Watkins to Canadian political economy. For a more recent analysis of its continued relevance, see the Canadian Centre for Policy Alternatives: https://policyalternatives.ca/sites/default/files/uploads/publications/National%20 Office/2020/04/Staple%20Theory%20at%2050%20-%202020%20version.pdf.

One of the empirical findings that emerged from Wilkinson and Pickett's landmark study *The Spirit Level* is that more equal societies tend to have less of an appetite for consumption. On an intellectual level, that makes intuitive sense because people don't have to spend as much of their incomes just to obtain the necessities of life, and it's among the reasons I've always been committed to decommodification. Removing things from the market is often the right thing to do for its own sake — healthcare, for example, is a basic need we should not be in the business of buying or selling — but it ultimately also means that more aspects of life are able to operate outside of capitalism's relentless consumptive logic.

You can trace this idea back, at least in the West, as far as the nineteenth century to John Stuart Mill and Karl Marx, who forcefully criticized capitalism for its commercialization of everyday life. There's an important ethical point here about the kind of society we want to create, from which a very practical political agenda quite naturally follows. I think you're right that the kind of deep commodification that accompanies the spread of markets has become pervasive in North America. It's now more or less taken for granted.

**LS:** It's always seemed to me that the real purpose of the neoliberal project was first and foremost to create a market society. Margaret Thatcher once said, "Economics are the method, the object is to change the soul," and I think she quite consciously hoped people would be rewired to think of themselves as economic creatures interacting through the marketplace. Part and parcel of making that vision a reality has been convincing people that the market is actually a very democratic space, because as consumers it's supposedly responsive to us in some way and we're voting with our dollars every time we make a purchase.

**EB:** Yes, that's a deep part of the mythology behind free-market fanaticism — that markets are somehow democratic. Even on its own terms that argument has never really made sense. If we're all voting with our dollars, the rich quite clearly have more votes than the rest of us. When it comes to the control of capital, that too is a matter of minority power.

**LS:** There was a constant tug of war in your early adult life between the two different roles you took on and the competing dispositions they involved. On the one hand, you were a newly practising politician with constituents to serve. On the other, you had a worked-out social democratic philosophy and a fairly radical political program that followed from it.

In the previous chapter, we talked about the ways Macpherson shaped your thinking, but you also attended a seminar of Michael Oakeshott's while at the LSE. There's an essay on your career by the political scientist Alan Whitehorn who writes about their respective influences as follows: "Among the lessons Broadbent took from Macpherson were the importance of class and the need to restructure society to foster the full growth of each individual. From Oakeshott he learned about people's reluctance to accept change, the fact that it takes time to persuade them to move to a new political position, and the need to respect different viewpoints." It strikes me as a succinct characterization of the two poles we've been discussing, and I'm curious if you think it's accurate.

**EB:** It is, broadly speaking, accurate. I had come to the LSE as a democratic socialist and ended up studying with the most eminent conservative thinker of them all. Oakeshott's seminar was the only one I attended on a regular basis, and I was quite taken by his famous metaphor about how the task of politicians is to keep the ship afloat on a boundless sea without setting course for any particular harbour or premeditated destination. My initial reaction was critical, because his metaphor seemed to imply a purely prudential imperative; he seemed to be leaving no room for ideology or philosophy. However, it turned out that he actually thought that those things could play a role when subordinate to other considerations or at least in conversation with them. Of all people, he cited Lenin as a case in point of someone who was ideologically driven but who also drew on historical precedents in navigating the future of the Russian Revolution.

One day in the seminar, I rather unimaginatively put to Oakeshott that his theory of politics allowed no space for innovation, and brought up the doctors' strike that had just happened in Saskatchewan over the introduction of universal healthcare. My argument was that, under his general formulation, it would be impossible to bring in a national medicare program, and he replied: "Mr. Broadbent, why is that?" asking if there had been any earlier experiments going on in Saskatchewan short of a comprehensive medicare program. Indeed, I said, there had been: among other things the Swift Current health plan had brought comprehensive medical and hospital coverage to residents in the southwest of the province in 1946, sixteen years before it would come to the rest of the province. Well, he argued, if there was already an established practice of using public enterprise to meet a demand then it could reasonably follow that the state could broaden its involvement and introduce something universal.

In any case, I think Whitehorn is basically right about the two impulses I learned to balance through a process of trial and error throughout my early years in Parliament. When I was thinking through a policy that would affect change in people's lives, I came to understand the importance of getting their views and understanding their perspectives. And if they were not as ideologically committed as I was on a given issue, that required an understanding of their position as human beings on my part and a tolerance and acceptance of difference. Showing respect was essential if I wanted to persuade them to move in another direction. Respect is fundamental.

# CHAPTER THREE

# The Balance of Power

*"Real social progress, in my view, is achieved by expanding the public sector, by providing more such facilities on an egalitarian basis so that our children can grow up in a non-competitive way, knowing that many of the essential requisites of a civilized society are provided by the community, as they are presently provided as a matter of right only to the children of the wealthy."*
— ED BROADBENT, response to the government's
Speech from the Throne, October 14, 1970

I f I had entered Parliament amid a general atmosphere of optimism and prosperity in 1968, the arrival of the 1970s quickly signalled a political landscape that was altogether more contentious and uncertain. The period of economic expansion that had spanned much of the sixties was beginning to ebb: Canada's rate of GDP growth dropping rapidly from 5.3 percent in 1969 to just 2.5 percent the following year.[1] Faced with sluggish growth and rising inflation, Trudeau and finance minister Edgar Benson began to tighten the screws of fiscal and monetary policy in an effort to stabilize prices. In equal measure, the rousing slogans of Trudeaumania quickly gave way to the language of discipline and restraint.[2]

This deflationary approach reflected the generally held view that higher prices are a greater evil than high unemployment in squeezing the public sector and putting a downward pressure on wages, the government's excessive emphasis on inflation thus embraced the conservative premise that the solution to the country's economic woes ran through cuts and layoffs — the flipside of which was a bounty of subsidies and tax concessions to private industry. Whatever progressive image Trudeau might have projected in 1968, it seemed that the cautious spirit of Mackenzie King liberalism was alive and well after all.

Other developments, both internal and external, compounded the general feeling of uncertainty and instability. Already spiking because of the increasing American demand for Canadian oil, high gasoline prices became a full-blown energy crisis in October 1973 when the Organization of Arab Petroleum Exporting Countries (OPEC) announced an embargo on exports, causing costs to skyrocket. With some 90 percent of its energy sector under foreign control,[3] Canada's economy proved especially vulnerable to exogenous shocks and fluctuations in the global market.

In the fall of 1970, meanwhile, extremists from the Front de libération du Québec (FLQ) kidnapped British trade commissioner James Cross, abducting and murdering provincial labour minister Pierre Laporte on October 17. A day earlier, acting on a request from premier Robert Bourassa and Montreal mayor Jean Drapeau, the Trudeau government had invoked the War Measures Act: granting authorities across the country sweeping powers to arrest and detain people without charge or due process. Reserved for instances of "real or apprehended insurrection," the legislation had never before been used in peacetime.

In the House of Commons — in what for me still is one of the greatest speeches of his life — Tommy Douglas made an impassioned and courageous intervention laying out the case for the NDP's opposition to the use of the act. Calling the occasion a "Black Friday for civil liberties in Canada," Douglas argued that the cabinet already had the necessary powers to deal with the situation and that Trudeau's chosen course represented a dangerous suppression of civil liberties. "The government, I submit, is using a sledgehammer to crack a peanut," he memorably told Parliament on October 16, 1970. "Right now, there is no constitution in this country, no Bill of Rights, no provincial constitutions. This government now has the power by Order in Council to do anything it wants: to

43

intern any citizen, to deport any citizen, to arrest any person or declare any organization subversive or illegal. These are tremendous powers to put into the hands of the men who sit on the treasury benches."[4]

Ahead of the speech, Tommy had met with Trudeau to learn what evidence he had to justify the invocation of the act. He reported back to the caucus that the prime minister provided no such evidence. A few days later I, alongside fifteen of my colleagues, cast our lonely votes against the War Measures Act, which was approved by the House 190–16.[5]

Though a handful of newspapers, civil libertarians, and Quebec opposition figures agreed with our case, polls at the time suggested overwhelming public support for the government's position. This support was probably founded in fear that violence would spread. Notwithstanding this concern, I remain convinced that the use of emergency powers represented an extreme case of overreach by the state and that the events that ultimately unfolded vindicated our opposition. As René Lévesque wrote in his memoirs: "Indiscriminately, union leaders, artists, writers, whoever had dared cast doubt upon official verities, or simply those the unleashed bloodhounds didn't like the look of, were thrown into the paddy wagons and put away. Deprived of their rights, beginning with habeas corpus, a great many of them were to remain in custody for days and weeks."[6]

Abuse of police powers, it turned out, also went well beyond the borders of Quebec. Just as Douglas had warned, authorities in Quebec seized upon the suspension of civil liberties to carry out arbitrary raids and arrests that had nothing to do with the FLQ. Throughout the rest of the country, the invocation of the War Measures Act also appeared to embolden repressive forces — Vancouver's conservative mayor, to take one example, publicly suggested that it might be an opportune moment to crack down on hippies, draft dodgers, and other "undesirables." A decade later, in 1980, as leader of the NDP, I tried without immediate success to convince Trudeau to replace or amend the legislation. In 1988, however, the War Measures Act was finally replaced by the Emergencies Act, a law explicitly subject to our Charter of Rights and Freedoms and considerably more constrained by checks and balances.

Politics is fundamentally about power, and who wields it will invariably determine the ends for which it is used. Across Canada, the events of the early 1970s offered living proof. On the splendid evening of August 30, 1972, forty-one-year-old social worker Dave Barrett led the NDP to victory in the province of British Columbia. Barrett's victory heralded not only the advance of Canadian social democracy beyond its origin on the prairies, but also its first crack at governing a wealthy and industrialized region. The decisive defeat of BC's ossified Social Credit regime (in power since the early 1950s) brought with it swift and tangible change — Barrett's government moving at a breakneck pace and passing new legislation almost every three days: a tenants' bill of rights, a guaranteed income for old age pensioners, and the public take-over of automotive insurance soon become a reality. Extending public ownership into the forestry sector, Barrett's cabinet used new resource revenues to expand social services, raise social assistance rates, and fund a province-wide kindergarten program.[7] On the heels of other recent victories in Manitoba and Saskatchewan, with the exception of Alberta, the NDP now governed every province west of Ontario.

Coming roughly a year after the October Crisis, the federal election of 1972 offered further evidence of democracy's transformative potential. Rolling out the self-satisfied slogan "The Land Is Strong" against a backdrop of unemployment and inflation, the Liberal Party had visibly lost the sheen of 1968 and proved unable to campaign with anything like the same confidence. The previous spring, John Turner (who had succeeded Benson as minister of finance) had announced a swathe of lucrative tax concessions to private companies[8] in the wrong-headed belief they would create jobs and significantly bring down unemployment. Railing against this and other Liberal handouts to big business, David Lewis aimed the NDP campaign squarely at "corporate welfare bums" and led the party to thirty-one seats, our best result to date. With 109 members, the Liberals were reduced to a minority caucus in the House of Commons barely larger than the PCs under Robert Stanfield, with 107 seats. (Social Credit and two Independents won the remaining seventeen seats.)

As I saw up close in my new role as caucus chair, the result was a Parliament quite unlike its predecessor, and one that brought about a perceptible change in the policies of the Trudeau government. When the House reconvened in January 1973, family allowances were tripled, plans for means-testing benefits were dropped, and Turner changed his position on the issue of unemployment.[9] The cause of these pivots was certainly no mystery. Forced to rely on the NDP for their survival in a minority Parliament, the Liberals were compelled to shift their priorities in a more progressive direction. What had been undesirable and unfeasible for the government only a few months earlier, it seemed, abruptly became both possible and worthy of action.

Perhaps most indicative of the NDP's newfound leverage was the creation of Petro-Canada: a publicly owned petroleum company with a mandate to reassert control over our vast oil-and-gas reserves, protect consumers from global market shocks, and ensure that benefits of natural resource wealth accrued nationwide to Canadians rather than to foreign shareholders. Adopted as NDP policy by delegates at the 1973 convention in Vancouver, the government stubbornly resisted the idea, even as the energy crisis worsened. Their intransigence persisted until just before the Christmas break when I delivered a message to industry and commerce minister Alastair Gillespie on behalf of the NDP caucus: that the Liberals could either create Petro-Canada or lose our support in the confidence vote scheduled before the holiday recess. Faced with the prospect of an early election, they conceded. The mood in the NDP caucus was one of elation.

The creation of Petro-Canada, like much of the NDP program, represented a union of hard-headed practical politics and social democratic philosophy. Perhaps more than at any moment since 1945, the end of the postwar boom was underscoring the extent to which the problems facing ordinary people were both systemic in nature and in desperate need of an activist response from the state. Global market fluctuations and sluggish growth exacerbated poverty and inequality which, in turn, worsened the human impact of unemployment and inflation. A foreign-owned petroleum sector run largely in the private interest, meanwhile, drove up energy costs while exporting resource wealth abroad. An emerging climate of fiscal restraint weakened the public sector while the wealthy and private industry were given tax breaks. The solution, as I argued at the time, lay in policies that promoted equality and lessened the overbearing pressure exerted by markets on daily life. From full employment and taxation to housing and industrial planning, the instrument for those policies was a progressive and interventionist state.

The parliamentary dynamic of 1972–73, however, was not to last. By the spring of 1974, the Liberal Party's standing in the polls had improved — likely as a result of the social democratic policies the Liberals had adopted from the NDP — and the government tabled a budget that was clearly designed to trigger an election. In Oshawa, I was somewhat apprehensive. In 1972, when Michael Starr had decided to challenge me for his old seat, I had appealed to the NDP's superb Ontario organizer Michael Lewis for help. The party then sent Jo-Anne McNevin: a seasoned organizer from BC who Lewis promised was one of the best in the country. Jo-Anne lived up to that reputation and returned to manage my third campaign in Oshawa with remarkable skill and efficiency. Whatever anxieties I might have had when the government fell that spring, they were quickly alleviated when the Oshawa polls reported on the evening of July 8, 1974 — delivering us a victory of more than 10,000 votes.

Regrettably, the same pattern did not repeat itself elsewhere. Campaigning against Stanfield's proposal for wage and price controls (that he himself would shortly introduce), Trudeau successfully manoeuvred his way back into majority government. For the NDP, the national result was a major disappointment. Not only was our caucus cut in half across the country, but David Lewis himself was defeated in York South.[10] Momentarily interrupted by the election of 1972, the Liberal Party's conservative streak returned, and we found ourselves back in the political wilderness.

---

**Frances Abele:** Your speeches and writing from this period suggest that you viewed social democracy as redistributive but also transformative. As an MP, you were making the case for particular interventions or policies in specific areas, but the larger theme is the need for a much wider renovation of the relationship between the economy and the state — the public sector ultimately taking on a more significant role in the economy.

**Ed Broadbent:** I have an Orwellian skepticism about the state being viewed as any kind of panacea. But I also believe it has a critical role to play and that its scope has been far too limited in liberal democracies, particularly when it comes to economic matters. That applies in both the senses you mentioned. Through progressive taxation and the provision of social needs in the form of government programs, the state can play a significant role in redistributing wealth — which in turn can transform both the market and the various areas of life outside of it. That was the social democratic project in the decades after the war: to modify the liberal capitalist structure that had been so inadequate during the Great Depression and put something better in its place. Progressive taxation was obviously one of the key modifications, as were socialized medicine, pensions, unemployment insurance, and the other innovations of the welfare state. Those changes were all hugely important, and there can be no doubt that they significantly improved the average person's quality of life.

However, it was becoming evident toward the end of the 1960s that the liberal welfare state model also had some significant deficiencies and limitations. One of those was the persistent and increasingly multinational character of corporate power — which was particularly relevant in Canada because of the extent of foreign ownership in the economy. Beyond that, there were a series of ongoing market failures that were still going unaddressed by the state. Among the first critic portfolios I was given after becoming an MP was housing, and it was immediately clear that there was an abysmal lack of affordable supply. Along with the tax system and persistent unemployment, the shortage of affordable housing was contributing further to poverty and inequality between people and regions.

In all of these areas, the Trudeau government was either content with the status quo or actively sought to move in a more regressive direction — especially after growth began to slow down and inflation started to rise. My argument was that we instead needed greater redistribution and also a broader transformation of the state's relationship to the economy.

**Jonathan Sas:** Perhaps we can talk about each of those areas in turn. During your first run in Oshawa, you partly campaigned on housing issues and became immersed in them as the NDP's housing critic. How did the critique you just described apply there?

**EB:** Housing was (and remains to this day) an absolutely textbook case of market failure, at least if we're beginning from the premise that the purpose of any economic model is to meet the majority's needs. There were, in my view, two basic and related problems. First, housing was being used by governments as a tool to stabilize the Canadian economy and manage the cycle of boom and bust. So, if a government wanted to be stimulative or create jobs, it would loosen the fiscal strings to invest in new housing and encourage the CMHC to become more active. In the inverse — as frequently happened throughout my years in Parliament — if it wanted to be deflationary, it would try to discourage construction. An instrumental approach like that is completely independent of the actual need for housing at a given time. No reasonable person would ever argue that the construction of schools (to take one example) should be determined by its inflationary or deflationary impact on the economy, and it makes no more sense to apply that logic to something as indispensable to human wellbeing as housing.

The second problem was the overwhelming reliance on profit-based incentives for financing. Around the time I was first elected, there was a broader legislative push underway to increase the involvement of market forces in housing. In 1967, for example, the Liberals freed up the bank rate for mortgages which had until then been fixed at 6 percent. Two years later, on the recommendation of minister Paul Hellyer, they similarly released the lending rate under the National Housing Act (NHA) so that it would be set by the market instead. When Ronald Basford, who was minister of state for Urban Affairs, introduced the Residential Mortgage Financing Act, he quite specifically said that its guiding principle was to "enhance the attractiveness of mortgage investment."[11] The result was that during the first five years of the Trudeau government, moderately priced housing virtually disappeared from the private market. That was obviously good for investors and speculators who made more money building more expensive housing. But it was catastrophic for low-income families who needed homes. This was the logical extension of treating housing principally as a financial asset or economic instrument rather than as a means to meet a basic human need. Housing should never be treated as a mere commodity.

In 1972, after the minority government was sworn in, we were able to work with Basford and prod him toward some positive measures including new emphasis on co-op housing. In Oshawa alone, there must have been five or six significant co-op projects with units for both low- and middle-income tenants that went up. This occurred right across the country. Unfortunately, the co-op emphasis, as well as funding for social housing and low-interest mortgage rates to ensure housing for low- and middle-income families would be available, would come to an end in the 1990s. The Mulroney government's 1993 budget eliminated federal funding for all new social housing (with the exception of on-reserve housing).

As a housing critic, I had proposed several potential solutions, all of which involved treating housing as a basic right as opposed to a fiscal instrument or investment vehicle. Key to that was isolating mortgages from other interest rates by placing certain requirements on banks in a manner that guaranteed low-interest-rate mortgages as part of their annual investment. The lower-than-market-rate mortgages would be allocated based on family income, going exclusively to those of low and moderate means. When the Liberals announced their intention to table a budget in the spring of 1974, in fact, one of the NDP's (ultimately rejected) conditions for continued support was the introduction of a subsidized NHA mortgage rate of 6 percent (others included an increase in the corporate tax rate and a new pricing system for commodities like oil, gas, and lumber).

**Luke Savage:** The issue of taxation is worth discussing in relation to this Parliament because Lewis's campaign against "corporate welfare bums" struck a chord during the 1972 federal election — and because the Liberals rejected the NDP's demand for an increase in corporate taxes in 1974. Taxation was a populist electoral issue, but it also touched on so many of the other debates that were happening because it was ultimately about how the state was going to respond to questions around inequality, unemployment, and inflation. One approach, which the Liberals tried, was to cut certain taxes with the view that it would have a stimulative effect: give companies tax concessions and (or so the argument goes) they'll invest the extra money in a way that will produce jobs or be otherwise economically constructive. The left's rejoinder to that idea has been that it won't have the stated impact, but also that conceiving of tax policy in that way inevitably increases inequality. Taxation is a primal political issue because it touches on so much else. Could you describe the contours of this debate during your early years in Parliament?

**EB:** Toward the end of the Diefenbaker years, there was a Royal Commission on Taxation chaired by Kenneth Carter. When it reported in 1966, some of the recommendations were quite progressive. After the Liberals formed government, they tabled a

White Paper that suggested certain changes to the tax system. The way that document was received by conservatives and business interests contributed, I think, to the impression it was a radical document. A leading Conservative from Alberta named Eldon Woolliams, for example, denounced it as a "Red Paper" (i.e., a communist proposal). I think Trudeau and Benson were inclined to accept that because they wanted to be seen as Robin Hood–like reformers who were taking from the rich and giving to the poor.

That kind of posturing was part and parcel of how the rhetoric of the Trudeau era — about a just society and so on — had the effect of obfuscating reality. When you look closely at what was actually being done throughout that period, on taxation and much else, you could see the language was intended to give ordinary people the impression there was some kind of serious reform effort underway. In fact, there was a consolidation of the basic class structure of Canada under Trudeau and in particular of the unequal distribution of income and wealth.

Without getting into the details of the White Paper, the essence of what was actually proposed was very moderate and was not intended to upend or significantly alter the ownership of wealth, though the Liberals were certainly very keen to give people that impression. While they recommended a new capital gains tax, they also introduced a series of income tax exemptions that benefited the rich. They took with one hand and gave back with another. These changes did not address indirect taxation, which at that time made up over half of all tax revenues. Such taxes are regressive by nature because everyone pays the same property or sales taxes regardless of how much they earn.

I believe there are four basic principles involved in a just and progressive tax system — all of which I advocated in response to the White Paper. The most rudimentary of those is that any system should be premised, first and foremost, on citizens' ability to pay. The Carter Commission proposed another concept that's related, which Carter called "a buck is a buck." The essence of that idea is that all income should be treated straightforwardly as income. There were, and still are, many kinds of loopholes that enable wealthy people to avoid paying their fair share of taxes, for example, on investment income. Such exemptions are not only unfair but they also undermine a third ingredient of any democratic tax system, which is redistribution. A market economy is always going to produce disparities of wealth and income, so taxation has to function as a major corrective to that imbalance.[12] (Walter Gordon's budget of 1965 had attempted to make the tax system more progressive. However, even this budget of moderate reform was attacked by Bay Street and the Liberal government capitulated.)

All of this inevitably raises deeper questions about what the state actually exists to do. That's why the other principle I advocated for had to do with how the revenues collected through taxation are actually used. If, as a society, we build public swimming pools, parks, and universities, then the average person will benefit from them just as much as the rich. If we remove pollution from our water and from the air; if we preserve and build livable cities; if we expand hospitals and fund medical research, then everyone benefits regardless of their income. By freeing people from the necessity to compete for everything they need, a society also frees them to contribute what they can. Every one of those public goods requires public investment, and the capital for that investment has to come from taxation.

Taxes were a significant issue for both ourselves and the Liberals throughout the electoral manoeuvring of the 1970s. But, notwithstanding that political dimension, I think the debate ultimately comes down to a more profound philosophical difference separating social democrats and liberals. Two decades later, Trudeau wrote an essay called "The Values of a Just Society," in which he dismissed the pursuit of equality as "adolescent" and argued instead that liberal capitalism creates "equality of opportunity" for all Canadians regardless of the economic region in which they lived or regardless of the language they spoke.[13] He held a kind of eighteenth-century liberal perspective that looked on the state as a neutral facilitator of individuals' private self-interests and little more. He also had a generally positive view of capitalism and thought that too much redistribution would undermine its productive potential.[14] He advocated means-testing of some social programs on those grounds when he first ran for the Liberal leadership and warned that we had to "put a damper on [the] revolution of rising expectations" in which people demanded more and more "free stuff."[15] There was an abundance of old anti-egalitarian liberal ideology at the heart of our policy disagreements.

**LS:** When you look into the kinds of things Trudeau was saying in those days, he seemed to see inflation as an almost spiritual problem and blamed it on this supposed culture of rising expectations. In 1972, for example, he remarked to a journalist:

> People are asking for more in every area, whether it be for welfare or for farmers, or for industrial workers, or for managers or entrepreneurs, health education, people want more. And I think this is a political reality that has overtaken most western societies. I think it came with the advent of television and mass communication; it's perhaps too much information of what the Joneses are doing and what we must do to live up to them. And this has caused the great inflationary push.[16]

I'm not sure how widely this aspect of Trudeau's thinking is remembered these days — perhaps because he's largely viewed as a progressive icon — but I wonder if you could comment on it a bit more in relation to the wider debate around inflation?

**EB:** There are several aspects to this that I think are worthy of comment. I respected Trudeau as a man and as a politician, but

I think it's disturbing that someone who had inherited millions of dollars was complaining that other people, wanting simply to improve their living standards, were the source of inflation. This demonstrated an insensitivity toward ordinary Canadians who were in a serious struggle to make ends meet.

I do think capitalism's inherent propensity to encourage endless consumption and engineer a feeling of permanent discontent is a problem for both ethical and ecological reasons, but I don't think that's what he was getting at. Trudeau didn't attribute the problem to our economic system or to the unequal distribution of income. Instead, he talked about personal demands arising from the impact of the media, the age of television, and even aspects of the welfare state. And I think he was seriously mistaken.

If we're actually interested in reducing that kind of artificially engineered demand for more stuff, the remedy is a more equal society in which people's basic needs are taken care of. Had Trudeau recognized the distinction between ordinary people wanting better lives and wealthy people protecting their investments, we could have had a very different debate. As Pickett and Wilkinson showed in their book *The Spirit Level: Why More Equal Societies Almost Always Do Better*, the greater equality there is in society, the less demand there is for more consumption.


**FA:** This also suggests that Trudeau thought inflation was the result of a demand for goods, which I think very few economists believe today. The inflation of the 1970s had more to do with rising fuel and other commodity prices, and the United States' monetary response to the recession.


**EB:** Yes, and his failure to recognize that came out later in the debate over wage and price controls — which he had campaigned against and then introduced in 1975. When I challenged him on the issue of growing corporate profits, his response was more or less that they were a sign of economic virility. But Trudeau felt the opposite way about higher wages, which were instead a policy problem to be managed.[17] He once berated some UAW workers in St. Thomas for their wage settlements, which he said were "screwing" the poor by causing inflation.[18] The fact is, when workers are organized, they *are* in a better position to weather inflation than others because they have more power to ensure their wages keep pace with the cost of living. All that means, from my point of view, is that more workers should be represented by unions. Instead of blaming unionized autoworkers for inflation, Trudeau should have taken steps to foster the expansion of unions in Canada.

**LS:** I suppose this brings us back to the issue of unemployment, because Trudeau, Benson, and Turner seemed to basically accept the view that a certain level was both necessary and acceptable to bring down inflation. How did that factor into all of this?

**EB:** It was during the Trudeau era that Canada began to shift away from something at least approaching full employment being the major economic priority of the government. Unemployment had been a huge concern after the Second World War, and many on both sides of the Atlantic thought there would be another depression in 1945 harkening back to the 1930s. Roosevelt's extensive reform program had significantly helped to bring down unemployment before the war economy eliminated it entirely. For that reason, and because the policies themselves were so overwhelmingly popular, aspects of that agenda, notably the Wagner Act — which opened the door for more unionization — were maintained afterwards. In 1944, the wartime government under Mackenzie King followed the U.S. example by amending the labour code to create a more favourable environment for unionization. King's government also embraced the idea of economic planning, creating the expectation that subsequent governments should maintain full employment as a key objective.

During Trudeau's first mandate, a certain level of unemployment came to be seen as acceptable — and the preoccupation of economic policy, especially under John Turner, became dealing with inflation with the explicit acknowledgement that it would lead to higher unemployment. (To this day, in fact, under the Bank Act, the mandate of the Bank of Canada is to deal with inflation but not employment. By comparison, the U.S. Federal Reserve, the American central bank, assigns a dual mandate to the Federal Reserve that includes the promotion of maximum sustainable employment.[19]) Successive NDP campaigns throughout this period mounted the alternative case for full employment. When Trudeau, after mocking Stanfield for suggesting them, finally brought in wage and price controls, we argued they would have the effect of controlling wages but not prices and that the economy would continue to hemorrhage jobs — which is exactly what happened. In spite of that failure, those years ultimately ushered in a new era of emphasis on controlling inflation, which has persisted to this day.

**JS:** There wasn't a coalition agreement or even a formal accord on matters of confidence between the NDP and Liberals after the 1972 federal election. Presumably, as caucus chair, you were closely involved in many of the day-to-day negotiations. How would you describe the dynamic? Was it generally collaborative or did it tend to be more adversarial?

**EB:** That Parliament was very challenging for the NDP caucus, and it was very demanding on David Lewis. In temperament, and in the best sense of the word, David was very aggressive: adeptly promoting alternative policies and engaging in philosophical debate. From day to day, we wouldn't be sure where the government might come down on a given issue and the extent to which we were collaborating was constantly in flux. Were we going to find agreement today, or was this an issue on which we should force a vote of confidence in the government?

On a case-by-case basis, I think it's often a matter of debate whether we were forcing the government's hand or merely shadow-boxing with them. There were clear instances in which I think the NDP and the Liberals together were really just implementing NDP policy. In other areas, I think the legislation that emerged was better than it would have been without us holding the balance of power — but it still fell short of what was actually needed: the bills concerned with foreign investment and foreign takeovers being one example, as well as the measures I mentioned related to co-op housing.

Another was the changes to the financing of elections contained in the Election Expenses Act. There had been a series of minority governments, which also meant more frequent elections. Elections, in turn, had become much more costly for parties to fund because television advertising was becoming so important. Given all of that, it's quite possible there would have been campaign finance legislation of some kind passed in that Parliament even if the Liberals had a majority. But the NDP's position certainly played a role in shaping the legislation so, for example, that the spending limits benefited new and smaller parties.


**JS:** The Liberals agreeing to establish Petro-Canada seems like a pretty clear case of the government passing NDP legislation less because they wanted to and more because it was the price of remaining in power.


**EB:** Yes, Petro-Canada is an interesting case. There was, as I've said, a nationalist sentiment during this time that pervaded the political culture. Alastair Gillespie and Herb Gray, for example, were sympathetic to economic nationalism. After Walter Gordon left politics, he teamed up with other Canadian nationalists to found the Committee for an Independent Canada.* Prior to the '72 Parliament, the Liberals had established the Canada Development Corporation and the Foreign Investment Review Agency in response to growing concerns about foreign ownership, so that kind of thing was certainly in the air.

Having said that, I know from my own involvement that the creation of Petro-Canada was an instance in which we compelled the government to do something it would categorically not have done otherwise — at least at that time. As caucus chair, I visited Minister Gillespie and told him we would withdraw confidence unless the demand for the creation of Petro-Canada was met. Our view was that a publicly owned Crown corporation in the petroleum sector would help bring down energy costs and provide a window into the industry. But the implications went well beyond that. Many of us in the NDP saw Petro-Canada as the first step in getting control of the whole energy sector and being able to shape our own economic destiny. A number of Liberal cabinet ministers were even thought to favour a greatly expanded role for Petro-Canada. It was rumoured, for example, that Governor General Romeo Leblanc favoured a public takeover of the whole sector.

Some years later, on the invitation of finance minister Mark Lalonde, I received a briefing about the company from a very able public servant named Ed Clark. He put to me that it would be better for Petro-Canada to face competition of some kind and not assume full control over the energy sector because a mixed model including a competitive component would be more efficient. That question notwithstanding, our thinking was that with the ability to set everything from environmental to investment policies, we would be able to create a more sophisticated and

---

* The founders of the CIC were Gordon, Abraham Rotstein, Peter Newman, and Max Saltsman. Claude Ryan and Jack McClelland were the founding co-chairs.

refinement-based energy sector — which would have represented a significant improvement for workers as well as consumers.

For my part, I was also interested in how the concept of worker participation might be applied. I used to point out, for example, that employees of Canadian National (CN) had no more rights overall than those at the privately owned Canadian Pacific (CP). This is why I thought Petro-Canada would be a good opportunity to put workers on boards and get them involved in the overall running of the company. Just because something is in the state sector doesn't mean it's going to be any more institutionally democratic or even socially beneficial than a market version of the same thing. But it should be, and I think that any social democratic government interested in pursuing public ownership needs to make it a priority.

For example, starting about the same time, Norway began to take control of its energy sector in stages, establishing a state-owned corporation with employee-elected board members (today's Statoil) and a sovereign wealth fund partly financed through oil revenues.* We had similar ambitions with Petro-Canada. However, over the following decade or so, both the Liberals and the Conservatives gradually dismantled it. I think that only adds to the argument that Petro-Canada represented a real project for the NDP and was looked on — like so much else in that Parliament — as more of an irritating necessity by the government that actually brought it into being.

**LS:** In the video documentary adaptation of Pierre Trudeau's memoirs there's a short clip of the two of you sitting in the House of Commons and talking about the legislation that emerged from

---

* Today Statoil and other publicly owned corporations dominate the Norwegian energy sector. The sovereign wealth fund reached $1 trillion a few years ago, the equivalent of about $192,000 U.S. dollars for every Norwegian citizen. See: "Norway's Social Wealth Fund Grows to $1 Trillion," *The People's Policy Project*. https://www.peoplespolicyproject.org/2017/08/23/norways-social-wealth-fund-grows-to-1-trillion/.

the 1972–74 minority Parliament.[20] You argue that "if it hadn't been for the NDP's presence, and the necessity of building a centre-left coalition as opposed to a different one" those things wouldn't have materialized. Trudeau replies, "You have no argument from me. I was not unhappy that I was given a political reason to do what very often my ideology wanted to do. I was on the left of the Liberal Party, and now I had a good argument: 'Geez, if we don't get the NDP with us we won't be the government anymore.'" In Trudeau's telling of the '72 Parliament, the NDP's presence helped him move where he personally wanted to go. What do you make of that?

**EB:** There's a funny story there, because the clip that appears in the film cut out my own rejoinder to that. Trudeau had said that this was the period he enjoyed most as prime minister. I asked why, if he'd enjoyed it so much, had he deliberately introduced a budget in 1974 that he knew we would vote down. His reply was just, "Well, that's realpolitik." And I think the Liberals' direction of travel after 1974, especially on economic issues, belies his characterization that the progressive course was actually his preferred one.

**JS:** There were of course other developments in the 1970s. One of the really significant NDP victories, in 1972, was Dave Barrett's win in British Columbia. That government was radical and ambitious, and elements of its program — including the public takeover of auto insurance — proved so popular that even many of the subsequent Social Credit and Liberal governments haven't dared touch them. What was your overall impression of Barrett?

**EB:** He was by far the most populist premier, and on a personal level he was easily the funniest. People on the left are sometimes seen as a bit dour and humourless, but that was never true of

Barrett, who could match Tommy Douglas's ability to pepper a speech with so many jokes and amusing anecdotes that people would often come away feeling great about being a New Democrat while mostly forgetting what the subject matter had been.

Not long before the 1972 provincial election, Lucille and I along with our son Paul had dinner with Dave and his wife, Shirley, at a restaurant on Grouse Mountain. At one point, he got up to do something and, turning to the table, asked, "Is there anything I can get you?" Paul, who was about eight at the time, replied that he would like some Chiclets. When Dave came back to sit down again and was asked to deliver the goods, he responded: "Look, young man, there is probably going to be an election called tomorrow, and if we win, I'll send you a whole crate!" Sure enough, when the BC NDP won a month later, we were back in Ottawa and my son asked, "Did Mr. Barrett win? . . . He owes me some Chiclets." Paul never did get his Chiclets, so Barrett began his premiership with his only broken political promise. Anyway, he was a likeable guy who was happy to kid around like that with a child. But as a politician, he was extremely tough and committed to live up to his promises.

**LS:** I want to ask about Barrett's populist style, which seems to have been an extension of ideology but also of personal temperament. He's said to have asked his cabinet at their first meeting, "Are we here for a good time or for a long time?" and the government's approach was to be as maximalist and unrestrained as it could — even if that meant the NDP was more likely to lose reelection. What do you think about that way of doing things? It strikes me that people in the average NDP provincial government feel they're lucky to be in power at all and often end up being cautious and preoccupied with respectability as a result — whereas Dave Barrett was incredibly aggressive in pursuit of his agenda and steadfast in his commitment to a more populist style in a way that presumably made him a lot of enemies.

**EB:** My own leadership style was certainly very different from Barrett's at the rhetorical level, but I shared his belief that you needed to put emotional heat behind the policy and not be purely cerebral. He was indeed very distinctive, but I think different NDP leaders have tended to reflect their provinces. If you look at people like Howard Pawley or Ed Schreyer, for example, they came from a very different political atmosphere in Manitoba. There was greater room for populist rhetoric in BC than there was in Manitoba. I had lunch with Schreyer when I first arrived in the House of Commons and came away very concerned by his conservatism on social issues. Back in Manitoba, though, he wasn't generally perceived as cautious. To a very real extent, I think the political context a leader comes from shapes the degree to which they're forceful or populist in their presentation, and that style isn't always totally interwoven with ideology. Tommy Douglas was outwardly more of a populist than Pawley or Schreyer, but he was also careful about policy implementation. He first formed a government in 1944 and did not bring in medicare until the 1960s when he judged the province was ready for it. In leadership, there's always a complicated interplay of policy, personal style, local circumstances, and ideology.

**FA:** Another important leader from this time was Robert Stanfield, whom I understand you admired. He obviously wasn't a New Democrat, but he was a very significant figure in federal politics during these years.

**EB:** Yes, I admired Stanfield and wish I had gotten to know him better. He was an immensely intelligent guy, which I suspect is something most Canadians don't know. Like Trudeau, he studied at Harvard but — unlike Trudeau — he actually completed his degree. (Jacques Parizeau once quipped that "Trudeau never completed a degree anywhere he went: the Sorbonne, LSE, or

Harvard!") Stanfield was a modest person and he really didn't care about seeming impressive, which I think was part of his problem politically. He once said something along those lines himself when someone asked him why he did not succeed as a leader (though I'm sure they put it more diplomatically than that). He answered, in effect, that he didn't want power enough, and I think there's some truth in that.

He'd come out of an authentic Red Tory tradition in Nova Scotia and, during his time as premier, the state was actually quite active in many aspects of the Nova Scotian economy. Just before the '68 election, he succeeded Diefenbaker as Progressive Conservative leader and everybody thought he was going to become prime minister. Then the Liberals elected Pierre Trudeau and Trudeaumania happened instead. Stanfield learned the hard way that timing is crucial in political life.

Something else about Stanfield that didn't come through in his public demeanour was his wry sense of humour. At the parliamentary press gallery dinner following the '68 election, for example, I remember him saying that if he'd had a meeting in Hamilton and walked across Lake Ontario to go to another meeting in downtown Toronto, the headline in the *Toronto Star* the next day would have been "STANFIELD CAN'T SWIM." True enough! Stanfield was by far the most humorous speaker at the parliamentary gallery dinners.

**LS:** I suspect that the biggest thing many people now associate with Stanfield is that famous photo of him fumbling the football in 1974 — an image now frequently cited as an example of how mass media and spectacle have trivialized democratic politics.

**EB:** Yes, I mean the irony is he had already caught the football two or three times! Of course, the press waited for him to drop it, and that was the picture they ran with so that's what he became known for. He was a slow speaker and had none of the flash of Trudeau, though he was every bit as intelligent. I really never got to know him as well as I would have liked to. When I retired, he had a dinner in my honour at his home. In addition to a number of my personal friends, there were Red Tories like Flora MacDonald and David MacDonald in attendance. It was a very thoughtful thing for him to do and, notwithstanding the ideological differences that existed between us, it was characteristic of his decency as a man. One of the last times I saw him was right after the 1993 election, when the Progressive Conservatives were left with only two lonely MPs. I ran into him on Elgin Street in Ottawa and expressed my sympathy. He looked me in the eye and said, "Oh Ed, it got rid of a lot of riffraff." I laughed all the way home.

**JS:** It wasn't an electoral disaster on anything like that scale, but what do you think went wrong for the NDP in 1974? The conventional wisdom, at least within NDP circles, is usually that the Liberals passed a whole bunch of popular measures under pressure and in turn got the credit.

**EB:** I think that's very much the accepted view, and it certainly played a role. It's not just the New Democrats who think that either. Tom Axworthy, a longtime confidante of Trudeau, wrote not long ago of that Parliament that "the more progressive the Trudeau government became in social policy on Lewis's urging, the more popular it became with voters. No longer could Trudeau be painted as a conservative clone."[21] I think this is in some ways just a built-in problem of minority government if you're the smaller party: the people who are actually in power tend to get the credit regardless of what they personally wanted (or didn't want) to do. That made the 1974 result both politically frustrating and tragic because David Lewis had fought so hard and done so much to maximize our position after 1972 and pry as much progressive legislation from the Liberals as he could.

**FA:** When Lewis lost his seat in 1974, the NDP caucus appointed you interim leader. In his history of the party, Desmond Morton wrote: "To Broadbent, the central problem of the NDP was its provincial orientation, between federal elections a national organization barely existed. The Federal HQ was dependent on contributions often far in arrears from provincial sections." It's at this point an obscure bit of history, but I understand you introduced a proposal at the 1974 NDP Federal Council meeting in Halifax to create some kind of central treasury, which the delegates ultimately rejected?

**EB:** What Morton says is absolutely true. In those days, the financial power of the party rested entirely with provincial memberships and the federal party was always playing second fiddle to the provinces. There was an agreement, renegotiated periodically, that a portion of what was collected by provincial parties from members would go to the federal party, which meant that we were dependent upon their fundraising and memberships. The NDP didn't exist as an independent federal entity, which was not a desirable situation for a national political party. Appealing to the new and more generous election financing laws we had just helped push through the minority Parliament, I fought an unsuccessful battle to give the federal party some structure and a more dependable financial base. All I ultimately managed to get was a higher percentage of funds and some access to provincial membership lists for fundraising purposes under certain conditions.

In general, I had a disagreeable experience as interim leader. Lucille and I had a young family and the demands on my time were draining. The job came with little real power, which made the task of negotiating between the different sections of the party quite difficult. The whole party, from the staff and MPs to the rank-and-file activists, was demoralized by our result in 1974. After all of the victories in that Parliament and provincial NDP wins across the country, things felt rather bleak.

**LS:** Insofar as either the Canadian public or just New Democrats remember it, I think the 1972–74 Parliament has occasionally been mythologized in a way that's counterproductive. For some, there seems to be a view that the role of a left party in Parliament is to goad the Liberals into doing things and keep them honest rather than to actively seek power in order to implement a comprehensively different sort of agenda. What do you think about that? It's been my experience that the 1972 minority Parliament, and perhaps the minority period that spanned the Lester Pearson years as well, are often cited by people who view the role of Canada's parliamentary left in those rather conservative terms.

**EB:** There are two aspects to that. I think it's true that a number of Canadians outside the NDP have come to believe that being the "conscience of Parliament" is a useful role for it to play, and they can point to examples like the 1972 minority Parliament. But my experience, by and large, was that the closer we got to political power, the more we could see how to use it for good. In those two short years, we really managed to advance our agenda. That gave us all the more reason to think that, if we won an election outright and governed independently of the Liberals, we could do so much more for Canadians. The real electoral task, as Tommy Douglas knew very well, was to win.

## CHAPTER FOUR

# The Rights Revolution

*"Social integration spread from the sphere of sentiment and patriotism into that of material enjoyment. The components of a civilized and cultured life, formerly the monopoly of the few, were brought progressively within reach of the many, who were encouraged thereby to stretch out their hands towards those that still eluded their grasp. The diminution of inequality strengthened the demand for its abolition, at least with regard to the essentials of social welfare."*

— T.H. MARSHALL, *Citizenship and Social Class*

*"I believe that even though the concepts of feminism may be radical, and even threatening at first to those who have not fully understood them, there is an integral connection between feminism and socialism . . . That is why we must insist on equal pay for equal work of value, and on an end to laws and practices which discriminate against women. That is why we must protect with all our strength the attack on Dr. Morgentaler, whose only crime was to provide women with medically safe abortions."*

— ROSEMARY BROWN, speech to 1975
NDP leadership convention

T he first political demonstration I ever attended was not actually in Canada. In the summer of 1964, my first wife, Yvonne, and I were holidaying in Maine. Amidst the growing momentum of the civil rights movement, we decided to head down to the Democratic National Convention in Atlantic City to join the protests outside the convention centre. This was a moment of intense political ferment, of radical possibility but also of great peril. The Civil Rights Act had passed Congress only weeks before. Earlier that summer, three activists had been abducted and murdered in Mississippi, and a coalition of civil rights organizations based there had organized a massive Black voting drive called the Freedom Summer. A delegation had marched all the way from Mississippi to protest the fact that the DNC's entire delegation from that state was white. I've never forgotten the faces I saw that day, or the courage of the older Black activists I witnessed in the crowd. That week was also the first time I heard people singing "We Shall Overcome," to this day an anthem to those fighting injustice and oppression.

It was the activism of African Americans, and the writing of James Baldwin, that drew my attention to broader issues of systemic racism. At this early stage, I knew more about the history, conditions, and aspirations of Black people in America than I did about Black and Indigenous people in my own country — although I was soon to begin learning about Canadian circumstances.

It can be misleading, of course, to assign excessive weight or significance to particular moments, memories, or people when accounting for the evolution of one's politics. In this, however, certain personalities — family, friends, colleagues, and activists — stand out for their outstretched influence. My socialist instincts, I can say with certainty, came directly from my mother. She possessed an intuitive egalitarian streak and an open and generous disposition. She was empathetic and loving throughout my formative years. She encouraged, by example, not only an acceptance of difference but a welcoming of it. Well before the feminist movement had really taken off, she was a strong presence in my life. I remember fondly and with respect that she was instrumental in changing the Boys Club across the street from my home to the Boys & Girls

Club. Later, when I was at the University of Toronto, I appreciated the warmth with which she welcomed international students into our home.

Another early memory comes to mind. One of my first encounters with gender injustice came during my high school days in Oshawa. Two especially bright female classmates had good grades and wanted to go to university, but their father didn't believe young women needed a university education, and they were more or less prohibited from going (I believe they ended up working in a bakery he owned instead). Here I was, excitedly on the cusp of attending the University of Toronto, and they were both being held back. This struck me as deeply unfair.

University life expanded my political horizons. As an undergraduate, one of the co-ops I lived in included students from the Caribbean and India who vividly discussed the brutality of British imperialism as well as Hungarian refugees from the Soviet oppression after 1956. Later, while at the London School of Economics, I attended an unforgettable lecture by the historian Eric Williams, who was soon to become the first prime minister of Trinidad and Tobago. Speaking to a packed hall, in an extraordinarily powerful address, he used a metaphor to describe Britain's attitude toward the colonies that has stayed with me to this day: "They take an orange, and they squeeze and squeeze and squeeze. When there's no life left in it, they throw it away."

The year 1974 saw two of the most influential politicians in my life leave public office: West German chancellor Willy Brandt, whom I'd go on to work closely with at the Socialist International, resigned after a close aide was revealed, devastatingly, to be an East German spy. And in my own party, the extraordinary David Lewis — one of the most important figures in the formation of the NDP and a pivotal influence on me — stepped down. These departures, imperceptible to me at the time, coincided with a historical turning point. It was to be the end of the postwar boom in the West — the Golden Era of capitalism that had consolidated a significant cross-political consensus in support of an expanding roster of social programs and public responsibility for full employment.

70

Having lived through the Great Depression of the 1930s and its political consequences, leaders across the political spectrum had come to believe that laissez-faire capitalism required balancing by a strong state. As a result, guarantees to health, housing, pensions, and employment became touchstones of democratic citizenship. Even as the economic turbulence of the 1970s increasingly threatened these rights, three decades of expanding equality had left an important sediment. It is my strong conviction that the growing social equality of the Golden Era, experienced in the daily lives of millions of people, helped generate a greater tolerance and generosity of spirit — fertile ground for the expansion of rights-based representative democracy.

Sadly, a common experience for many women and people of colour was one of prejudice and disadvantage. The demographics of Canada in the late 1960s and early 1970s were drastically different than they are today. Canada was then an overwhelmingly white country, still predominantly made up of those of British and French origin. While the Trudeau government had ushered in its official multiculturalism policy in 1971, Canadians of European origin still accounted for 96 percent of the 21.5 million people in the total population that year. In 1971, there were only 35,000 Canadians who identified as African or Black in the census, a number that would grow to 250,000 by 1991. Similarly, the population of those who identified as Asian grew from just 121,000 in 1971 to 1.6 million in 1991. These demographic shifts were principally due to changes in immigration policy. While Canada's overtly racist immigration laws had undergone some changes in the 1960s, the Immigration Act of 1976 opened up our borders substantially to non-white immigrants and set the stage for the much more diverse population we have today.

Meanwhile, massive shifts were also taking place in the workforce. Women's labour force participation, for example, grew from just 39 percent in 1968, when I entered the House of Commons, to 75 percent when I left — a shift that had profound implications for the lives of Canadian women and the political power of feminist organizing.

Over the course of several decades, powerful social movements would transform the struggle for equality and shake up the entire political landscape by exposing the shortcomings of liberal democracy and advancing their demands for the recognition and expansion of rights. In Canada, for example, the newly formed National Action Committee on the Status of Women (NAC) was fighting to see the recommendations from the 1970 Royal Commission on the Status of Women implemented. These currents had a major impact on the NDP, as NDP women were active in the party, and also prominent in NAC and the wider women's movement. At the 1973 NDP Convention in Vancouver, feminist activists were determined to shape party policy. They overcame some resistance and hesitancy in the party ranks. Delegates voted for the NDP to hold its own national women's conference the following year. In July 1974, that conference endorsed a decidedly feminist policy agenda. One result was the appointment of a women's organizer, Judy Wasylycia-Leis, who also later served as my executive assistant. Judy went on to a distinguished career in the federal and Manitoba legislatures, where she served in Cabinet and as a new mother, broke ground by breastfeeding at work. In common with many other NDP women — Margaret Mitchell, Muriel Smith, Grace MacInnes, Pauline Jewett, Mary Humphrey, and others — she led by advocacy and example. As a result of their work and that of allied men in the party, reproductive rights, equal pay, and action on violence against women were henceforth central to what the NDP stood for. The women's liberation movement, of course, was part of a broader constellation of social forces at that time challenging the status quo. The peace movement, the gay and lesbian rights struggle, the fight for racial equality — and in Canada, the mobilizations to assert Indigenous rights — would come to shape my worldview. Initially, I had mostly restricted my work to issues of class, workers' rights, and combating the marketization of life. (A key plank of my 1975 leadership campaign, for example, was that *the* socialist issue of our time was the need to break corporate power.) Due to the organizing and mobilization efforts of rights-driven activists through the 1970s and 1980s, my thinking broadened. I came to understand that the issues they were raising, like those of class inequality, constituted practical problems that could be best addressed by democratic socialist solutions.

It was during my time as party leader that I clarified and refined my conception of rights in a democratic society as I responded to social movements within and outside the party. I would come to advocate for a more expansive vision, particularly when it came to cultural and group rights. Imaginative and responsive, our caucus played an important role in bringing the demands of social movements into the House of Commons, into election debates, and into policy and law.

---

**Luke Savage:** Your political life has been animated by a strong critique of class- and market-based inequalities. But, beginning in the 1960s, there was a growing awareness on the left that such a critique had limitations on its own. When did you begin to think seriously about what might be called group or collective social rights, and how did that thinking evolve as an MP, NDP leader, and beyond?

**Ed Broadbent:** This is an important discussion, and it has profound implications for how the NDP reacted to social movements pushing for their rights during my leadership. Moreover, it was ultimately formative in how we were able to help shape the Constitution Act of 1982.[*] Small-l liberalism — which is to say, the ideology as opposed to the party label with a capital L — came to be expressed in the 1980s by people like Margaret Thatcher and Ronald Reagan. But a version of it was also championed by Pierre Trudeau, notably in the now-infamous 1969 White Paper, which proposed to make the assimilation of First Nations the official policy of the Canadian government. As I've remarked already, Trudeau espoused an individualist, eighteenth-century liberalism. He always rejected the notion of cultural, social, and economic rights as *rights*. I would argue that conservatives and liberals have tended to embrace these rights not as rights, but as aspirations. They see them in purely political and civil terms, extending to the economic sphere only insofar as it implies the right to own property or participate in the marketplace. I would

---

[*]    See Chapter Seven: The Great Patriation Debate.

argue that the CCF/NDP have often been more serious and committed defenders of individual rights than either the Liberals or the Conservatives. Both the internment of Japanese Canadians during the Second World War and the War Measures Act come to mind.

It was a Canadian social democrat — John Humphrey, a professor of law at McGill University — who first drew together the amalgam of secular and religious values that subsequently emerged in 1948 as the Universal Declaration of Human Rights. Taken along with its companions, the Covenant on Economic Social and Cultural Rights and the Covenant on Civil and Political Rights, the result constituted a deeply social democratic global objective. Social democrats see social and economic rights — access to decent employment, healthcare, education, pensions, food, a union, among other things — as rights of citizenship: that is, as rights as important for human development as civil and political rights like freedom of association and freedom of speech. In the daily lives of many people, I would argue that those are what make political and civil rights real and accessible to begin with. It's in the same vein, I think, that social democracy has extended its analysis of inequality into the domain of broader cultural and group rights — including Indigenous rights, linguistic rights, and others that find their origin in the fulfillment of particular groups. Put another way, social democrats ultimately view group rights as necessary antecedents of many civil rights that are essential for individual freedom. People can only realize their political and civil rights within a social context, which ultimately implies the need for recognition of particular groups and the context-specific struggles they face or have faced.

Social democrats support both the rights that underpin an equal claim to a life of dignity and the social context to support the full development and flourishing of human beings in a democratic society. For Quebeckers, this flourishing may reasonably include French cultural institutions and access to other communal experiences in the French language. For an Indigenous person, the ability to live off their land, speak their language, and practice their culture. For women, it could include interventions that target sex-based discrimination that serve as barriers in their day-to-day lives.

**Frances Abele:** That is an important philosophical point. Can you speak a little more about the actual political struggles that came to shape your ideas?

**EB:** I've always reacted strongly in my social democratic core to class issues. This was much more than simply intellectual engagement. I think it was a product of growing up in an industrial town like Oshawa. On feminist issues, however, it was really more on-the-job training for me. I was taught a great deal by women in the NDP like Grace MacInnis, Pauline Jewett, Margaret Mitchell, Alexa McDonough, Judy Wasylycia-Leis, and Rosemary Brown to name a few. Demands from the women's movement while I was leader — for pay equity, child care, anti-harassment protection — became understandable not just as matters of class but also as critiques of the status quo power arrangement between men and women. Identifying such injustices in government institutions and policies, and then rectifying them through affirmative action in hiring and other measures — this kind of analysis of power was something I came to understand and promote.

I'd like to pause here and reflect on how different things were when I entered politics. A year before I was elected in Oshawa, I attended the NDP convention in Toronto. One of the resolutions that was being debated concerned putting an end to an existing law under the Criminal Code of Canada that permitted a married man to rape his wife. It was still, by law, a conjugal obligation of women to submit themselves to the desires of men. This was on the heels of a 1964 amendment to the Civil Code of Quebec that granted married women legal autonomy from their husbands, a result of feminist agitation during the Quiet Revolution. That's just a small sample of the institutionalized inequality that prevailed only fifty years ago. As Simone de Beauvoir said, women were indeed the second sex, subordinate to men in so many ways.

In 1967, NDP MP Grace MacInnis introduced the first abortion reform bill in the House. This was two years before the limited and inadequate liberalizations that Pierre Trudeau as justice minister would usher in. Trudeau's law stipulated that abortions could only be performed in a hospital if a committee of doctors determined a mother's life was in danger. Support for a women's right to choose was NDP policy before I joined and something I was supportive of from the beginning. But even within the NDP, the right to abortion remained contested.

**FA:** An early political encounter with women struggling for equal rights must have been getting to know Bev McCloskey, Maurie Shorten, and other women in the UAW Local 222 in Oshawa. With the support of Oshawa MPP Cliff Pilkey, they led a successful campaign to have a prohibition against discrimination on the basis of sex added to the Ontario Human Rights Code. For these women, the amendment meant that the union and General Motors were finally forced to remove gender discrimination from their contracts so that women were able to work anywhere in the plant for equal pay.

**EB:** I'm glad you raised this. I have immense respect and affection for the remarkable Bev McCloskey and Maurie Shorten. These women, and others in Local 222 who helped form the Women's Committee, took on the struggle for gender justice in the UAW. They were just ferocious and unyielding in getting rid of sex discrimination in union contracts. The UAW and General Motors had an unholy alliance classifying jobs by sex and preserving certain jobs as off-limits to women. The seniority rule, a cornerstone union principle, was being applied plant-wide within sex-based job categories — meaning men with less seniority could (and would) be hired back by GM before women.[1] And while these women had some allies, they faced a lot of resistance from their union brothers in trying to rectify this.

Their story ought to be made into a movie or documentary. It illustrates how feminist activism in the trade union movement promoted broader social progress. The Ontario Human Rights Code at the time outlawed discrimination on the basis of race, colour, creed, and national origin, but not on the basis of sex. Now, Bev and Maurie were also active members of the NDP. And they lobbied, organized, and convinced their local MPP Cliff Pilkey — a one-time Local 222 president — to present a bill at Queen's Park barring sex-based discrimination in employment. Bill 83, An Act to Prevent Discrimination in Employment because of Sex or Marital Status, became law leading to an amendment to the Human Rights Code in Ontario to include sex. I think it was Bev McCloskey who got the phone call from GM when they finally adhered to the new legislation and negotiated a contract without these discriminatory seniority rules.


**FA:** The rising women's movement in the late 1960s and early 1970s was multifaceted, and its currents washed through the New Democratic Party. The Abortion Caravan in 1970, when a group of feminist activists travelled across the country and came to Trudeau's doorstep with a coffin, comes to mind. The caravan, which grew into a broad protest in the thousands against discriminatory abortion laws, culminated in women chaining themselves to seats in the House of Commons.


**EB:** I remember the Abortion Caravan quite vividly. NDP MP Andrew Brewin was asking pointed questions in the House of Commons concerning federal restrictions on access to abortion the day the members of the Caravan chained themselves in the gallery. The Caravan had a major impact, dominating news coverage and ultimately keeping the heat on the Liberal government, helping to challenge its restrictive approach to abortion access. The work of the Caravan coincided with the courageous work of Dr. Morgentaler and others who were operating safe abortion clinics despite the criminalization and risks from, frankly, violent opposition amongst some citizens. Later, the NDP was instrumental in fighting for the inclusion of Sections 15 and 28 guaranteeing gender equality rights.* The landmark 1988 Supreme Court decision in R. v. Morgentaler ruled that the abortion provision in the Criminal Code was unconstitutional because it violated women's rights under Section 7 of the Charter. Together with NDP MP Dawn Black, who had been a leading voice on the national stage on abortion, I spoke at a celebratory rally on Parliament Hill after that case was decided.

**Jonathan Sas:** The feminist movement had a marked impact on the 1975 leadership contest. What stands out in your memory?

**EB:** Especially during my early years as leader, the feminist movement was growing across the country and was very strong in the party. The 1974 NDP women's convention came at a special historical moment — leading up as it did to the International Year of the Woman — and it had energized a lot of the membership. NDP women were also very active in organizations outside the party, organizations like the National Action Committee on the Status of Women, the Voice of Women, Wages for Housework, and others that were bringing feminism into mainstream political debate. Rosemary Brown, the first Black woman elected to a provincial legislature in Canada, decided to run, and her campaign created a lot of excitement. She ensured feminist issues were a key

---

\* See Chapter Seven: The Great Patriation Debate.

feature of the race, but I maintain it wasn't terrain of any profound philosophical disagreement between us and more a difference of emphasis.

In any case, I grew to have great respect for Rosemary and she ran a very strong second. I asked her to run for us federally just a few years later. Often, when I visited Vancouver, we would meet and talk about feminist politics and she would bring issues to my attention, such as getting women in more positions of power in the party, and of course getting more women to run in winnable seats. As I reflect back now, it strikes me how odd our interactions during the 1975 leadership were. Anyone who knows the history of political parties and leadership contests knows that this kind of collegial, amiable relationship is not typical.*

Intellectually and morally, I came to believe that any serious equality-seeking program necessitated feminist interventions, whether they be affirmative action in hiring, public support for child care, or the expansion of reproductive rights. In other words, these aims were, as feminists within the party insisted, part and parcel of a modern social democratic orientation.

**JS:** In addition to the women's movement, what were some of the other important flashpoints during your time as leader?

**EB:** The 1981 Toronto bathhouse raids, and the inspiring community pushback against "Operation Soap" by the Toronto police, come to mind. That was a turning point on the matter of gay rights. When I entered politics, there simply wasn't acceptance of open homosexuality. Gay men and women faced discrimination on our streets and in places of work. The bathhouse raids,

---

* Rosemary went on to sit in the British Columbia legislature until 1986, after which she taught at Simon Fraser University and finally became chief commissioner of the Ontario Human Rights Commission.

however, were so outrageous that gay people with the support of many others fought back, defending their rights. Within the NDP, Svend Robinson was a forceful and sometimes lone voice in our caucus on gay rights. Not only in the wake of the bathhouse raids, but throughout the AIDS epidemic, he brought the demands of the gay community forward. In 1988, Svend became the first openly gay MP in Canadian history.

**JS:** Feminist and gay rights activists were engaged in important struggles. So too were civil rights activists and anti-racist organizers. They faced a stubborn narrative of Canadian openness and tolerance as compared to the U.S. Black and Indigenous activists in Canada today talk about how the U.S. comparison helps distract from the racist foundations of Canada, whether it's colonization, residential schools, or the fact of slavery in early Upper and Lower Canada. James Baldwin's searing publication *The Fire Next Time* came out in 1963. That same year, novelist Austin Clarke wrote his own withering critique of anti-Black racism in Canada in *Maclean's* magazine.[2] There were voices exposing the Canadian reality, which could sometimes be overshadowed by an emphasis on what was going on in the United States.

**EB:** Yes, and I think it's telling that the piece by Clarke did not have the same impact in Canada that James Baldwin's work had in the U.S. Our preoccupation with the open violence in the United States partially obscured our seeing what the reality is in Canada, a dynamic that arguably persists to this day. My understanding, however, did begin to change late in the 1960s. In 1969, Black activists and their allies in Montreal, and students at Sir George Williams University, organized a large protest against racial discrimination. Five West Indian students believed they had been unfairly graded by one professor and that both the university and the professor had failed to respond to their complaints. As the protest unfolded, hundreds of students occupied a university building for thirteen days and Montreal became a locus of struggle for racial justice. As a new member of Parliament, I travelled to Montreal to meet the students. It was clear that racism was involved, something the University never conceded. The occupation ended in open conflict with police and the arrest of several student leaders.

We still live in a country where denial of racial inequity remains, where it occurred to the prime minister in his youth to parade about in blackface, where Black people are more likely to be unemployed or living in poverty and where they are many times more likely than other Canadians to suffer police violence.

**FA:** Your time as an MP and particularly as NDP leader also saw radical changes in Crown-Indigenous relations. Resistance to the White Paper remains a key reference point today for contemporary Indigenous movements, from Idle No More to LandBack.

**EB:** I was involved in responding to the aptly named White Paper. We as a caucus reacted very strongly in defence of Indigenous people, who we believed had special rights arising from the treaties and their original sovereignty. Even in this early period, I was advocating for the existence of Indigenous rights that were different from, and indeed preceded, the rights of settlers who came much later to this part of the world. I came to understand then that citizenship for Indigenous peoples in Canada was necessarily more layered. It required the exercise of rights to their language and culture linked as they are intrinsically to the land. But I must admit that it wasn't until the constitutional period leading up to 1982 that I got fully engaged on what was referred to then as Aboriginal rights issues. That was the first time that I really found myself grappling with the political reality of Crown land in Canada, and with an understanding of what was called the land question.

**FA:** Resistance to the White Paper was important, but there were other key moments of resistance to Crown policy along the way. The 1974–1977 Berger Inquiry into the Mackenzie Valley Pipeline — and the response of Dene, Métis, Inuvialuit, and other northerners to the inquiry — was formative for you and the NDP. That inquiry was a reckoning for how the left thought about the political economy of the country.

**EB:** That inquiry was very important in showing that the development philosophy of which that pipeline was a part was not only depriving Indigenous northerners of their land rights but was also handing those resources over to foreign control and benefit. Thomas Berger was also very helpful in both 1980 and 1982 as intellectual support for our position on Indigenous rights in the Charter battles. He had a major impact on the NDP — both on myself as leader but also earlier on BC members of the caucus. Berger played a significant role in the history of our country.

**JS:** We're having this discussion about Indigenous rights as the graves of children killed at Indian Residential Schools are still being uncovered around the country.

**EB:** I share the horror, but not surprise, over the discovery of these graves. And we will almost certainly uncover more. It's quite telling in terms of the politics of the period we're talking about that I was largely unaware of the Indian Residential Schools. What I now understand as cultural genocide was not a part of the constitutional debates. Certainly, what was going on in those schools was known by some politicians and officials, particularly those at the national level in what was then the Ministry of Indian Affairs. It was also known in some provincial governments. But it was not the prominent political issue that it has since become. The discussion of land rights at this almost completely abstract level was what took place between Trudeau and me and in the House of Commons. But the terrible lived experience of the kids in these schools was not, to my recollection, part of the debate — or something there was broad awareness of from politicians on either side of the rights issue.

**FA:** By part of the debate, do you mean making the connection between state policies like the Indian Residential Schools and the issue of dispossession?

**EB:** Yes, the theft of the land in one way or another by the settlers from Indigenous people, and related to that, the rights that had been there at one time and had since been abrogated, ignored, or denied. For thousands of years this country was theirs alone, until by violence, stealth, and the law, our ancestors managed to get control of their land. Those of us in the NDP who were working to advance the recognition of First Nation rights were largely referring to the historic treaties, but there was also an awareness of unceded land in British Columbia that had been denied by federal courts and needed to be recognized again.

It was a generation of people who had been through those schools who ultimately fought back for their land that ignited a nationwide movement for Indigenous rights. These terrible things had been done to them and their communities, but they were not defeated.

**LS:** We've been talking about group and cultural rights in relation to a number of different things, but one of the unique features of Canada is the complexity of its federal system. Was this a problem you confronted as leader in trying to advance Indigenous (or other) rights?

**EB:** Canadians are going to have to get accustomed to this fact: Indigenous peoples have rights to make decisions that are going to affect them and their land. Practically, I think this will mean the proliferation of regional agreements with nations as they self-determine and assume their jurisdiction. Some Indigenous nations will readily reach an agreement for certain kinds of resource development. Other nations right next door may not. We will have to accept that legal pluralism and the possibility of conflict: hopefully, of course, nonviolent conflict, and the kind that may be worked out in tribunals or new arrangements set up when we finally do the hard intellectual work of carving out real government and decision-making authority for Indigenous peoples. Canada is going to become more decentralized with the implementation of Indigenous rights. And I, for one, don't mind that if we handle it carefully and responsibly in a manner informed by respect for the cultural and social rights of all people in this country.

**JS:** We are living through a moment where a very shallow representative politics has supplanted more radical redistributive approaches to justice. But at the same time, we have to account for the fact that progress on many elements of rights-based citizenship occurred during the neoliberal era.

**EB:** Marriage equality, access to abortion, and many other important rights are vociferously defended by many neoliberals. Neoliberalism can incorporate a lot of rights, so long as the primacy of the market mechanism isn't threatened. I find this to be a wholly inadequate response to today's conditions. By this I don't mean to downplay the importance of identity politics. The battles today over trans rights, or barriers to abortion access, for example, matter immensely for freedom and equality. But it remains my firm belief that substantive equality still requires a fundamental change in the distribution of power and wealth in society along class lines. The task of social democracy must be to fiercely battle economic inequality and corporate power, but also go beyond that. In addition to redistributive policies, strong unions, and the provision of universal social and economic rights, we have to develop specific policies for women's rights, for the implementation of Indigenous rights, and to counter systemic discrimination against racial minorities — policies that shift power. And I'm proud that the NDP when I was leader took this position. We were offering a very different vision for the country than the Liberals and Conservatives.

**CHAPTER FIVE**

# Ordinary Canadians

*"The great enemy of clear language is insincerity. When there is a gap between one's real and one's declared aims, one turns as it were instinctively to long words and exhausted idioms, like a cuttlefish spurting out ink."*
— GEORGE ORWELL, *Politics and the English Language*

*"A dissident intellectual who philosophizes in his study about the fate and future of the world . . . has a different kind of freedom than a politician who moves among the complicated social realities of a particular time and place."*
— VÁCLAV HAVEL, *Summer Meditations*

*"To be a socialist . . . is to make an act of faith, of love even, toward this land. [Socialists must] sense the seed beneath the snow; to see, beneath the veneer of corruption and meanness and the commercialization of human relationships, men and women capable of controlling their own destinies."*
— MICHAEL HARRINGTON, *Fragments of the Century*

There is a tension at the heart of all leadership in democratic societies. Democratic leaders are expected to take risks and stake out new ground in important public debates. Doing so with legitimacy or effectiveness, on the other hand, necessarily means speaking to the aspirations and preferences of large numbers of people and persuading them to come along for the ride. "It's important to lead in politics," Tommy Douglas used to say, "but when you look over your shoulder you have to be sure there's someone behind you."

In the NDP, the basic challenges of leadership come with several layers of complexity. Like Canada's other two national parties, the NDP is an electoral organization that competes for votes and political power. By design, however, it is also a democratic movement committed to both profound social change and an ideology in constant tension with many of the ruling ideas in the society around it. When grafted onto Canada's already intricate federal structure, these unique qualities make leading the NDP a distinctly difficult task.

If I had not fully grasped this reality when I agreed to be interim leader after David Lewis's departure, the role certainly impressed it on me with uncomfortable haste. As an ordinary MP, I had typically been able to concern myself with two or three major areas of focus at any given time. Being leader, even on a temporary basis was, by comparison, a quantum leap in responsibility. If there was a fishing disaster in Nova Scotia, a crop failure on the prairies, or a complicated legislative item before the House of Commons, it was now my job to respond in some way. And while it was generally understood that I couldn't be an expert on everything, I at least had to be reasonably well informed. The resulting workload was more time-consuming than anything I had experienced in political life before. My wife, Lucille, and I were raising our two young kids, Paul and Christine, and with the complexities of the role of interim leader piling up, it was not one I was keen to make permanent.

Though parts of the media and some inside the party mistakenly believed it was a stunt or ploy, I was thus being sincere when I announced at a meeting of the NDP's federal council in January 1975 that I would not be standing for the leadership at the coming convention in Winnipeg that July.[1] Only after weeks of urging by people like David Lewis and Charles Taylor, and Lucille's encouragement (she had encouraged me to run from the very beginning), was I persuaded to change my mind. The race, to say nothing of the task beyond it, proved every bit as demanding as I had imagined it would be. But I was aided along the way by the support of MPs like my friend Bill Knight* — and by the presence of a rival candidate with the exceptional qualities of Rosemary Brown.

Throughout my early years as leader, it became increasingly clear that the creeping sense of uncertainty and instability that had defined the first half of the decade was going to persist. South of the border, Richard Nixon had been toppled by Watergate, and the United States had been defeated in Vietnam. Riven by internal division throughout Britain's so-called Winter of Discontent, the Labour government of James Callaghan fell in a 1979 confidence vote and was subsequently defeated by Margaret Thatcher. Canada, as ever, had its own particularities. Under the leadership of Stephen Lewis, the Ontario NDP reduced the province's ruling PC dynasty to minority status and formed its first social democratic Official Opposition since 1948 (a development soured by the defeat of the Barrett and Schreyer governments in 1975 and 1977). In 1976, René Lévesque led the Parti Québécois to power in Quebec, ultimately setting the stage for its 1980 referendum on independence and the protracted Canada-wide struggles over patriation, Meech Lake, and Charlottetown.

I believed that rising anxiety and conflict about the future of Canada, whatever their sources might be, were inescapably related to Canadians' broader sense of economic justice and well-being.[2] With unemployment remaining high[3] and the Trudeau Liberals rediscovering their conservatism after the 1974 election, it was becoming evident that the gains made by working people in the postwar decades — let alone those of the recent minority Parliament — could no longer be taken for granted. When I first entered political life in 1968, the welfare state, and the consensus around it, were more or less accepted by non–social democrats. Amid ongoing economic dysfunction, and what would in retrospect mark the

---

* Bill would go on to be my chief of staff and a trusted friend and political advisor from 1982 to 1987. In 1988, he was federal secretary and our national campaign director.

beginning of a concerted global drift toward the ideological right, they were now increasingly up for debate.

Broadly speaking, the debates were a continuation of those that had begun in the early 1970s. With the Canadian economy facing protracted unemployment and heavy job losses in the manufacturing sector, the critical questions for the federal government became how best to increase productivity, restore competitiveness, and stabilize prices. There could certainly be no doubt that Canadian manufacturing was less productive than its American equivalent, that it was trailing in terms of research and development, or that this unhappy status quo was resulting in a severe trade deficit.[4] The immediate question, on which all of the resulting policy responses depended, was the cause.

An increasingly ascendant school of thought continued to popularize the idea that Canada's economic woes were primarily the result of excessively high wages. When I cited figures in October 1977 in the House of Commons that showed more than a million people were out of work, Trudeau replied:

> [In] manufacturing generally Canadian workers are productive but only 80 percent as productive as the American worker in manufacturing. At the same time, the average wage rate for the Canadian worker in manufacturing is 7 percent higher than that of the American. If the leader of the New Democratic Party thinks about that he will understand that this means our costs are higher and that we cannot compete with our main competitors in the market, the United States. If we cannot compete, that means we cannot continue to invest and if we cannot continue to invest, it means we cannot continue to create jobs.[5]

For me, the more significant source of inefficiency was that the bulk of our manufacturing sector had never been designed to be competitive in the first place. Beginning in the 1940s, successive federal governments had opted to help finance postwar growth by selling off parts of the country's resource base.[6] In the export-dependent and heavily foreign-owned economy that resulted, many factories had become little more than warehouse-assembly operations whose real purpose was to generate profits in corporate offices abroad. Multinational companies typically supplied their Canadian subsidiaries with ready-made technology, machinery, and components from elsewhere — and kept the benefits of scientific research and technological development for themselves. Directly responsible for our considerable trade and balance of payments deficits, this branch plant structure also meant a significant loss of well-paying jobs and other social benefits for Canadians. Without good jobs, and without a viable economy to sustain it, a viable welfare state would in turn become ever more difficult to maintain, let alone expand.

Unsurprisingly, the various policy remedies for Canada's economic problems diverged as sharply as the competing explanations of their cause. For some, the solution lay in the further loosening of trade tariffs and deregulation of markets. Channelling this view — in an argument that presaged the eventual case for free trade with the United States — a February 1982 editorial from the *Globe and Mail* stated the logic as follows: "There is only one permanent solution to the massive layoffs in Canada's manufacturing sector. The nation's manufacturers must become competitive with their foreign counterparts. Winners must replace the losers."[7] The alternative, as I put to Canadians after becoming NDP leader, was an ambitious reorientation of economic priorities with a view to reclaiming our economic destiny. The means for achieving that goal was an imaginative industrial strategy.

I firmly believe that the most serious task of any political party in a democracy is the pursuit of power, and that this principle is no less applicable to a party like the NDP. Like other moments before it, the minority Parliament of 1972–1974 had once again given Canada's socialists a taste of what could be achieved from a position of influence, but it had also demonstrated the limitations of our continued third-party status. The NDP, like the CCF before it, had been created to build a new and more equal kind of society. Until a majority was mobilized behind it, this vision was always going to remain elusive. From the outset of my leadership, I set out to make the NDP the governing party of Canada. That pursuit was not corrupting. I viewed it as a moral imperative.

To champion a socialist vision in a capitalist world is, in a sense, a strangely paradoxical act of faith: unless you are prepared to lose majorities you will compromise your core beliefs, but to act on the basis of belief or program alone, without regard for the feelings and commitments of the majority in society, does both a profound disservice. You must show people the respect they deserve. In the real world of democracy, people have short-run problems they need solved, and most have little interest in grand political projects or ideological abstractions. Above all, what they want are results. The task, as I saw it, was thus to communicate a social democratic vision to ordinary Canadians as plainly and directly as I could in a way that would be attractive and relevant to their daily lives.

Though I became leader in 1975, the next federal election did not take place for nearly four years. In the intervening time, however, several developments ensured that the coming campaigns would be markedly different from those that had preceded them.

The introduction of cameras into the House of Commons signalled both the growing influence of mass media in politics and a newly unmediated relationship between citizens and politicians. Before 1979, there had only been a single televised federal debate. Throughout the course of my leadership, they would become a significant element in every campaign, and sometimes played more than a negligible role in determining its outcome. In a break with the format of the televised debate of 1968, in which Tommy Douglas had been given less speaking time than either Trudeau or Stanfield, in 1979 I was afforded the right to participate on equal footing with the other leaders. The increasing influence of television was certainly not without its downsides, but nevertheless afforded me a new and very direct medium for communicating social democracy to Canadians.

The 1979 election would be the first of three over the next five years. With a boost from the new election finance legislation that had been enacted in the 1972–74 minority Parliament, the NDP entered the campaign with a full slate of candidates for the first time in its history and finished it with an improved share of the popular vote in every province and territory except Quebec — roughly matching what was then our best ever result in 1965. Though well short of what I had hoped for, we elected twenty-six MPs, representing a good cross-section of Canada. This cohort included newcomers such as Svend Robinson, Ian Waddell, and Pauline Jewett in BC and Bill Blaikie and Bob Ogle on the prairies. Retaining the seat he'd won for the NDP in a recent byelection, Fonse Faour — the first CCF or NDP member ever to represent Newfoundland and Labrador — was also reelected.

The 1979 election returned a minority Conservative government led by Joe Clark. Clark's tenure was ultimately short-lived. With Pierre Trudeau announcing his retirement and the Conservatives tenuously positioned, I began to consider the possibility of prompting an early election if the opportunity arose (even if the prospect of immediately fighting another campaign worried many of my own advisors). The moment soon presented itself when the Clark government tabled its first — and, as it turned out, only — budget. With the Conservatives struggling and the Liberals rudderless, we decided that our finance critic, Bob Rae, would introduce a sub-amendment indicating lack of confidence in the government. Needing the votes of Liberal MPs as well, I shared the wording of our motion with their interim leader, Allan MacEachen, in the Commons lobby. "We can live with that," he replied, and — with the critical abstentions of five Quebec members from the small Social Credit Party — Clark's government was duly toppled by a margin of 139–133.

MacEachen, as it turned out, was not to be outfoxed and, to my surprise, he used the sudden election call to coax Trudeau out of retirement. The Liberals, who had faced a string of particularly embarrassing byelection defeats[8] and fought a visibly poor campaign the previous year, fared better this time — in part by keeping Trudeau himself out of the spotlight. Trudeau, for his part, found his abrupt return rewarded with another majority. While the NDP made further gains and elected 32 MPs, the more significant breakthrough I had sought remained frustratingly elusive.

With the Canadian body politic still dazed from the intensive constitutional wranglings of the early 1980s, and some of the party's western sections still dissatisfied with my endorsement of Trudeau's patriation effort,* we entered the first months of 1984 facing a series of decidedly ominous polls. In what seemed like another bleak divination, I took a painful tumble down the stairs at home and badly bruised my back. On the same day, the Liberals' new leader John Turner decided to call a snap election.

---

**Frances Abele:** Your election as NDP leader signified a generational shift in Canadian social democracy. Tommy Douglas and David Lewis had both been active in the CCF, while you had not. Douglas, J.S. Woodsworth, and many of the other prominent figures in the CCF/NDP had also come out of, or at least been influenced by, the progressive Christian social gospel tradition and had lived through the Great Depression. How do you think this generational divide manifested itself in terms of your own outlook and leadership style?

**Ed Broadbent:** First, there was a difference in rhetoric. Earlier eras of politics on the left had often been characterized by a kind of sweeping rhetorical style. Mine was of a more skeptical age. I thought that earlier rhetoric had the potential to bury the substance of political arguments in abstraction. When I first entered politics as an MP, my instinct was to lay out arguments as straightforwardly and analytically as possible. Gradually, however, I came to recognize that simply telling the truth is insufficient and that arousing people's emotions is an important obligation of leadership. Tommy Douglas, for example, had a very impassioned speaking style honed during his days as a Baptist minister — but there was a basic humanity to his speeches that always shone through even if he was singling out particular targets for attack.

---

* See Chapter Seven: The Great Patriation Debate.

My own rhetorical style as leader was obviously quite different, but examples like his helped me grow more comfortable with the idea that I needed to engage people on an emotional level as well as on the basis of reason.

**FA:** You alluded to this already, but from the 1970s onwards, there was a passing of the torch to a new generation of political leadership that was not a direct product of the 1930s. The men (and increasingly women) who were being elected to Parliament had all come of age taking certain features of the modern state, and the existence of social democratic parties, for granted — whereas the generation of Douglas and Lewis had been part of the very struggles that brought them into being.

**EB:** My peers and I felt more like we were fighting from within the welfare state settlement of the postwar years rather than battling from without. There was understandably something of an outsider identity among those belonging to previous generations of the social democratic left, but I didn't feel like an outsider and that was a significant difference. I felt at home as a democratic socialist in Canada, in large part because those in an earlier generation had been so successful in embedding our tradition and its values in the hearts and minds of many Canadians. My task wasn't to fight for that tradition's legitimacy, but to help it flourish.

**FA:** Speaking of generational differences, Stanley Knowles — who first entered Parliament in 1942 by succeeding Woodsworth as MP for Winnipeg North Centre — served throughout the Coldwell, Douglas, and Lewis eras, and was still there when you became leader.

**EB:** Yes, and as longtime House leader he actually became my seatmate after the 1975 leadership convention. Stanley was incredibly helpful. I would instantly turn any questions of parliamentary procedure over to him — both because he knew the system inside out and because he was adept at using its rules and mechanisms to our advantage. He was an extremely loyal and committed member of the CCF and NDP, but he was also very devoted to the civic culture and decorum of Parliament. He could give passionate speeches, but like Douglas's they never carried a hint of personal animosity toward political opponents.

I learned a great deal from Stanley. But to continue the theme here I think he and I also had some real differences in outlook as social democrats from different generations. He was an incrementalist who had learned to work the system to win important concessions in social programs. By comparison, I think I was a lot more impatient for change and felt strongly that getting those kinds of concessions wasn't enough. We ultimately had to break through so that we could make the rules from a social democratic perspective — not just improve those made by others.

Incidentally, after ill health forced Stanley into retirement, Trudeau did something quite exceptional for him by creating the new position of "table officer" — which gave him a permanent seat on the floor of the House immediately adjacent to the Speaker so that he could follow the proceedings whenever he wanted. No one else had ever received such an honour. It was a generous gesture on Trudeau's part to recognize Stanley's distinguished career as an MP spread over many decades.

**Luke Savage:** Obviously you learned a good deal from observing the leadership styles of your elders and colleagues in the House, but other things clearly informed your outlook as well. One of your intellectual influences quite early on was George Orwell, but we haven't really discussed his writings on language yet. Were your views on rhetoric at all influenced by or reflected in those?

**EB:** Yes, and as a young MP I once gave each of my colleagues in caucus a copy of his brilliant 1946 essay *Politics and the English Language*. I had been influenced by Orwell's belief that concentrated power, whether in the state or the capitalist economy, has to be challenged and made accountable. But he was also one of the twentieth century's great critics of linguistic and rhetorical deception. He was particularly observant about the various ways language can be wielded by those trying to shape public opinion — whether politicians, intellectuals, or media figures — to obfuscate and mislead. Orwell believed that elites in any system are likely to be self-serving and that linguistic hyperbole is typically their preferred instrument because it can be so effective in disguising their true objectives. The solution, as he argued in his distinctly stubborn and unpretentious way, lay in the use of plain and direct language stripped of any adornment.

From quite early on, I acted on this idea. I knew I needed to use concrete language and draw from a political vocabulary that would resonate with ordinary people. For example, when I talked about decommodification, I don't think I ever actually used that technical term in a speech. I did use it in explanatory texts and academic papers. But applying the concept in practice meant speaking very directly about how it related to a particular issue — in the case of housing, how we could require banks to put a certain percentage of their portfolios directly into low-cost housing average people could afford. I thought that style of argument would be something any ordinary person could find relevant. I took this approach to political language long before I became leader — including in my objections to some of the rhetoric in the Waffle Manifesto.*

Something else I share with Orwell, and tried to practise as leader, is the belief that any serious program or agenda must be premised on the concrete hopes and desires of ordinary people before it moves to general answers. He was particularly wary of

---

* See Chapter Two: Ideology and Respect.

the kind of theoretical abstraction that begins with systems and proceeds to the lives of ordinary people almost as an afterthought. That skepticism made him very suspicious about the political judgement of many intellectuals in his day. He was scathing about their tendency to suffocate meaning under layers of strained symbolism and cumbersome prose.

Even as I became more comfortable with rhetoric, and with the idea of arousing people's emotions, I believed that social democracy must be explained and pursued in specifically clear language. I used to say to my caucus colleagues: remember that we're here because we believe that social democracy is right, it's truthful, and that it wants to do good for the people of Canada; so, if you're defending our position on something, just explain that position clearly and honestly and the public will respect it.

**FA:** How did you approach the task of being leader in your relationship with the caucus itself?

**EB:** That was certainly on-the-job training. There was no specific effort on my part to study how other leaders worked with caucus, but I did have a kind of apprenticeship when I was elected caucus chair. It's a key political position because you have to mediate between the leader and the rest of the caucus, explaining one's position to the other and mobilizing people to come together as a team. Often, that means keeping the caucus on track to support where the leader is going. They need to trust the leader and believe he listens to them. The master of that kind of leadership, incidentally, was Brian Mulroney. Throughout all of his ebbs in the polls, he never faced a serious revolt in the PC caucus. And it's because he managed to pay such close attention to members and their concerns.

Bill Blaikie once described my own approach as one of "intellectual persuasion." As an academic, I had learned to use rational argument. My appreciation for the importance and power of such an approach deepened during my time as caucus chair. After I became leader, I continued to try to get people onside that way rather than by way of threats. It's a more desirable and effective route regardless. However, an NDP leader in Opposition doesn't have much power to threaten people anyway (beyond basic things like removing an MP from his or her critic portfolio). You really do have to govern by agreement in caucus. However, I remember the debates sometimes being difficult for Indigenous MPs like Wally Firth who came out of a different decision-making tradition, one that was more consensus-based and didn't involve the same kinds of swift up and down votes. In general, my goal in any debate was to get 80 percent on a given issue rather than 50 plus one so that the caucus would feel good about itself and not be divided. Occasionally the votes were closer and it just couldn't be avoided.

Caucus was very helpful for me in making decisions because the conversations were an opportunity to hear different views and because the members could keep me informed about what was happening in different regions of the country. How, for example, was a particular policy being received in Regina or Halifax as compared to Oshawa or Toronto? You learn very quickly what a vast and complicated country we have because the differences are invariably reflected in the caucus. Ignoring that diversity of views just sows the seeds of future trouble.

**Jonathan Sas:** There's a particular caucus story you've mentioned in private that I don't believe has ever been printed or discussed anywhere, which involves one of the meetings being bugged . . .

**EB:** That happened back when I was caucus chair. At the time, I was carrying a copy of Mao's *Little Red Book* around with me as a joke. On the day in question, during a particularly raucous caucus debate, to inject some humour, I started reading out a section on how to deal with dissidents. As it happened, there was privacy legislation being discussed in Parliament that concerned the media. Unknown to us in the caucus, the meeting was being taped by CTV because they wanted to prove how easy it was to bug a caucus room on Parliament Hill. So, they got me on tape quoting from Mao Zedong to the caucus. Later in the meeting, I reached under the table and discovered the bug. Needless to say, some colleagues were very nervous about what would happen if my use of Mao's *Little Red Book* were to hit the press. They were notably not happy about my sense of humour.

It's funny to tell that story in retrospect, and in part, it illustrates a generational difference. A number of MPs came out of an earlier period in which there were concerted attacks on the legitimacy of the CCF and the labour movement and in which they frequently had to deal with the charge of being communists. For me, it was just a joke, but socialists of an earlier generation had a very different attitude and were understandably anxious about being red-baited. Subsequently, on the instructions of the Speaker, the tape recorded by CTV was destroyed.

**JS:** There was a generational shift underway when you became leader, but there were also a number of parallel developments that presumably had a significant impact on the actual nature of the job when it came to things like how campaigns were fought. TV coverage of politics, for example, became ubiquitous in the 1970s and 1980s as did the use of polling. To what extent were you actively conscious of the impact of developments like these on politics?

**EB:** I became very conscious of the importance of TV, and of the broadcasts from the House of Commons in particular because they allowed us to speak directly to families at home in a way that was relatively unfiltered by the media. When the Cable Public Affairs Channel (CPAC) came into being, for example, it allowed me to speak across the whole country and also to address people in regions where we didn't have any MPs. I became increasingly aware of the need to get good soundbites into question period because I knew they would be more likely to get picked up by the networks and even make their way into national news. I think I did become fairly adept at honing our message in a way that would punch through.

On the whole, I believe that the introduction of televised proceedings in the House has been good for democracy. It's led to plenty of abuse too, of course, and plenty of outrageous, foolish, and misleading rhetoric. But, on balance, if an MP has an issue to raise, whether they're from Moose Jaw, Prince Edward Island, or Toronto, raising it in the House of Commons now gets much more play back home and elsewhere than it did before the age of mass media. It has a greater chance of influencing the political agenda of the government.

I am ambivalent about polling, which was present in those days but has now become ubiquitous and elections have increasingly been turned into horse race–driven spectacles. Coverage has become more and more about who's winning the competition: which horse is ahead in this race? What do the other ones have to do to catch up? There used to be a poll maybe every ten days throughout a campaign, but between 1984 and 1988, the number of public polls conducted quite literally doubled.[9] For campaign purposes, the NDP simply didn't have the resources to do its own sophisticated polling so we depended on public opinion polls to get a picture of the party's standing.


**FA:** Did it bother you to have to tailor your remarks and speeches in the House for televised consumption?


**EB:** It didn't bother me — and, in fact, I generally found it very desirable for getting points across. I once had an exchange with

Trudeau, for example, about the cost of living.[10] He could be disdainful and often came across badly in those moments, so I would sometimes try to provoke him. One day, I decided to ask him in sequence if he knew the price of a pound of butter, a loaf of bread, or a dozen eggs. He quite predictably didn't know the answer to any of them, and his dismissive reply became a news item that in turn allowed us to put the government on the defensive over the cost of living.

**LS:** There seems to have been a consensus at the time that the growth of TV coverage was benefiting the NDP and your leadership personally. A 1977 *Toronto Life* article by Norman Snider included the complimentary words: "A tiger in debate, Broadbent's national recognition began to improve when Canadians began to see the actual confrontation . . . Television loves a drama and Broadbent hammering away began to become a staple of the national news."[11] TV was influential beyond the House, though, and I'm wondering if you're of the same opinion regarding the various televised leaders' debates you participated in? I'm not sure what people made of those at the time, but they've always seemed like more substantive viewing than their equivalents today.

**EB:** I'm somewhat reluctant to comment on questions about whether politics was more substantive in the past because it often seems like self-serving nostalgia. But I do think TV debates used to be better and that there's been a general dumbing down of television coverage more broadly. Policy is shortchanged in answers in comparison with manner of delivery. Indicative of that is that the news is now described by the networks themselves as a "show" rather than a program. That goes hand in hand with the draining of substance from public discourse and political debates more broadly.

As to whether those TV debates hurt or helped the NDP, I think the answer is mixed. Going into the 1979 federal election,

I remember being somewhat apprehensive because it was my first national campaign as leader. But, in the event, I found that I enjoyed campaigning because it allowed me to talk about the things I believed in. That was especially true of the leaders' debate. Mordecai Richler afterwards remarked that it had featured "two men and a boy,"[12] and that was generally how we were described: Trudeau and I were said to have conveyed the impression of being serious and competent while Clark was seen to not have been on his mark.

Then again, there was that moment in the 1984 debate when Brian Mulroney famously hit Turner with that line about patronage appointments ("You had an option, sir"). Just prior to his departure, Trudeau had made a slew of patronage appointments and foisted them on Turner for ratification. He had handed his successor a poisoned chalice and Turner had no choice but to drink it. Anyway, when Mulroney delivered that line, I knew he had just "won" the debate because it was such an obvious retort and had been so effectively delivered. Predictably, they kept running that clip on the news throughout the next week. Every night, Canadians saw Turner looking hopelessly defensive and Mulroney looking triumphant in his opposition to such patronage. This turned out to be misleading. It helped him win the election, however — once in power — Mulroney continued the practice of patronage appointments.

Incidentally, many years later, Turner invited me for dinner at Stornoway, the official residence of the leader of the opposition. We discussed various subjects, but at one point Trudeau's undermining action in forcing him to make those patronage decisions came up and was still clearly a painful memory.

**JS:** I've always been pretty aghast at how widespread patronage politics are. They're corrosive to public trust and the legitimacy of institutions and yet have been incredibly normalized.

**EB:** That's true, and I think it's something of a hangover from an earlier era. As someone who was new to politics in 1968 and hadn't come up through either of the old party hierarchies, I never could quite understand how or why the people of Canada had come to accept such a high degree of crass patronage. Occasionally, this would end up backfiring on the government. In 1981, Trudeau wanted to get Jim Coutts, his principal secretary and close political advisor, into Parliament so he appointed the sitting MP for Spadina (which was then considered one of the safest Liberal seats in the country) to a sinecure in the Senate and called a byelection. We nominated Dan Heap, who was a rebellious Anglican priest and popular municipal councillor. I can still remember campaigning in the riding armed with the slogan "Put the Boots to Coutts!" And we did just that. Heap had a good reputation in downtown Toronto, and that helped a lot, but I think disgust at Trudeau for treating a seat in the House of Commons as if it were a mere stepping stone for one of his advisors was an important factor in the victory.[13]

The Senate, of course, is in a universe of its own when it comes to that kind of thing and I quite happily campaigned for its abolition. A reporter once asked what I'd do about the place and I replied facetiously that I would turn it into a gymnasium with twelve hours a day of compulsory calisthenics for the Senators.

**LS:** Speaking of the Senate, one of my favourite stories is that when Mikhail Gorbachev was on an official tour of Parliament Hill during the 1980s with the then-minister of agriculture Eugene Whalen, he apparently had the Senate explained to him and replied, a bit perplexed, by asking how citizens in a democratic country could possibly put up with legislators who were appointed for life.[14]

To turn back to the 1979 election, the other major event from the NDP's point of view was being endorsed by the *Toronto*

*Star* — Canada's largest newspaper.[15] This had never happened before (and has only happened once since). For years the *Star* had been endorsing NDP policy ideas put before Parliament, but typically endorsed the Liberals during elections. In 1979, they decided to be more consistent. The editorial is a bit of a strange artifact in that, among other things, it also criticizes the NDP for its close association with unions. What did you make of that endorsement? Was it an electoral boost?

**EB:** Beland Honderich, the *Star*'s publisher, put me through a veritable Ph.D. oral exam ahead of that endorsement. Two, in fact, in the form of a couple of very long conversations. He obviously took the role of the paper very seriously. I also know that George Bain, the *Star*'s bureau chief in Ottawa, played a role in convincing him. Bain was an intelligent and witty man. In the wake of Trudeaumania back in the late sixties, when he was the *Globe*'s Ottawa bureau chief, he was one of the first members of the press gallery to get off the Trudeau bandwagon. He had also been critical of the invocation of the War Measures Act. As head of the *Star*'s bureau in Ottawa, he told me he was going to recommend that they endorse us — specifically on the grounds that they needed to start practising what they preached. They needed to be consistent and endorse the NDP.

As to what the endorsement meant in practice, I think our candidates in the Toronto area certainly got a boost. Even if people didn't actually get around to reading it, the fact that the largest newspaper in the country had endorsed us was good news. I'm not sure newspaper endorsements directly affect how anyone votes, but they can definitely be a shot in the arm for the morale of campaign activists. Other papers picked up on the fact that the *Star* had endorsed us too, so there was a bit of a positive snowball effect.

Something interesting that came up in conversations with Honderich was the prospect of changing the NDP's name. I had always used the terms democratic socialism and social democracy interchangeably and mentioned to him that I'd been tossing around the idea of changing the name. It didn't take long for others to persuade me not to pursue that because it could have easily become a divisive intraparty debate similar to those the Labour Party had over removing Clause IV of their constitution, which dealt with the question of nationalization. When I did raise it internally, friends within the party basically said, "Well, there goes Ed again. Next thing you know he'll be introducing the Socialist International Rose as a symbol." (In fact, I rather mischievously tried to get it on the agenda at the 1988 NDP convention without success . . .) To this day, I wish God could reach down from the heavens and retroactively give us a different name without it requiring a big and divisive debate. My personal preference would be the Social Democratic Party. In any case, the *Star* never endorsed the NDP again during my leadership. In 1980, Montreal's *Le Devoir* did endorse us.

**LS:** Something the *Star* did approve of was your proposal for an industrial strategy. That was, in many ways, the NDP's flagship economic policy when you became leader, and when the party first rolled it out in 1978 the *Star* ran a favourable editorial about it.[16] On the other hand, I understand that some of your political and campaign advisors thought it wasn't a winning issue, in part because it was perceived as complicated to explain and didn't seem to break through in the 1980 election when you had strongly emphasized it.

**EB:** NDP strategists, who think about campaign more than policy, argued that the industrial strategy was not, to put it euphemistically, a vote-winner. Within the party, there was some inevitable conflict between the leader's office and bodies like the federal council — which housed the election planning committee mandated to prepare our platform and manage our organizing efforts.

Some certainly believed the industrial strategy was too complex and thought people weren't all that interested in the kinds of longer-term goals and objectives it encompassed.

I've always respected people involved in that kind of campaign work, which is essential in any democracy. But I strongly disagreed in this case and wanted to campaign on an industrial strategy because I firmly believe that something like it has to be front and centre for a social democratic party like the NDP. Our job, as I saw it, was to offer a broad-ranging view of the national economy and demonstrate that we had proposals far-reaching enough to change and improve the circumstances of a majority in Canadian society. Social democracy is fundamentally about challenging the dominance of market mechanisms, and any party or movement that seeks to do that is obligated to say what it would put in their place.

There was a strong policy argument to be made about how an industrial strategy could help us deal with our economic challenges. But as a political issue, I thought it was an important point of distinction between the NDP and the other parties. Liberals and conservatives generally prefer to be responsive to markets as opposed to trying to influence them. They tend to go along with national and global economic currents in a somewhat ad hoc way and, by extension, are perfectly happy to let them shape the destiny of a country. Social democratic parties, on the other hand, can and should be trying to intervene constructively in the framework of markets to roll back their noxious elements to the greatest extent possible — and replace them with politically agreed upon alternatives.

For an open economy like Canada's, that meant reckoning with the limits of a Keynesian stimulus approach as the deficit grew, and offering more than just redistribution as a response to the pressing macro-economic challenges of the day — including stagflation, sluggish private sector investment, and rising unemployment. It meant we had to address the serious imbalance that had developed in our economy in which we were living off raw resources, selling them to companies abroad, and then buying back a huge surplus of manufactured goods. For example, it seemed inconceivable to me that places like Germany or Japan (to take two other countries with big automotive industries, for example) would allow their manufacturing capacities in the automotive or any other major sector to just wither away as a result of market forces — and an industrial strategy of some kind was integral to their policymaking for exactly that reason. Because the power of multinational companies was growing, I knew we would eventually need to create mechanisms of some kind through which states could cooperatively control their behaviour.* In the meantime, we had to develop our national economy into something that didn't place a constant downward pressure on workers' wages, export wealth abroad, or create a massive trade deficit.

The idea was to get the federal cabinet involved in an ongoing sector-by-sector analysis with a view to reorienting Canada's economic priorities using a combination of taxes, tariffs, strategic investments, and other policy tools. In the end, we'd have a very different kind of economy in which all sorts of goods — furniture, petrochemicals, machinery, etc. — would be manufactured here. Those plans were laid out in detail in various policy documents we published, but the basic case I made on the campaign trail boiled down to the idea that it was time for our resources to be owned by Canadians, controlled by Canadians, and put to use for Canadians.

**FA:** Whether or not your message about the industrial strategy broke through, one phrase you regularly invoked that seems to have resonated quite strongly was "ordinary Canadians." Can you walk us through where that originated and how it figured in your message more broadly? Were you ever tempted to say "working class" instead?

---

\* See Chapter Nine: Globalization and the Struggle for Equality.

**EB:** To begin with the last part of the question, the short answer is no. Even growing up in Oshawa, which was a very working-class town, people didn't refer to themselves that way. It was just not the language they used. I likely first ran into that phrase when I began studying at U of T and was interacting with academics there who used it. It was never a term I thought would be effective in communicating. Something else that was in general usage was "working families," but that always sounded like a slogan tailored for campaign purposes. I never felt that way about "ordinary Canadians" at all. It came very naturally to me. Strictly speaking, I think the phrase originated from my friend the American pollster Vic Fingerhut, who worked with the NDP during the 1980s. I was so comfortable with it that it didn't feel like a slogan or cliché.

Something that was my idea, and an extension of exactly the same message, was referring to Turner and Mulroney as "the Bobbsey Twins of Bay Street" while launching our 1984 campaign in front of two giant towers on Bay Street in downtown Toronto. On the face of it, things looked rather bleak in that moment going into a campaign well back in the polls. But I relished the opportunity to fight an election on the theme of whose interests were going to be represented and whose side the parties were ultimately on — wealth and privilege on the one hand, or ordinary people on the other. That went to the heart of so many of the policies we were campaigning on, like introducing a minimum tax on the rich who in many instances were paying nothing. I think that idea — of whether a party or party leader represented ordinary Canadians — resonated with people because it reflected a widely shared view throughout the country even if not everyone who held it ultimately voted NDP. And the Bobbsey Twins line became ubiquitous throughout that election. I used it again and again and it got picked up by the journalists who were following the campaign.

Another reason the Bobbsey Twins reference struck was that it happened to be a truthful description of Mulroney's and Turner's backgrounds: one, after all, had been a corporate executive and the other had left politics for nearly a decade to work as a Bay

Street lawyer. I remember saying that it was like having a choice between Visa and Mastercard: they might have looked different on the outside but in reality, they were functionally interchangeable — and the interests of ordinary Canadians were going to be unrepresented as a result.[17] I once modified it a bit by saying "Actually, they're not the same" and rattling off all of the different directorships and corporate ties each of them had. More than anything else, I'm convinced that getting that message across was the main thing that propelled us in that campaign — which we began at around 10 or 11 percent in the polls and finished at nearly 19. The Liberals bled almost a hundred seats. After all the difficulties and challenges of the early 1980s, we lived to fight another day.

**JS:** The effectiveness of something like "ordinary Canadians," especially when paired with that Bobbsey Twins message, is that it's broad and inclusive but also specific enough to distinguish the constituency it's describing from the ones it's targeting. Whatever people think "ordinary" means, they know what it's not: the person with power pulling the strings or sitting up high in those towers.

I suppose the NDP's success during your time as leader is connected to your personal popularity as leader, which often exceeded the popularity of the party. This was also reflected in NDP strategy, which tended to foreground your leadership. We've talked about your approach to political language and rhetoric, but how do you see the role of personality in politics?

**EB:** I don't think these things can really be separated from one another. The personal dimension is just an inescapable fact of democratic politics. Most people are not engaged by abstract theory or even the details of important policies. But they *are* motivated by the person who believes in those things. The substance of what you're saying as a politician matters a great deal. Because, even if people don't remember the precise details, they will remember whether you sounded convinced of your own arguments and whether your attitude seemed to be one of honesty and respect for different views. Showing respect is very important.

This goes back to the internal debate we had about the industrial strategy. Gerry Caplan, who was the NDP's federal secretary at the time, never thought I should be talking about it. Part of his case was that he didn't think people would believe us. Strategically speaking, I thought that was a circular argument because if we never talked about the issue and didn't explain it in at least some detail, people would obviously never come to believe in or accept it. Caplan also felt it was too intricate and complicated as a policy to campaign on. I disagreed, and not only because the industrial strategy was important to me on a philosophical level. The polling that showed I was personally popular as a leader is relevant here. I believe it wasn't possible to distinguish those perceptions of me from the actual substance of what I was saying. Insofar as people found me to be on their side or viewed me as an honest politician, I think a good part of it had to do with them hearing me discuss complicated issues in a way that didn't oversimplify but didn't use overblown language either.

Whether they came to support the party because they loved the specific elements of the industrial policy is another question, of course. But the values that lay *behind* an idea like that, and the way I expressed them, are to me inextricably linked. One doesn't just talk in a vacuum and people don't respond in one either.

**LS:** We've spoken a lot about questions of political rhetoric, campaigning, and leadership. But it's probably worth noting the NDP had a pretty far-reaching platform in all three of the elections we've discussed — beyond the industrial strategy.

**EB:** Something that's particularly satisfying about looking back at the NDP program from these years is how much emphasis it put

on the various issues that had been raised by the feminist movement. The 1984 leaders' debate on women's issues was a historic
first for Canada. And, as unbiased as I'm not, as a result of all the
feminist activism that had taken place inside the NDP, I felt that
I had a clear advantage over both Mulroney and Turner, who were
more or less representatives of the male chauvinism of the age and
struggled to master the basic language of gender equality. That
really came out during the debate. Virtually every major women's
organization said afterwards that I won the debate. The point I
want to emphasize is that that was in large part because of the
feminists in the NDP who had pushed, agitated, organized, and
propelled the party forward on women's issues.

I don't know how many votes the debate or our measures
on pay equity and gender equality ultimately counted for, but it
brought joy to my heart to look back on the platforms from that
era — and also at the updated version of the Regina Manifesto we
passed at the 1983 convention.*[18] It's not a very well-known document, but it remains a powerful statement of the values we were
fighting for. If you look at the key affirmations in that document,
the first one states: "Socialists around the world share as their
goal a society from which exploitation of one person by another,
of one class by another, of one group or sex by another, will be
eliminated. We believe in a society where each person will have
the chance to develop his or her talents to the fullest. This ideal,
a society based on equality, within a world of equally respected
nations, is the major aim of democratic socialism."

Another is: "We affirm our belief that aboriginal peoples have
the right to shape their own future out of their own past and to
possess the institutions necessary to survive and flourish." And
the one after that reads: "The women's movement has challenged
us to fulfill the socialist commitment to end sexual discrimination, unequal pay and opportunity and violence against women.
The crisis of technological unemployment and changes in the

---

\* A complete version of the 1983 Manifesto is included in the Appendices.

family must be met by socialists so that women as a group are not victimized." The next: "The right to participate in the trade union movement, including the right to organize, to engage in collective bargaining and the right of workers to withdraw their services if necessary are fundamental in a democratic society. Workers' rights in the workplace must be defended and indeed strengthened."

These are four key affirmations that I'm very proud to see in the 1983 Manifesto — an important statement of principles that, if realized, would have transformed the lives of ordinary Canadians for the better.

## CHAPTER SIX

# Social Democracy without Borders

*"Democratic socialism should never stand on the side of colonialism and racialism. In each individual instance we must stand on the side of the poor and oppressed peoples and give our support to the continued struggle for liberation in Southern Africa. It is not only a question of contacts and dialogue but of identifying ourselves with the liberation struggle of the oppressed majority of this planet."*

— OLOF PALME, address to the Congress of the
Socialist International, Geneva, 1976

*"Socialism without human rights is like Christianity without Christ."*

— WILLY BRANDT

*"The necessity for a form of socialism is based on the observation that the world's present economic arrangements doom most of the world to misery; that the way of life dictated by these arrangements is both sterile and immoral; and, finally, that there is no hope for peace in the world so long as these arrangements obtain."*

— JAMES BALDWIN, *No Name in the Street*

I n late 1976, the Socialist International held its thirteenth postwar congress in Geneva. Elected to lead the organization by unanimous vote, former West German chancellor Willy Brandt outlined his vision to the assembled delegates. "We should recall the continuity which for many decades has been at the root of our struggle for peace and freedom, for justice and solidarity," Brandt remarked.

> The simple laws of morality and justice which should rule the relations between individuals ... should also be applied as the supreme laws to the relationship of nations. And it is laid down in the statutes for the First International [of 1864] that the emancipation of the working class, thus the large disadvantaged strata, was neither a local nor a national but a social task which involved all countries in which modern society exists. Who among us would deny that we were given a compass here that has not become obsolete despite the impressive achievements made by the labour movement, the social democratic parties, and the trade unions, and despite fundamental changes that have become characteristic of the relations between states in this part of the world?[1]

Both Brandt's comments and the occasion that inspired them were characteristic of a deep internationalist tradition carried forward from the earliest stirrings of the socialist movement in the nineteenth century. Though complicated by the organization of the world into nation-states, internationalism has played a significant and, in many ways, concomitant role in left politics from the very beginning. To be a socialist, after all, is also to be a universalist: committed to the dignity, equality, and rights of every human being regardless of where they were born or on which side of a border they happen to reside.

This high-minded sentiment, of course, has always been much easier to theorize about than realize in practice. The First International mentioned by Brandt in his address was riven with ideological tensions and split barely a decade after its creation. Its successor, meanwhile, collapsed as the workers of Europe succumbed to nationalist fervour and faced each other across no man's land from the putrid trenches of the Great War. Founded in 1951, the Socialist International I knew began as a loose association of affiliated socialist and social democratic parties from around the world. Under Brandt's inspiring leadership, it came to serve as an important forum for deliberation, debate, and action in global affairs.

This success owed much to his own internationalist vision, which sought to expand the organization's membership and focus and diversify its European character. The very conference that elected him president was an example of this vision in motion. In his remarks to delegates, Brandt called on the International to make common cause with parties and movements throughout Asia, Africa, and the Americas. Swedish prime minister Olof Palme, meanwhile, used his address to condemn South Africa's apartheid regime and express solidarity with independence movements in Mozambique, Angola, and Guinea-Bissau. The Congress also passed a host of resolutions concerning Latin America and welcomed new delegations hailing from several continents — two developments that anticipated the International's deepening engagement outside the western hemisphere in the ensuing few years.[2]

Such engagement was important on its own terms, but it also constituted a critical thrust of an ambitious global strategy. From the outset of his tenure, Brandt's overriding objective was to promote the democratic socialist model as an alternative to both the rip-and-run capitalism of the United States and the authoritarian communism of the Eastern Bloc, particularly in newly postcolonial societies at risk of becoming theatres for destructive superpower competition. In the context of the Cold War and its bipolar climate, this was an urgent and challenging task — further complicated by the ambient rightward drift of global politics toward the end of the 1970s. In the 1990s, Bill Clinton and Tony Blair would speak about a market-driven Third Way. But a full two decades earlier Brandt had helped to give the phrase a very different, and altogether much more laudable meaning, one that sought to reduce the impact of markets and advance social and economic rights.

Brandt's distinctive internationalist outlook flowed quite directly from lived experience. As a German born to a social democratic family in 1913, his trajectory had exposed him to some of the century's bleakest moments and also its greatest hopes. He was involved with the Socialist Youth Movement in Lübeck from a very young age, and his antifascist activity in the 1930s put his life at risk and ultimately compelled him to flee the country. Stripped of his German citizenship by the Nazis and for a time stateless, Brandt made a home in Norway and crossed over into Sweden when Oslo fell to the Wehrmacht.

There, he became secretary of an ad hoc "Little International" consisting partly of socialist exiles from occupied Europe (among them was Bruno Kreisky, another key figure in the Socialist International and the future chancellor of Austria). Brandt himself would later cite his exile in Sweden as politically formative, remarking in a 1971 speech in Stockholm: "I am indebted to Sweden not only because for five years I found refuge here; not only because I learnt much here; not only because . . . I have experienced what is meant by Swedish altruism; but also because, on the way toward an understanding between West and East, I received most valuable support from this country."[3]

Neither a Stalinist sympathizer nor a hardliner vis-à-vis the Soviet Bloc, Brandt embraced openness and détente while mayor of Berlin and hoped that it would eventually lead to reunification. As SPD chancellor of West Germany, he pursued a policy of Ostpolitik and sought to end the rival Christian Democratic Party's freeze on relations with the East.* Having himself borne witness to the horrors of authoritarianism, he had an instinctive solidarity with people resisting oppression and consequently used his position as president of the Socialist International to support democratic forces in Greece, Nicaragua, South Africa, and beyond.

---

\* In his speech to the Socialist International Congress hosted in Vancouver in 1978, Brandt's willingness to speak out on Soviet repression while still pursuing his careful diplomacy with East Germany shone through. He remarked that "democratic socialism furthers demands for freedom and fosters the experience of human rights. We will continue to speak out when people are being tortured — particularly when that is happening under the misused name of socialism." See: Socialist International Congress 1978, Vancouver, *Socialist Affairs* (January/February 1979).

Through my role in the Socialist International, I had the privilege of working closely with Willy Brandt for more than ten years. Along with Tommy Douglas, he became the other great inspiration in my political life. Though the NDP had maintained a nominal involvement with SI since its founding, Brandt's ambition to expand outside of Europe led him to invite me to serve as a vice president and to become a more active participant when I became leader. Like much about his tenure, the idea was actually somewhat novel. Though many of Europe's social democratic leaders had historically taken on the role at one time or another, most had also been heads of government — making my own presence as the recently elected leader of a North American third party fairly unorthodox.

On a personal level, Brandt was to me the living embodiment of what socialism should be all about: warm-hearted, generous, politically principled, but also open-minded and non-dogmatic. Practically speaking, his experience as the former mayor of Berlin and leader of a major industrial power meant he also had a great deal of insight into the inner workings of government. Through my role as vice president, I was introduced to many others to which the same applied: Kreisky and Palme, two of Brandt's leading collaborators; Joop den Uyl of the Netherlands; François Mitterrand; Irène Pétry of the International Council of Social Democratic Women; Michael Foot and Neil Kinnock from the British Labour Party; Gro Brundtland, Norway's first female prime minister; Michael Harrington of the Democratic Socialists of America; Shimon Peres of Israel; and Bernt Carlsson of Sweden (who served as the secretary of the Socialist International).

As a Canadian, I found the discussions at SI meetings deeply engaging. Forging connections with like-minded leaders from around the world, I learned how various social democratic models worked and about the policy debates found within the different national parties. I also travelled extensively throughout South and Central America, where our efforts to promote social democracy ran up against the reactionary course being pursued at the time by the United States.

**Jonathan Sas:** Your vice presidency at the Socialist International coincided with your leadership of the NDP, but is far less well-known or well-documented than other parts of your political career. How would you broadly characterize the SI and its work during the period in which you were involved?

**Ed Broadbent:** The work of the organization during that time was in a very important sense the extension of European social democracy in its golden age. The figures I met through the Socialist International were not just people with whom I shared common ground. They were people who represented the movement at its apogee and who had — alongside their immediate predecessors — laid the foundations for the modern welfare state and the practical realization of economic and social rights. During the postwar decades, this project represented the main challenge to the capitalist order as it was then constituted in many Western countries.

Many of the European leaders involved in the Socialist International had lived through the economic turmoil of the 1930s and had seen first-hand the kinds of outcomes that unbound markets guaranteed: both for ordinary people and for liberal institutions that had been ill-equipped to beat back the fascist threat. The solution, for them, was to confront the market mechanism and carve out a broad set of social and economic rights: to healthcare, education, pensions, housing, decent employment, and other social goods.

This was the struggle that had defined the left for at least two generations of politicians in labour, socialist, and social democratic parties in the decades after the Second World War. And it's important to remember that it was not only a challenge to the existing liberal order in North America and Europe, it was also an explicit rejection of the kind of centralized and bureaucratized state socialism that had been established in Eastern Europe (and in many cases directly imposed by the Red Army). That was the wider context for the work of the Socialist International while Brandt was president, and also very much the impetus for his wider mission to offer a constructive global alternative to both the American and Soviet models.

As for the activities of the organization itself, they were a mixture of debate, discussion, and direct material support that would be offered in various countries. Even as early as the mid-1970s, the formal and plenary sessions were already becoming like bureaucratized UN meetings in that leaders would make speeches that had already been typed up and sent out as press releases in their home countries. But on the final day of a conference, there would be leaders' meetings that I found particularly useful in my capacity as a social democratic politician: these meetings typically had an open agenda, meaning they tended to feature free and no-holds-barred discussions or debates. There would be frank sharing of information about how different parties were responding to conditions in their own countries. There would be detailed discussions about income policy, taxation, labour rights, electoral strategy, and a whole range of issues, generally giving a broad sense of what seemed to be working or not working.

All of that was quite useful on its own terms, but it was ultimately in service of Brandt's overriding strategic goal of promoting social democracy or democratic socialism as an attractive alternative to the rival models championed by the two Cold War superpowers. That necessitated expanding the Socialist International beyond its traditionally European scope. To that end, Brandt scheduled gatherings further afield: memorably in Japan, where he actually reached out to two competitors (the similarly named Democratic Socialist and Socialist parties) and asked them to host, in Vancouver in 1978, and Lima in 1986.

Vancouver, incidentally, is where I first properly met Brandt. The NDP acted as the host for the Socialist International Congress that year,[4] and it was the first time the organization had ever met outside Europe.* Working with Willy as the hosting chair, I had to navigate for the first time the intricate dealings of a big international conference. This proved especially interesting because that conference was also where the Sandinistas made their debut on the world stage. Armed with revolutionary rhetoric, their large delegation scared the bejesus out of the good citizens of British Columbia and some of my NDP colleagues. The Sandinistas had recently overthrown the authoritarian government of Nicaragua. They consisted of progressive priests, social democrats, Leninists, and a host of other political tendencies. At this point in history, they acted cohesively to depose a tyrannical regime. Later on, their conflicting tendencies from within would lead to significant policy conflicts and ultimately to another authoritarian regime.

Central America became an important area of focus for the SI under Brandt's leadership — among other things because it was such a significant front in the battle between U.S.-style capitalism and authoritarian statism. Our work there often brought us into direct conflict with the Americans, who were supporting some truly vicious regimes in places like Guatemala and El Salvador. The SI got the leaders of social democratic parties and movements throughout the region involved in its meetings, but it also in some cases offered them direct financial assistance. In the short-term, the goal was usually to call worldwide attention to the horrendous human rights abuses going on in these heavily militarized countries. But we also tried to foster a vibrant civil society and the kind of constitutional development and growth of representative democracy that would protect basic civil and political rights — while opening the door to the economic and social kind in the future.

All of it was very much an uphill battle. Because of their social democratic agenda, leaders like Guillermo Ungo in El Salvador

---

* The Vancouver Congress had a major focus on several areas: disarmament; redeploying military spending to development support for the Global South; and with Willy's leadership, debate over how the conflict between East and West implicated divisions between North and South.

were attacked as foreigners in their own countries. The danger some of our partners faced could also be even more serious than that. A friend from El Salvador, for example, travelled to Guatemala one weekend and never returned. They found his Volkswagen near the border, and he was almost certainly murdered by the ruling right-wing junta there. I met some truly courageous people in the course of that work, many of whom were quite literally risking their lives by getting involved with democratic movements.

**Frances Abele:** A major site of the superpower competition you've been talking about was Cuba, which experienced a popular revolution during the 1950s and then a failed invasion the following decade that was organized and financed by the United States. How did it figure in your work at SI and elsewhere? Where do you see its place in the broader geopolitical context we're describing?

**EB:** Cuba certainly stands out as an interesting case, and it was distinct from other communist administrations (like those in Eastern Europe) because its government was the product of an indigenous revolution rather than a phoney one imposed from outside. I supported Castro while a student and was pleased to see Batista overthrown. I, like so many others around the world, was optimistic and thought that he would bring democracy to Cuba. In various capacities — as an MP, as a vice president at SI, and later as head of Rights and Democracy — I ultimately had three encounters with him and got a chance to see what he was like up close.

The meetings were all a number of hours long and covered a tremendous swathe of ground. During the first two, I made a point of not discussing domestic politics in Cuba or raising questions about what was going on internally. At the time, what interested me was Castro's analysis of Central America and the extent to which he and his movement were involved there. One thing I'd say about the meetings is that I never subsequently learned he had lied or misled me on anything, which mattered because I was trying to obtain an accurate picture of what was actually going on in Nicaragua, Guatemala, and other countries in the region. Much of what he had to say simply reinforced what I already knew, but in retrospect, I think those meetings were fairly constructive and went smoothly. He was the head of a communist party and government, whereas I was a social democrat, and we never discussed what significance those allegiances might have to our relationship. It just never came up.

The third meeting, which was in 1991, went very differently. By that time, the Soviet Union — which had been a major ally and source of material aid for Cuba — was disintegrating, and Castro was well aware of what that meant for Cuba, that is, the disappearance of subsidies upon which the economy depended. For some members of the Socialist International, this created an opportunity to move Cuba in a more democratic direction. The Spanish social democrat Felipe González had scheduled a meeting in Madrid for the following year to celebrate Columbus's so-called "discovery" of America. The idea was that Castro could attend the meeting and announce certain democratic reforms, including free elections. In return, certain social democratic governments would provide financial assistance that would compensate for the economic damage done by the American embargo.

I put forward this proposal to Castro. I raised the question of financial assistance quite specifically with him because the Americans had importantly not been invited to Madrid: it would be Latin American governments only, and he had said in both public and private that he wasn't going to yield to Yankee pressure to have multiparty democracy. I also tried, as forcefully as I could, to make a multipronged case that accepting the offer would ultimately be in his own long-term self-interest. First, I argued that (outsider as I was) my strong hunch was that if elections were held at that time, he would probably win. I also made the case that the Cuban revolution, which he very much symbolized, had been genuine as compared to what had until then prevailed in Eastern Europe — and that, by extension, a major reason the various Soviet satellite states were breaking up was that they had never been genuine revolutionary societies. For that reason, I argued, he should probably hold an election sooner rather than later if he and his successors wanted to avoid the same fate.

The argument didn't go over well. In fact he rejected it outright. The conversation (which went on for at least three hours) had been on thin ice already because I had raised the case of a Cuban social democrat named Elizardo Sánchez who publicly supported the government's social programs but wanted it to hold free elections. I had heard that the local Defence of the Revolution committee was terrorizing the residents where Sánchez's mother lived: making noise twenty-four hours a day by beating pots and pans around the house. I had hoped Castro would intervene to stop the harassment. When I raised the issue, he just said, "Sánchez is a worm and we are not going to be making any concessions" (or something to that effect). The meeting was a failure and I never saw him again. It was the one and only time our relationship had gotten acrimonious. But it was also the one and only time we had broached the subject of domestic politics and the question of democracy in Cuba.

**JS:** He was a famously charismatic figure, and was known for great command of history, politics, and many other fields. What was he actually like when you were dealing with him in person? And what was your overall impression of him?

**EB:** I think that he was, at heart, an authoritarian figure. He was interested in providing universal healthcare and education — which they did to a very high standard for a developing country — but he had no interest in promoting free discussion, freedom of association, or anything that might lead to the government being challenged. That attitude, which isn't one I respect, revealed itself in parts of our conversations where he positioned himself as an authority on absolutely everything. He certainly was an autodidact and had a remarkable level of knowledge about a wide variety of subjects. On one occasion he sent me back to Canada with a giant bundle of medications to treat a medical condition I had (and, I would add, with some particularly fine cigars).

There was a certain generosity of spirit on his part that came through in an encounter like that. But it also showed his irrepressible desire to become master of every topic. I heard from others that, no matter what department of the government he was dealing with, he always had to be the dominant figure in policy discussions. To me, there's an intellectual arrogance implicit in that behaviour and in his cruelty in the Sánchez case. Someone who did not support him was too readily considered contemptible.

**Luke Savage:** I suppose the common rejoinder around Cuba and the absence of free elections would be that Castro was concerned they would make the country more vulnerable to the efforts directed at it from within the United States. Because, in addition to the embargo, there were numerous assassination attempts on Castro and the U.S.-backed invasion of Cuba at the Bay of Pigs. He was presumably also thinking about what had happened in places like Chile, where the Allende government was overthrown in a violent coup. Given all of that, do you think Castro had a leg to stand on in rejecting the offer along with multiparty elections? To what extent do you think the repressive climates that took root in twentieth-century communist countries were endemic to, or the result of, outside pressure being applied by capitalist powers?

**EB:** It's a complex question, and one I think I would rather entrust to historians as opposed to political scientists. The answer is also going to be somewhat dependent on the country being discussed. If we're talking about the USSR, I simply don't know enough to offer a definitive answer about the extent to which the repressive direction of travel from the 1920s onward was endemic to communist institutions and practice, as opposed to being a response to pressure and interference from Western capitalist powers. Some of it clearly was, but I can't offer much of an opinion as to exactly how much. What I can contribute is my own bias that the Bolshevik leadership, up to and including Lenin himself, had a marked authoritarian propensity. Given that, I think a lot of what occurred had to do with the ruling order within the USSR itself, and not just the hostile response elicited by the Russian Revolution.

When it comes to the Americas, which were the part of the world where I was most involved through the Socialist International, my judgement is more categorical. There, I would argue that American foreign policy has been repressive, particularly during the 1980s when Ronald Reagan was president. There was a marked ideological aggression coming from conservative parties across the West in those days, and in Central America, it manifested itself in a total intolerance toward even the most mildly progressive initiatives coming from democratic forces. Once there was a hint of anything like that, the logic of the Monroe Doctrine immediately kicked in — the imperative to protect American commercial interests in the former colonies to the south. And, as we saw in Reagan's funding of the Contras, those guiding American foreign policy were willing to go against their own laws in order to pursue their right-wing crusade. That was ideologically driven at the highest level, and I don't think it reflected any genuine pressure coming from the American people at all.

Turning back to Cuba, I think that the question is a somewhat complicated one to answer. Castro had every reason to be suspicious after the Bay of Pigs invasion, which of course the Americans had organized and which was a flop. There is today a big state security apparatus in Cuba designed specifically to keep the Americans and the CIA out. Still, as I had tried to persuade Castro, there was good reason to believe his project could survive if he went ahead with the institutions necessary for multiparty elections. For one thing, nearby countries like Costa Rica had managed a degree of pluralist social democracy and, in that particular case, had actually done so without even having a military. Its former president, Óscar Arias, won a Nobel Peace Prize for his efforts to make peace in Central America.

I came to think that much of Castro's talk about the Americans was self-serving and based on the domestic utility of the argument. Because Cubans remember the Bay of Pigs, the direction Castro took afterwards would be forever justified by him as a necessary defence against an external threat. When I was first elected to Parliament, I remember meeting Cuba's former ambassador to Canada a few times, a guy who had been one of only two people from his law class in Havana who had stayed to support the revolution. Despite having that background, he was among those who indicated to me, clearly but discreetly, that some in the government favoured an opening up of Cuba's political system but didn't dare engage on the question in public for fear of reprisal. If Castro had opted to move in a democratic socialist direction, I think he would have found allies not only among many of the leaders in the Socialist International but also in countries like Canada.

**FA:** We've been talking about the right-wing anti-communist ideology you saw at work throughout the region, but what about business interests? Don't you think that a lot of what lay behind American foreign policy was simply the protection of capital?

**EB:** Oh, undoubtedly — particularly in Latin America given the kinds of resources there and the American business interests who want to control them. But it's still an open question as to how far the American state would have gone in that regard if different people had been in control. What if, for example, George McGovern had somehow won the '72 presidential election instead

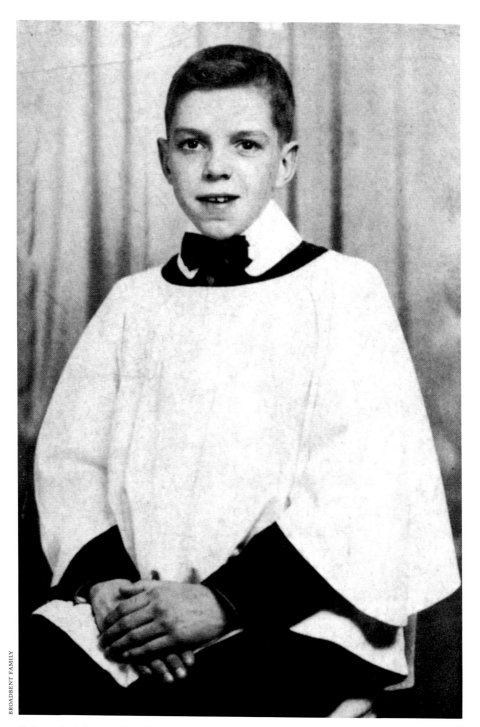

Ed as choirboy at St. George's Anglican Church in Oshawa.

ABOVE: NDP leadership candidates in 1971: Frank Howard (L), James Laxer, John Harney, David Lewis, and Ed. David Lewis was elected leader.

LEFT: Ed with his mother, Mary Broadbent, at his 1972 nomination meeting in Oshawa.

CP

Party leader David Lewis and House leader Stanley Knowles flank Ed who is chairing a caucus meeting after the 1972 election; the NDP won thirty-one seats, up six from the previous election.

Tommy Douglas and Ed meet in 1975 on Parliament Hill.

RIGHT: A close race for leader in 1975. Ed narrowly defeated Rosemary Brown, who later became a regular advisor on BC politics and women's rights.

BELOW: Ed with Oshawa office staff Bev Johnson and Nester Pidwerbecki. Ed was the first member of Parliament to establish a constituency office, initially paid for by Ed's salary and support from UAW local 222.

LEFT: Ed addressing the 1975 NDP convention after being elected leader.

Ed speaks with Willy Brandt, president of the Socialist International, while advisor Robin Sears stands in the background. Ed served as vice-president, and was a close collaborator of Brandt.

Ed supporting women workers at the Fleck plant in Ontario striking for a first contract. The miserable working conditions, low pay, and company resistance to any bargaining made this a particularly bitter strike. The workers were successful, winning a pay raise and application of the Rand formula.

RIGHT: Campaigning by motorcycle in British Columbia for Ray Skelly and Karen Sanford in 1979.

BELOW: Ed, Pierre Trudeau, and Joe Clark just before the 1979 election televised leaders' debate.

Lucille and Ed take a break from campaigning during the 1980 federal election.

Lucille, Paul, Christine, and Ed — the Broadbent family walk in Strathcona Park, Ottawa.

Ed with Parliament Hill staff on assistant Anne Carroll's birthday.

In Parliament on the occasion of the final vote on 1982's constitutional package. Ed was a strong supporter of the package and the Charter of Rights and Freedoms.

LEFT: The end of the 1984 campaign. Ed rides away on a bicycle given to him by campaign workers in Oshawa. Ed won all seven elections he contested in the riding.

ABOVE: Ed pays his respects to his sister-in-law, Sharon Broadbent, an ardent campaign worker in Oshawa.

Ed supporting striking Canada Packers workers in 1984.

Ed campaigns in Halifax with Alexa McDonough in 1984. McDonough was leader of the federal NDP 1995–2003.

IF ED BROADBENT HAD BEEN A USED CAR SALESMAN...

HONEST ED'S USED CARS

THE DOOR RATTLES THE RADIATOR LEAKS AND WE'VE TURNED BACK THE ODOMETER...

" I want to vote for Broadbent but I'm afraid he might win "

Meeting with newly ascended Pope John Paul II to discuss the political turmoil in Central America.

Michael Manley, former prime minister of Jamaica, and Ed meet there to discuss conflicts in Central America.

Ed with longtime senior staff George Nakitsas, Anne Carroll, and Bill Knight in one of many meetings in Ottawa hotels.

Ed campaigns for Ruth Grier, a longtime friend, in 1987. Grier would soon go on to be a cabinet minister in Ontario's NDP government.

ABOVE: Ed meets with King Juan Carlos of Spain during the King's work to help shepherd the country's democratic transition following the death of fascist dictator Francisco Franco.

LEFT: Ed campaigns on Bay Street in 1988. While Ed focused on the interests of "ordinary Canadians" he called out his challengers' allegiance to the financial elite.

Meeting with Benazir Bhutto, leader of the opposition in Pakistan, to discuss the human rights situation in her country.

LEFT: Ed with Elizabeth Spehar, Latin American specialist at Rights and Democracy, and Fidel Castro, president of Cuba, in Havana in 1991.

BELOW: Meeting with Bill Clinton in the White House to discuss the shipment of arms by the Chinese government to the military regime in Myanmar. Clinton agreed to issue a press statement condemning the shipment.

Ed with Desmond Tutu, the Dalai Lama, and others. Ed led a delegation to Thailand to campaign for the release of Aung San Suu Kyi and her reinstatement as the elected head of the government of Myanmar.

Campaigning with Jack Layton in 2008.

Old friends: Ed chats with political philosopher Charles Taylor and United Steelworkers president Ken Newman at a Broadbent Institute event.

Greeting Bernie Sanders onstage at a 2017 event in Toronto.

Receiving an honorary doctorate, with good friend and longtime political advisor Terry Grier, founding president of Ryerson University, now Toronto Metropolitan University.

of getting swamped? There was at one point a more liberal wing of American politicians who might have been less likely to react with the same violent hostility toward countries trying to nationalize their own resources. It could well be the case that the American state would still have gotten involved in protecting business interests even with different actors in power. But, quite apart from the pressures exerted by capitalist enterprises themselves, I think ideology played a significant role in shaping the aggressive U.S. policy toward Latin America in that era. I don't think any capitalist forces were pushing Ronald Reagan: he was their willing handmaiden.

That potentially raises other complicated questions about the role of ideology in determining political outcomes as opposed to that of material self-interest or raw power. My own view, in relation to this and also much of what we've been discussing here, is that ideology is significant.

**LS:** During his second run for president, there were numerous attempts to smear Bernie Sanders for having supported the Sandinistas during the 1980s and for a few totally innocuous comments about literacy rates in Cuba. Given that kind of thing, I'm curious whether anyone tried to red-bait you over your international work or use it against the NDP?

**EB:** The short answer is no, or not that I can recall. Joe Clark once gave a totally irrational red-baiting sort of speech in Alberta, but that's the only thing that really comes to mind. Prior to my SI days, I did experience something faintly analogous at the local level when my opponent Mike Starr chided me for referencing Scandinavia so much and trotted out some statistics about the high suicide rates in Sweden, demanding to know why I wanted to bring a foreign system like that to Canada. As it turned out, I happened to know that Swedish suicide rates had been as high or higher before the Social Democratic Party had come to power, meaning there was no correlation between the two and replied to him to that effect. Though I suspect there were a few stronger examples of that kind of thing, the red scare tactics associated with the 1950s had largely dissipated by the time my generation entered politics.

**JS:** It sounds like your involvement with the Socialist International had fairly low visibility in Canada as compared to your other work. Was it something you communicated much to the public or incorporated into your own political messaging as a party leader? It strikes me that the component of SI's work that was critical of American foreign policy potentially rhymed with the nationalist sentiments that were prevalent in Canada at the time. Olof Palme in particular was quite vocal in his criticisms of the U.S. over Vietnam. Perhaps you can tell us about your relationship with him as well?

**EB:** The old cliché that all politics is local definitely applies here. Tommy Douglas, David Lewis, and myself were all openly critical of U.S. policy over Vietnam. But it did not play a central part in our domestic politics or messaging, and neither did the SI when I was involved in it. There were always domestic politics to think about, and those tended to play a much bigger role. You're right, though, in bringing up Palme's critical attitude toward the United States, which was characteristic of the SI's orientation. He would give speeches that were often perceived as deeply anti-American, but he was simply calling for more independence in both domestic and foreign policy, and making the case that countries should resist the economic and other pressures exerted by the United States on the one hand and the USSR on the other. As prime minister of Sweden, he had to think very seriously about these questions because the Soviet Union was right next door.

Incidentally, speaking with Palme always underscored the extent to which every country has its own unique perspective on foreign affairs — a truism often borne out in our discussions at SI as well. When Pierre Trudeau announced his retirement, he went on a global peacenik tour which many of us felt was more of an exercise in conscience-cleansing. Because Palme had been very active in pursuing disarmament and trying to lower tensions between the superpowers, I asked him how he felt about his dealings with Trudeau. To me, Trudeau's approach to bilateral relations with the United States in particular had always seemed excessively conservative as compared to Palme's. Palme's reply was that he didn't have to live with the U.S. as his neighbour. He intended this as a serious remark, his point being that there are major pressures on any Canadian prime minister that complicate things because of our country's location and the disparity in relative strength between Canada and the U.S.

That kind of nuance was quite characteristic of Palme's approach in general. He also had a good understanding of the United States, partly from having spent a year at Kenyon College in Ohio (he actually wrote a senior honours thesis on the United Auto Workers). He spoke with a very North American style of English which was less stilted than was common for European politicians in that era. I didn't know him well, but he was a remarkable man who was always determined to emphasize issues of equality in his political agenda and was looked on as a class traitor by many in the very Swedish aristocracy he'd come from. Other than at SI meetings, I never saw him. Even through that limited contact, it was obvious that he had both a firm intellectual grasp of theory and an ability to explain socialist ideas in a legible way. I especially admired that about him, and I have no doubt he would have succeeded Willy Brandt as president of the SI had he not been assassinated.

Probably the most moving public funeral I've ever attended was Palme's. The Social Democratic Party itself organized the memorial and there were people of all political persuasions there from across the world. The orchestra played Mozart, and a group of singers from Finland who had campaigned with him performed what I can only describe as a hymn to social democracy. It was at once a deeply sad and joyful occasion.

**JS:** Sweden pursued a radical form of social democracy and introduced a significant proposal with the Rehn-Meidner Plan* — which in many ways channelled many of the ideas and themes around industrial democracy that interested you. The SI may not have been a major part of your political message in Canada, but did your work there inform your thinking about domestic policy vis-à-vis industrial democracy, economic planning, or anything else?

**EB:** I certainly learned a great deal from the policy discussions and major debates that happened at SI meetings, and it was always fascinating to hear about what social democratic governments were implementing or trying. When it came to adapting ideas about industrial democracy, economic planning, or other serious domestic policy areas, I always had to grapple with the realities of Canadian federalism. So much control over the Canadian economy and over our natural resources rests with the provinces, which made it difficult to neatly transpose the kinds of things that were being done by social democrats in more centralized states. Sectoral planning, for example, was a staple of left-wing economic thinking in Europe but would be a huge challenge for a party like the NDP to take up in government.

I think the bigger influence of the SI on my thinking had to do with exposure to people like Brandt, Palme, and Kreisky. These were men (and they were mostly men at that point) who

---

* The Rehn-Meidner Plan, named for its authors, was an approach to management of the economy on Keynesian principles to foster low inflation, full employment, high growth, and income equality. A distinctive feature was the solidarity wage policy, in which wages rose with economic growth.

not only embodied the values I believed in but had devoted their lives to forming governments and making social democracy real with legislation. Thinking back on my early experience in the federal NDP caucus, a few of my colleagues had really seemed to internalize a particular idea about what the role of the NDP was, and they were, at the very least, agnostic on the question of trying to win government. That was most strongly illustrated by Stanley Knowles, who was convinced that even if we did not expand beyond a handful of MPs, we could work vigorously in Parliament and have a positive impact.

I wouldn't call this view complacency, but I did think some were too comfortable in the idea that the NDP existed primarily to be the conscience of Parliament. That probably sounds overly critical, but I don't mean it that way. Sociologically speaking, I think this perspective was probably born of the fact that neither the CCF nor the NDP had ever wielded majoritarian power in Ottawa. In the absence of that kind of power, you have to look for other ways of advancing your agenda — and, since leaders of the movement going back to J.S. Woodsworth and M.J. Coldwell had been quite effective in that regard, I think some came to see being the conscience of Parliament as a perfectly satisfactory role. That was not, however, my own view. And being in the company of people who had real experience wielding state power at the SI only impressed on me further the importance of trying to win a parliamentary majority as opposed to just pushing other parties to do things.

**LS:** Beginning in the 1970s, there was a generalized shift of global politics to the right that eventually captured many of the traditional social democratic and labour parties as well. By the time Brandt had taken up the presidency of the SI, for example, Germany's Social Democratic Party was already going in a more conservative direction under Helmut Schmidt and the British Labour Party moved further to the right with every subsequent election after Margaret Thatcher's victory in 1979. Did you encounter any early versions of the so-called Third Way philosophy that dominated during the 1990s or any figures who were attracted to it?

**EB:** There were not a lot of them, though they did exist. Within the SI, during my time there, they were a minority faction and a far cry from what eventually came after me in the 1990s. Despite what was happening globally, the milieu of the SI itself largely stayed anchored in the left social democratic orientation that Brandt embodied. People like Tony Blair and Gerhard Schröder, of course, ultimately took European social democracy in a more conservative and market-centric direction, but that was a little later, and that's at least part of the story of the SI's eventual decline after Brandt's departure. For much of the 1980s, I think, the most visible ideological revolution was happening on the right.

Illustrative of that, and also an ominous harbinger of what was to come, was the 1983 formation of a new conservative analogue to the SI: the International Democrat Union. Prior to that, the only major international body on the right was the Christian Democrat Union, whose founding principles incorporated an acceptance of economic and social rights. The ideologues of the new right in the 1980s, notably Thatcher and Reagan, rejected them explicitly and excluded them from the IDU charter.

Before the Third Way turn really happened within the SI itself, there was another problem, which was that the SI bureaucracy — in a careless move simply to expand — accepted a lot of parties from Africa and Latin America without properly checking on their social democratic (or even just democratic) credentials. This led to contentious fights about who should be included. These conflicts ultimately contributed to the decline and breakup of the Socialist International.

**FA:** Looking back on the SI during Brandt's tenure, it's quite remarkable to see the expansive political imagination social democracy had in the fairly recent past. How would you characterize Brandt's legacy?

**EB:** Broadly speaking, the organization had real international heft under Brandt. He could go practically anywhere in the world and be met by the head of government. And indeed, when I travelled, the fact that I was a vice president at the SI actually meant something. The social democratic alternative Brandt was championing also attracted considerable attention. That all withered away very quickly after his death. Pierre Mauroy, who had been French prime minister under François Mitterrand, succeeded him and was a classic, bureaucratically oriented guy who took the organization nowhere, and its influence dissipated. The important truth, which Willy would have conceded, is that the SI never became the force in world affairs he had envisioned, notwithstanding the influence it had on me.

When I retired from leading the NDP, I nearly ended up working for him full-time as an advisor. It had been the view of some leaders within the SI that Willy was too captured by the bureaucracy of the organization, which is something I think he felt himself. There was a discussion between him, me and one or two of the other leaders about how he needed an adviser in his office concerned specifically with political rather than bureaucratic questions. He would have been happy to have me take up a position like that, but the financing for it was not forthcoming, and there was also some resistance to what was seen as preferential treatment for a Canadian in the SI's top office. It's regrettable because I would have enjoyed working for him immensely. He was an extraordinarily decent and courageous man who had a tremendous impact on my political outlook and on my life.

## CHAPTER SEVEN

# The Great Patriation Debate

> *"So what Canada got with the Charter was a dramatic package of guaranteed rights, subject only to those reasonable limits that were demonstrably justified in a free and democratic society . . . All of this flowed from Lord Sankey's admonition to the Canadian Supreme Court in 1929 that the word 'persons' in the Constitution included women: 'The British North American Act planted in Canada a living tree capable of growth and expansion . . . Their Lordships do not conceive it to be the duty of this Board — it is certainly not their desire — to cut down the provisions of the Act by a narrow and technical construction, but rather to give it a large and liberal interpretation.' And the 'living tree' has been our guiding constitutional interpretive approach ever since."*
>
> — CHIEF JUSTICE ROSALIE SILBERMAN ABELLA,
> *Freedom of Expression or Freedom from Hate*

Modern states stand or fall by one basic test. Citizens must instinctively ask themselves not merely what is good for me, my region, or my ideology, but also what is good for us. No people can live together in a democratic community if they do not respond in this twofold way. Citizens must be able to look at their compatriots in distant, even alien, regions and ask not simply, "What share of this is mine?" but also, "What can we do together?" Debated in the abstract, such questions are challenging enough. Posed amid the complex realities of an intricate federal society, they carry an existential weight.

It's perhaps unsurprising, then, that the years leading up to the patriation of Canada's constitution and the entrenchment of the Charter of Rights and Freedoms were among the most intense and difficult of my political life. Throughout the early 1980s, the high-stakes business of constitution-building aggravated the regional, social, and linguistic tensions endemic to the federation while exposing significant ideological differences in my own party. Forging consensus within the NDP, a daunting task at the best of times, became an enterprise more delicate, and volatile, than ever before.

In principle at least, there was initially some reason to think that it might be otherwise. The CCF had committed itself to patriation back in 1932 and officially adopted the idea of a constitutionally entrenched bill of rights as party policy in 1944. While premier of Saskatchewan, Tommy Douglas had passed the country's first Human Rights Act, guaranteeing basic civil and political freedoms and prohibiting discrimination on the basis of either race or religion. The protection of individual rights in constitutional form, in other words, was deep in the bedrock of Canada's democratic socialist tradition.

Political practice is rarely a straightforward matter — a fact that the heady debates surrounding patriation would bring into sharp, and at times blinding, relief.

Though its outcome fell short of my ambitions in bringing down the Clark government, the federal election of February 1980 produced an arrangement of MPs that would afford the NDP important leverage. Returning to power with a majority, the Trudeau Liberals won seventy-four of Quebec's seventy-five seats but failed to elect a single MP west of Manitoba. For the NDP, the reverse applied: our House cohort increasing from twenty-seven to thirty-two without any representation east of Ontario. Disappointed as I was about the result, I knew the prime minister would now have to seek out the NDP's support for any serious constitutional effort.

It therefore came as no surprise when Trudeau proposed a meeting shortly after the election. What was a surprise was the meeting's actual purpose: to invite the NDP to join a coalition government. "You are concerned about a national energy policy, as I am. You've broadly supported constitutional change," he told me. "And I know you're sympathetic to a charter of rights. You're concerned about having a clarification in the constitution on jurisdiction over resource development, as I am. You have a lot of seats west of Ontario, and we have virtually none. I think it would be very helpful for you to come into the cabinet and work from within." Surprised, I responded that I'd want five or six additional NDP cabinet ministers to come with me — at least a couple of them being in major portfolios. Trudeau's direct reply indicated the seriousness of his offer: "You've got them." Pressing the issue a bit further, I posed a few hypotheticals and informed the prime minister that I would think on it.

Though the offer had an obvious political logic from Trudeau's perspective, my own attitude upon leaving the room was far more circumspect. As junior partner to a majority party, the NDP would be bound to cabinet decisions but ultimately unnecessary to the government's survival — with or without our support, Trudeau's majority would remain intact and our influence would be severely limited. This was my major concern. I was also aware of the risks historically associated with national (coalition) governments, calling to mind the example of Britain's Ramsay MacDonald in the early 1930s and the feelings of betrayal his coalition with the Tories and Liberals had elicited throughout the Labour movement. I was skeptical, but I did consult a few colleagues who agreed with me that the answer had to be no. In rejecting his proposal, I nonetheless indicated to Trudeau that I saw a potential for common ground on both energy policy and his rights agenda, at least under certain conditions.

When Quebec's referendum on sovereignty association delivered a clear victory for the federalist side a few months later, the prime minister proceeded to pursue his long-standing ambition: the patriation of Canada's constitution from Great Britain with a new charter of rights. Unable to secure the necessary support from the premiers at a First Ministers' conference that September, Trudeau decided he would act unilaterally. The following month, I met with him again and agreed to offer the NDP's public backing of the effort in principle — provided he accept some amendments to the Charter and affirm provincial jurisdiction over natural resources. These were significant concessions, and both of us hoped that the latter in particular would be favourably received in the west. As it turned out, the country's sole NDP premier — Allan Blakeney of Saskatchewan — was far from persuaded.

I supported patriation and the Charter as a matter of principle. For one thing, since my days as a high school student, it had struck me as absurd that Canada should have to go to another country to amend its own constitution. More importantly, it had been a long-standing commitment of the CCF/NDP, and some of Canadian history's darkest episodes — Japanese internment, Duplessis's Padlock Law,* and more recently the imposition of the War Measures Act — demonstrated the clear need for a charter of rights. By offering Trudeau the NDP's backing with conditions, I thought we would ultimately be in a stronger position to influence the process and assert key demands like the inclusion of clauses protecting gender equality and Indigenous rights. Over the coming months, amid challenging debates in caucus, party, and country alike, I was comforted and encouraged by the support of respected figures in the federal NDP like Tommy Douglas, David Lewis, and Stanley Knowles. Whatever the limitations of the constitutional process might be, I saw it as a worthy endeavour firmly in accordance with party history and social democratic principles.

---

**Luke Savage:** Upon returning to power in 1980, Prime Minister Trudeau made patriation a key political priority. Can you describe what your thinking was when it became clear he was determined to go ahead? Did you have any concerns, either with the idea in principle or in how you believed the effort was actually going to play out?

---

* The 1940s law, introduced by the Union Nationale government of Maurice Duplessis, gave Quebec's attorney general broad repressive powers against individuals accused of vaguely defined communist or Bolshevik activities.

**Ed Broadbent:** I looked carefully at the initial package. I believed it was worth struggling for, particularly because of the two additional commitments Trudeau offered: to accept amendments to the list of rights that were going to be protected in the Charter; and to provide constitutional language that would clearly establish provincial control over resources. Patriation and a charter of rights were long-settled as NDP policy, so with those conditions attached I was comfortable offering him our support in principle and believed that we could make the package desirable for Canada as a whole. After the 1980 referendum, I had thought it important that some initiative should be taken to address Quebec's concerns, including survival of the French language and control of the provincial economy. As it turned out, Trudeau's initiative was not especially designed to appeal to Quebec — though it wasn't obvious at the outset that they would ultimately refuse to sign on. Given their frequently expressed concern about the need for clarification of provincial control over resources, I mistakenly hoped the NDP government in Saskatchewan would be supportive. Trudeau hoped for the same result.

**Frances Abele:** It seemed to me at the time, and I suppose I was not alone, that most of the premiers were focused very narrowly on protecting provincial jurisdiction and powers, ignoring the advances that could be inscribed in the Constitution for the protection of rights. Is that a fair assessment?

**EB:** Yes, the premiers very quickly began squabbling about jurisdictional questions and failed to see the larger picture or understand the need for Canada to get its own constitution with a reasonable amending formula. That was long overdue for the country, which needed a stronger entrenchment of rights than was provided in the Bill of Rights passed by John Diefenbaker's government. This process was ultimately about enshrining fundamental rights in the constitution and obtaining real nationhood.

It seemed to be hard for many of the premiers to rise to the occasion. The exceptions were Bill Davis in Ontario and Richard Hatfield in New Brunswick, who both gave their early support to the constitutional initiative. The former was especially important because it would have been inconceivable for Trudeau to have gone ahead without the support of the largest province. Hatfield was a committed nationalist and promised to get French entrenched as an official language in New Brunswick. Aside from those two, at the outset anyway, most of the premiers seemed exclusively pre-occupied with questions of provincial jurisdiction. Once we got into that area, there were many variations and conflicts among them about what set of rights they wanted to include. For example, the NDP government in Saskatchewan, after a long process, supported and worked hard for a section on Aboriginal rights,* whereas Conservative governments were more focused on an effective notwithstanding clause which they saw as maintaining the historical strength of provincial legislatures and Parliament vis-à-vis the courts.

There was understandably strong opposition to unilateral action by the federal government, but in their response, the provinces diverged significantly. They focused on specific components within the package, as opposed to seeing the initiative as a broad and important national objective. As the battle carried on, public opinion increasingly swung behind the Charter of Rights: the more people learned about it, and the more it was amended to

---

\* The term Indigenous, rather than Aboriginal, is now the preferred umbrella term many Indigenous people, communities, and organizations in Canada use to refer collectively to the many original peoples and nations of North America. Aboriginal remains in use when speaking to the body of Canadian law made by Crown courts and legislatures. Aboriginal rights, for example, refer to the unique constitutional rights of First Nations, Inuit, and Metis peoples as enshrined in the Constitution Act, 1982. Indigenous law, in contrast, refers to the legal orders — the customs, practices, traditions, and governance — rooted in Indigenous societies, existing independently of colonial laws.

incorporate and recognize further rights, the more it attracted public support.

**FA:** There was some philosophical opposition to the idea as well. One contrary view was that the entrenchment of the Charter of Rights and Freedoms was inadvisable because it shifted power away from elected members of Parliament toward unelected judges. Were you concerned about the potential democratic implications?

**EB:** Allan Blakeney and I, as two social democrats, differed strongly on this issue — and one of his major stated worries was that unelected judges could strike down progressive laws, as regularly happens in the United States. I was aware of the democratic issues involved in having a strong charter of rights. But I did not ultimately see the idea of an embedded charter as at odds with democracy, and key figures in the federal party — including David Lewis, Stanley Knowles, and Tommy Douglas — shared my view. We saw Supreme Court judges, at times of public passion, as more likely — with a strong charter — to protect the rights of citizens than an elected body like the House of Commons, subject to the direct pressures of the electorate. In short, we believed that a well-written charter would protect Canadians against the kind of draconian measures taken during the Second World War when thousands of Canadian citizens of Japanese descent were incarcerated, had their property confiscated, and had their fundamental rights denied.

To go back to Blakeney, the continuing negative response of the Saskatchewan government, even after it became clear that Trudeau was going to accept an amendment with wording meeting Saskatchewan's desire for provincial control over resources, was one of the great disappointments of my public life. To this day, I still don't really know what the root of the problem was. We

secured a critical concession from Trudeau right from the beginning and those in the Saskatchewan leadership of the party have
still never conceded that important truth about constitutional
change in 1982. It is possible that Premier Blakeney simply did
not accept the need for a constitutionally entrenched charter of
rights, preferring instead the Diefenbaker model.

**Jonathan Sas:** Within the NDP, this period was arguably the most
contentious during your tenure as leader. Were there moments in
which you worried about it affecting your ability to keep the party
together or believed the process was going to fail?

**EB:** On the latter part of the question, there were several moments
— especially when we were waiting for the court at various stages
to issue rulings on the package — in which we feared that it would
all come apart or see the whole package thrown out. There was
definitely a real concern about party unity too, and it particularly
concerned me to be in such a public dispute with the most traditionally CCF/NDP government of them all (Saskatchewan). On
the positive side, we had what was probably one of the best debates
of the entire constitutional process at the 1981 NDP convention
in Vancouver. It went into considerable detail about what was
involved in the package, and I thought it was a vigorous discussion.
In the end, there was a vote that went approximately two-thirds
in favour of my position in supporting the package. A majority
of westerners were on our side too, including a large majority in
British Columbia, a majority of Manitoba, and I suspect maybe
even a majority of individual delegates from Saskatchewan —
all of which was boosted by strong support from the sections in
Ontario and Atlantic Canada.

The debate within the NDP certainly had a lot to do with
principles, but extraneous regional tensions also came to the
surface. I resented being attacked as an "eastern" leader, even

though I had done a lot to try to build bridges between the east and the west. I did not appreciate it when politicians from Saskatchewan and Alberta tried to portray the constitutional changes simply as the "Trudeau package." Trudeau was unpopular on the prairies, and using his name only undermined public understanding of the substance of what was being proposed. Alberta premier Peter Lougheed was popular in Saskatchewan and, when he was initially not onside, the Blakeney government was reluctant to move far away from his position on the issue. In addition, there was always the danger that more than three or four Saskatchewan MPs would go offside in the caucus. I had to hope that the rest, the majority, would hold solid — which they did. And because of the strong backing I got from our MPs in British Columbia, I couldn't really be characterized as anti-Western.

On a personal level, it was an extremely difficult period, and people like Tommy and David really helped keep me sane. Dave Barrett and I would often talk privately about things over the phone and that was a great help as well. Lucille, as always, was a voice of unstinting courage and optimism. But there's no denying that those were challenging times. Having said that, it never occurred to me to abandon the constitutional direction we had taken, even during the most contentious moments.

**FA:** Can you comment on the judicial issue more specifically? As a committed social democrat, it seems that you might have shared some concern about having a charter that unelected people would be charged with interpreting.

**EB:** That's complicated by the very nature of democracy itself. In any democracy, there is in practice a range of rights pertaining to things like free assembly, speech, and competitive political parties. If you accept the need for those rights as a given, there's also good reason to want some protective mechanism to ensure their continuity. In that sense, far from being a denial of democracy, I think an embedded charter of rights can be seen as integral to it. I thought that it would be best to entrench that set of rights in the constitution and hope that the judges would be better protectors of them than politicians caught up in the passions of a particular moment. It was, in that sense, an act of faith in our democracy, and I didn't see any evidence in the Canadian tradition that I thought warranted significant concern about judges making decisions at variance with the Charter's provisions as long as they were clearly spelled out.

Since 1982, in fact, I would argue that rights have been expanded by court decisions rather than narrowed — including in one area that's very important to me: namely, the right of workers to form a union and engage in free collective bargaining. Another example would be the gradual, and admittedly still imperfect, broadening of the meaning of Aboriginal and treaty rights entrenched in Section 35.

**JS:** Let's talk about Section 35. The NDP used its leverage to help get that into the Charter.

**EB:** We did, though importantly there was also immense pressure coming from Indigenous people themselves to make sure their rights were recognized in the constitution. The Constitution Express, with dedicated leaders like George Manuel, saw thousands of Indigenous people come to Ottawa to fight for their

---

* The Constitution Express was a movement of Indigenous activists and community members led by Grand Chief George Manuel, then president of the Union of BC Indian Chiefs, to ensure that Indigenous title and rights would be affirmed in the Constitution. Beginning in Vancouver, supporters joined the express as it made its way across the country, garnering the attention of the wider Canadian public and galvanizing the broader Indigenous rights movement. By the time it reached Ottawa, there were a thousand strong participants.

rights and influence the consultations. That pressure is what ultimately led to Section 35, which recognizes "existing aboriginal
and treaty rights" in the Charter, and it was felt strongly by myself
and my NDP colleagues. During the battle for Section 35, I can
vividly remember having in my office at one point the heads of
the national Indigenous organizations who had been engaged in an
intense struggle for the affirmation of their rights to be included in
the Charter. It was one of a number of similar meetings when rights
were thoroughly discussed. I had been involved in responding to the
infamous White Paper in 1969, just one year after I was first elected.
As a caucus, we agreed with the objections raised by Indigenous
peoples on the grounds that they had rights of citizenship, but also
special rights arising from their original presence on the land.

The struggle over the White Paper notwithstanding, it wasn't
until the Constitutional period of 1980–82 that I became fully
engaged with what were then referred to as Aboriginal rights issues
and properly recognized their centrality to the political reality of
Canada. A good part of my initial thinking came from discussions
within the caucus itself, particularly with British Columbia MPs
like Jim Fulton, Jim Manly, Ian Waddell, Svend Robinson, and
others like Tom Berger (they were all, of course, being educated
by Indigenous leaders, and organizations like the Union of BC
Indian Chiefs, which had formed in response to the White Paper).
Because of those experiences, I had a solid grounding ahead of my
discussions with Trudeau on the importance of a clause like what
we eventually got in Section 35. I contended in those meetings
with Trudeau that Indigenous rights existed long before European
settlers had arrived regardless of what our constitution said. The
federal government also had a responsibility to honour the treaties
made with the Crown.

Trudeau rejected those arguments on philosophical grounds.
His resistance came from his eighteenth-century liberal perspective on individual rights: that rights for all citizens had to be the
same, that equality equals sameness. For Trudeau, you could not
have differentiated rights for different parts of the population —

a notion we had previously seen embodied in the White Paper. It's to his credit as a politician that he eventually came around to accept Section 35, something he conceptually and philosophically didn't agree with but recognized was essential to getting the constitutional package passed.

**JS:** The struggle to get those rights into the Constitution opened up a whole new era of legal action that has since come to shape the country's politics and future. But courts are only one avenue, albeit an important one, for the Indigenous rights struggle. In your view, what would genuine self-determination within Canada require, and what kinds of new decision-making or even legal frameworks do you think are necessary?

**EB:** That's the big question coming for the federal government, but for the provinces as well. Both, as representatives of "the Crown," have to be involved in serious negotiations with Indigenous peoples about their rights and how they're actually going to be implemented. I think there will be very different models. The Nisga'a reached one kind of settlement decades ago by concluding negotiation of a modern treaty which secured their land rights and established a form of self-government. I suspect and hope other Indigenous nations will reach other types of settlements in the coming years.

It's incumbent on governments to take what I regard as a social democratic attitude toward collective rights: that is, to understand the necessity for Indigenous peoples to exercise real control over their land. Nations can't shape their own destinies unless they have the land to which they're entitled, to provide a foundation for the fulfillment of those destinies. I don't think we should underestimate the difficulties here, but it has to be done.

Strangely enough, it's one of the areas that I am somewhat optimistic about right now. Seeing the attitudes of non-Indigenous Canadians toward Indigenous issues — which I think are more open these days — gives me some hope we'll see progress. These are the most favourable conditions for change in my lifetime. But, as always at historical hinge points, it could go either way. Things could turn sour, or there could be some blossoming of agreements in different parts of the country with different groups of Indigenous people implementing their rights and assuming their rightful jurisdictions.

I think that the inclusion of the wording that we put in the Constitution had a greater impact than many of us thought it would. But we also knew that the courts would have leeway in terms of interpreting that and consequently hoped that Section 35 would broaden out (rather than narrow) the scope of rights. By and large, I think it has.

**JS:** Provincial NDP governments have checkered records on Indigenous title and rights, where often resource revenues have taken precedence over securing consent for projects. Here, we might think of the Notley government in Alberta's support for the Trans Mountain Pipeline or the Horgan government in British Columbia on LNG (liquified natural gas). Why do you think that is and what is the path forward from a social democratic perspective?

**EB:** Take the issue of the connection between Indigenous rights and the development of resources: I think that on the one hand, provincial governments — whether it's in Alberta, BC, or anywhere else in Canada — have a profound and deep constitutional and moral obligation to respect Indigenous rights. Insofar as provinces wish to make agreements with private companies to develop resources, the parameters for those agreements should be negotiated at the outset with the involvement of Indigenous people. They have to be involved in setting out the parameters and ultimately have to offer consent (or not) for a project to move forward, because it's their land. Historically, some Indigenous nations are in favour of development on certain land while others are not. And there isn't an easy way of squaring the circle when there are divisions among and within Indigenous nations and provincial governments.

Philosophically, I would like to see the integration of decision-making with full participation of Indigenous groups — and, for example, with unions and businesses, if there's going to be a private development. There's no way of predicting what the outcomes will be or should be from that process. The process itself should determine the outcome, and all the participants should be able to conclude that they had an effective say, but also that the rights guaranteed by the Constitution and the UN Declaration on the Rights of Indigenous Peoples have been properly recognized. So that's got to be the starting point. Furthermore, there must not be militarized RCMP operations against Indigenous people. Any injunction enforcement should be by unarmed police officers acting in a civil matter, and certainly not in a brutal one.

I think there are important aspects of these decisions that are not mere nuances. They go to the heart of whether you respect the dignity of other people, whether they're Indigenous peoples or others.

**FA:** Going back to your point about the Charter and the courts, it is also applicable to LGBTQ rights. The 1995 Supreme Court decision rooted in Section 15 prohibits discrimination on grounds of sexual orientation, even though sexual orientation is not explicitly mentioned in that clause.* That's due to a single phrase ("and, in

---

* The full text of Section 15 reads: "(1) Every individual is equal before and under the law and has the right to the equal protection and equal benefit of the law without discrimination and, in particular, without discrimination based on race, national or ethnic origin, colour, religion, sex, age or mental or physical disability.

   (2) Section (1) does not preclude any law, program or activity that has as its object the amelioration of conditions of disadvantaged individuals or groups including those that are disadvantaged because of race, national or ethnic origin, colour, religion, sex, age or mental or physical disability."

particular") which precedes the list of specific grounds of discrimination that are listed in the section. When the Charter was being drafted and debated, did you anticipate that the courts would end up protecting minority rights in a way that was not explicitly specified?

**EB:** Yes, which was again part of my rationale for supporting it. Both the Charter and the package as a whole were referred to a House of Commons committee that held public hearings. Those enabled a broader public participation which was important and a lot of questions were raised during that period that were not part of the initial discussion. As leader, I ensured that we had different people on the committee, depending on the specific rights that were under discussion. For example, Neil Young from the Beaches riding in Toronto was active on the issue of disability rights and Pauline Jewett was a leading advocate of what came to be Section 28, which guarantees equal application of the Charter regardless of gender.

**FA:** This might be a good moment to talk more generally about different theories of jurisprudence. Canada's legal tradition has generally followed the "living tree" understanding of the Constitution, in which decisions made by the courts take into account the changing circumstances of history. The courts have, on occasion, innovated, building upon the arguments with which they've been presented in order to find a new settled law. That's in contrast, among other things, to the originalists you see represented on the U.S. Supreme Court. It seems that you view the "living tree" understanding of the Constitution as a good thing?

**EB:** I think the living tree analogy is an excellent one, both in terms of normative theory about jurisprudence and in terms of what actually happens in the Canadian experience. The evolution of the meaning of certain words and clauses was exactly what I had argued over with Trudeau. For some time, he kept arguing with me and others about the question of Aboriginal rights and asking what precisely they meant. Can we define them, exactly? My response — then and now — was that we could leave it in large part up to the courts. The court decisions in non-Indigenous law had evolved over time in the British common law tradition. There has been, in other words, an ongoing elaboration and extension of the meaning of key clauses and phrases. The absence of a precise definition at the time of inclusion in the Constitution allows the courts to find an interpretation that makes sense to the people at a given time and based upon legal arguments presented by Indigenous litigants.

This has happened in relation to Section 35 and with respect LGBTQ rights. It has also happened in relation to the rights of workers to organize trade unions — a right that is not spelled out in the original document but was subsequently recognized in a historic judgement written by Chief Justice Beverley McLachlin. Relying upon the constitutional guarantee of freedom of association, that judgement gives a deep and broad-ranging right to workers to organize.

In comparison, look at the country to the south of us, where there are originalists on the Supreme Court. I would say they have a "dead stump theory" of constitutional evolution as opposed to a living tree. Those justices, who are evidently out of touch with the democratic majority of the population, insist on giving their own interpretation of the original meaning of an eighteenth-century text. Surely, a highly literal reading of such an old document cannot have an appropriate meaning in a democratic country centuries later.

**FA:** On the subject of workers' rights, it is striking that the Constitution makes no reference to the right to organize. That has sometimes been attributed in part to the lack of engagement by the Canadian Labour Congress and other representatives from organized labour. Similarly, it appears the NDP did not press this issue. As a result, those critics argue that what we have is a liberal rather than a social democratic constitution. This characterization might sound a little unfair because a lot of the provisions have been good for workers. But what about the right to organize?

**EB:** It's true that we did not push for a specific category of workers' rights to be included and in retrospect, I regret that. But, as Albert Camus argued many years ago, a liberal constitution can provide the political and civil rights that can in turn be used in democratic political struggle to win social democracy. And, because of how the living tree model has ended up enshrining workers' rights, that is in effect exactly what has happened. I agree that it would have been preferable to have the right to organize explicitly included in the original package. But because of how the document was designed and subsequently interpreted, that right has been guaranteed anyway.

**FA:** One analyst, Larry Savage of Brock University, attributes the absence of organized labour in the patriation discussions to the CLC not wanting to step on the toes of the Fédération des travailleurs et travailleuses du Québec (FTQ) and cause friction in the labour movement. That seems like a singularly uncourageous choice when the prize might have been getting workers' rights into the Constitution. It also would have made it more difficult for the NDP to pursue that objective because there were no wider social forces pressing for it. There is an interesting contrast here with the cases for provincial control of resources and Sections 28 and 35. The NDP had the benefit of other actors and social forces pressing for those things, but not on workers' rights. It seems like a big omission by the CLC, based on questionable judgement.

**EB:** Yes, but I think their involvement would have torn the wider labour movement apart, because the Quebec labour movement was not supportive of the package. If the CLC had endorsed the package in principle, and started to work on improving it, the result could well have been a major split. Still, on a personal basis, CLC president Dennis McDermott supported my position on patriation on more than one occasion and was critical of the position taken by some in the western provincial parties. But it is true that, by and large, organized labour stayed out of the constitutional conversation.

Incidentally — given what I think their reasoning was — the constitutional process did produce a big schism between the federal NDP and our section in Quebec. There was mutual respect between both sides, but also very deep disagreement about how we should proceed. The NDP was, by definition, in a constant battle with sovereigntist forces in Quebec by virtue of being a federal party. But many sovereigntists were social democrats, and most Quebec social democrats at that time were probably sovereigntists.*

**FA:** I suppose there's always a strategic consideration involved from a sovereigntist perspective, and it applies for the Indigenous movement too: do you accept a flawed or partial victory on the understanding that it's going to be a platform from which you can struggle to get more? Or do you refuse to participate and forgo the opportunity of partial victories because of the risk of co-optation?

**EB:** Indeed, though from my perspective I came down quite firmly on one side of that question, even if there was the potential risk of co-optation. I knew that I would rather be in there fighting for

---

* See Chapter Eight: National Questions.

something flawed that I could agree with in principle rather than standing back — and that goes to the root of my early endorsement of the package after discussing it with Trudeau. Once it became clear there was going to be an openness about resource control, amendments to include additional rights in the Charter, and the possibility of a decent amending formula, I was content to work from within. Obviously, that consideration might be different depending on where you're situated, though the Indigenous movement certainly opted to make its presence felt rather than sit on the sidelines.

**LS:** I'm curious what you think Trudeau's imagined endgame was regarding Quebec? In his book *Federalism and the French Canadians*, there's an address that he gave to the Canadian Bar Association in 1967 in which he says that a "Constitutional Declaration of Rights" (which I guess was the terminology being used at the time) could help establish unity in Canada.[1] There's an argument to be made that the Charter process ultimately did the opposite because Quebec didn't sign on — and the subsequent efforts to obtain its signature, first through Meech Lake and then through Charlottetown failed as well. The trajectory of events, or so the argument might go, at least, culminated in the 1995 referendum — which was about 50,000 votes from breaking up the country. What do you think was Trudeau's view of Quebec in the context of these negotiations? Did he believe he could get René Lévesque to sign on? Or did he think that it didn't matter?

**EB:** I'll deal with one part of the question first: all of those things did indeed happen after patriation, but it doesn't follow that patriation or the Charter was the cause or that either can be blamed for sowing any subsequent disunity. Still, it's a serious and complex question that raises important issues associated with political action. As a political leader, you can never know for sure what all the consequences of your actions are going to be. Instead, you hope that a number of the short-run specifics you're most concerned about will have the intended effects. Even then, there can be a substantial degree of uncertainty built in.

We could not be certain, for example, that the entrenchment of Aboriginal and treaty rights would have the desired implications once the courts dug into the issue. I'm not a lawyer, though I had done work in political theory and followed legal opinion, so I knew there was historical justification for the recognition of Indigenous rights. But how they would be precisely interpreted in the future is something I could not predict with total confidence, and nor could anyone else. Trudeau's reluctance to proceed was partly about that lack of absolute clarity. And it was true: those of us on the other side of the issue didn't possess a crystal ball but were hardly working in a vacuum either. We knew that there were written treaties and commitments made by the Crown. And, as in the case of almost all major political decisions, you decide your position based on the most important particulars and imperatives at the time and hope that things will work out for the best.

As far as Quebec is concerned, I cannot tell you exactly what Trudeau thought would happen, but I suspect he did not think Quebec would end up signing on. My hunch is that he probably decided he would put the Charter on the table and that Quebec could take it or leave it. I expect he also believed it was within federal jurisdictional authority provided that the right number of provinces got on board, even if Quebec wasn't one of them. (The federal government had referred the matter to the Supreme Court, and at the time, both of us expected it to come down on the federal side of patriation.) He likely thought the best thing was simply to do it and that, in the end, Quebeckers (if not their politicians) would come to accept it. When you think about it, the Quebec Charter of Human Rights and Freedoms (Charte des droits et libertés de la personne) is substantially the same as the federal. For my part, I didn't expect René Lévesque to sign on. But I also hoped I was wrong; I had a high regard for him, his social democratic values, and for most of his policies. But I suspected his belief in independence for Quebec would be stronger, even if there were some who believed he was insufficiently committed to the sovereigntist cause.* In the end, it's kind of a mug's game to try and judge the motives of other people, especially politicians. It's ultimately actions that matter.

**JS:** What about developments in Western Canada after 1982? An argument could be made that the Reform Party emerged in good measure as a response to the big federal and constitutional wranglings of the 1980s. And it strikes me that the politics of regional identity that were so present throughout the 1990s sucked up oxygen and populist energy that might have been channelled into issues of socioeconomic inequality and instead went somewhere else. Perhaps that partly explains the electoral frustration of the NDP in the 1990s?

**EB:** When it comes to the Reform movement, I think it was more anti-Trudeau and anti-Quebec than anything else. I do think that many people in Western Canada in particular objected to asymmetrical federalism and felt that the federal parties were not meeting their political desires adequately — not just the NDP and Liberals but the Conservatives as well — and Preston Manning successfully presented himself as a spokesperson for Western grievances. I didn't think much of Manning's politics, but I do not believe that the forces that gave rise to them should be dismissed. People in Western Canada were indeed feeling left out, though I don't think the Charter had anything to do with that.

---

\*   See Chapter Eight: National Questions.

**FA:** Despite resistance in the West, eventually all of the premiers except for Lévesque supported the package. Was it the amending formula that finally brought Peter Lougheed and Allan Blakeney in?

**EB:** The inclusion of the notwithstanding clause was certainly very important to both of them. Trudeau did not agree with it, but he came to see it was a necessary evil because it was an essential requirement to get everything else approved. At the time, I did not agree with it either but, like Trudeau, saw the political necessity of its inclusion. In thinking about it subsequently, I have come around to believing that the notwithstanding clause could make sense, under certain circumstances, to protect desirable social policies of either order of government from being undermined by a court.

Take, for example, the case of cigarette advertising. Federal legislation to prohibit cigarette advertising was challenged in the courts on free speech grounds and, had the challenge succeeded, we would have had a circumstance in which the rights of free speech were given precedence over the right of the government to legislate on social policy. The decision did not go this way but it could have. If it were up to me in such circumstances, I would have used the notwithstanding clause to protect the right to legislate for healthcare.

**JS:** Another matter is the inclusion of property rights, which do not appear in the Constitution. While we do not have a social democratic constitution as such, the absence of the right to private property seems significant.

**EB:** There was a Conservative motion to put private property rights in the package, seconded by a Liberal cabinet minister. Two members of the NDP, Svend Robinson and Ian Waddell, made sure that the motion would not even be referred to a committee and successfully filibustered until it was withdrawn. The NDP was strongly opposed to it. Fortunately, others quickly realized the folly of including it as well. There are so many reasons to be concerned about that. If we had included property rights, the courts could start talking about corporations having certain rights because of the property connection that the owners have with capital. There could have been interminable battles, say, for municipal, provincial, and federal governments trying to take action on the environment and being sued by companies for violating constitutionally enshrined property rights. There might have been endless legal wrangling, not to mention a tremendous restriction on the exercise of public power.

Property rights (of a kind) were included in the Universal Declaration of Human Rights (UDHR) and in two international covenants concerned with civil, political, social, and economic rights. There the language is more about the right to individual ownership (for example, owning your own home) as opposed to state ownership of the instruments of production. Those are very different notions, and conservatives who invoke property rights typically emphasize the former. I don't know for certain what was behind the references in the UDHR, but I suspect it may have been informed by the experience of totalitarian governments: the Soviet Bloc on the one hand, and the Nazis on the other, who ripped up existing property rights — not simply those of big corporations but also those of ordinary people (farmers in Ukraine, for example). There can be an argument related to basic human dignity to preserve the right of ordinary people or families to own property.

However, I was very much against including any reference to property rights in the constitution because of the potential negatives associated with it and the strong potential for them to be in conflict with other rights. Besides, the right to own your own home or family farm is already protected under common law. Constitutional entrenchment was not necessary.

**LS:** In a different sense, Conservatives won a version of these rights a few years later in the form of international trade agreements that created supranational tribunals and dispute resolution mechanisms that supersede the power of individual states.* That's an entirely different discussion, but I would argue events since have only strengthened the case against giving property rights any kind of constitutional status.

Taking things back to the realm of the personal for a moment, after the negotiations concluded, Trudeau ended up giving you a prominent spot in the procession at the signing ceremony — ahead of the premiers. What was the story there?

**EB:** My placement in the procession was his way of saying thanks, I think. After all was said and done, and we finally got the constitution passed, Trudeau offered to make me a member of the Privy Council and the process was very typical of the man. Instead of calling me on the phone or requesting that I come to have a word with him in his office, Trudeau sent Michael Kirby down to my office to ask me if I would accept this honour. Clearly somewhat embarrassed, Kirby commented that only his boss would be so impersonal. I accepted, of course. I knew Trudeau well by this point and was not surprised. After that, he did follow up by ensuring I would precede the premiers in the procession on the day of patriation itself. He was that kind of guy. Apart from Jean Marchand and Gérard Pelletier, he had pretty cool relationships with everybody else in his cabinet. Intimacy and friendship were not there on a widespread basis, even with people he respected.

**LS:** Trudeau retired from politics ahead of the 1984 election and you didn't face him in any further campaigns or debates. Were the two of you in touch at all after his retirement? You shared that

---

\* See Chapter Eight: National Questions.

funny story about running into Robert Stanfield after the 1993 federal election.* Did you happen to bump into Trudeau again?

**EB:** I did indeed: in Montreal, when I was at Rights and Democracy.** Shortly after I took on my role there, we organized an international protest against the military junta in Myanmar over its refusal to recognize the election of Aung San Suu Kyi. I wanted Trudeau to join us in support of the initiative because he had, by this point, acquired a positive international reputation. He turned me down — not out of personal animus but because, he said, if he accepted one request of this kind, he would be under constant pressure to accept more. He said he didn't want to do that kind of thing — he just wanted to retire. I respected that, but I was also disappointed. Plenty of former politicians remain active in national or global affairs after they've left office. Jimmy Carter, for example, probably has a better reputation today than he had when he was actually president because of his post-presidential work. Willy Brandt is another obvious case in point. But Trudeau was serious about his retirement, and I respected that.

**FA:** After patriation, there was a general aura of exhaustion with constitutional issues and a discernible feeling of deflation in many quarters about what had been achieved. That's reflected in the title of a collection of essays about the process that was published in 1983 (*And No One Cheered*) and it's the theme of most of the articles in that book. My impression is that history has since overtaken this judgement. Among other things, the Charter now has widespread support. Assuming you agree, can you talk about what might account for the shift in both perception and received opinion about it?

---

\* See Chapter Three: The Balance of Power.
\*\* See Chapter Nine: Globalization and the Struggle for Equality.

**EB:** I think the living tree metaphor applies here as well. The battles of 1980–82 left real scars, but they were worn far more by the politicians involved than by the population at large. Those debates were intense and often incredibly personal. In the NDP and elsewhere, tactical and procedural differences frequently transformed into much deeper ideological conflicts that ended up affecting relationships in the long term. That was especially true among federal and provincial leaders who had been at odds. We also felt it within the federal caucus itself in ways that were sometimes hard to get over. Speaking for myself, it was one of the great contests — and most difficult challenges — of my entire political life.

To this day, I deeply regret the absence of Quebec and believe it was not inevitable. But the country ultimately got an embedded Charter of Rights informed by twentieth rather than eighteenth-century values — a living document open to change and progress. For exactly that reason, I think, a large majority all across Canada support the Charter of Rights and Freedoms. In the end, it was a battle worth fighting.

## CHAPTER EIGHT

# National Questions

*"In contemporary Canada, the elites of politics, business, education, and certain other professions have contacts across the country. But farmers and blue collar or white collar workers in Quebec, say, have only a dim inkling of what their counterparts are like in other provinces, and little sense that they have much of significance in common with them. A program of reform that comes to grips with certain common problems could create a sense of common purpose across these barriers; but it would at the same time divide Canadians within all regions and groups along the lines of their political option. A division between left and right would tend to close the gap between French and English, Easterner and Westerner."*

— CHARLES TAYLOR, *The Pattern of Politics*

A few years after his retirement from politics, former Liberal cabinet minister Walter Gordon published a book called *Storm Signals: New Economic Policies for Canada* in which he grappled with the question of the country's economic independence. Both in his analysis and his recommendations, Gordon's thinking was characteristic of a strand of Liberal nationalism that took seriously the problem of foreign ownership while seeking to address it from within the confines of the private sector. As minister for energy, mines, and resources, for example, Alastair

Gillespie had once suggested that Canada respond to the issue by creating its own multinationals to compete with their American equivalents. Gordon dismissed this idea as naive. But, as I noted in 1975 in my review of *Storm Signals* for the *Globe and Mail*, much the same was true of his own proposal, which amounted to the bizarre suggestion that Parliament pass a resolution politely asking the owners of large Canadian subsidiaries to gradually sell their stakes to businessmen north of the 49th parallel.[1]

As a dedicated nationalist, Gordon was genuinely alarmed about the extent of Canada's deepening cultural and economic integration with the United States — and, while a senior member in the government of Lester Pearson, he had played a significant role in getting the issue onto the national agenda by urging the creation of the influential 1967 task force on foreign ownership chaired by Mel Watkins. As an ideologically committed liberal, however, he rather breezily dismissed the policy solutions advocated by democratic socialists on the grounds that they required too much state intervention.[*]

In this respect, *Storm Signals* was characteristic of a deeper philosophical divide separating business-oriented nationalists like Gordon from those of us on the left who were equally concerned about the dangers of continental integration. For many liberals, the goal of maintaining Canadian independence has been distinct from a wider project of economic democracy and social equality. From the earliest stirrings of my own nationalism, the two have always been inextricably linked.

On the eve of the 1988 federal campaign, the mood in the NDP was one of optimism. The previous summer, we had enjoyed a trifecta of byelection victories: Marion Dewar in Hamilton Mountain, Jack Harris in St. John's East, and Audrey McLaughlin, who became the first federal New Democrat ever to be elected in the Yukon.[2] The single greatest source of elation was a slew of national polls showing the NDP ahead of the other two major parties for the first time in its history.[3] (A surge that notably included a 25 percent showing in the province of Quebec.[4])

---

[*] See Chapter Three: The Balance of Power and Chapter Five: Ordinary Canadians.

Contributing further to our buoyant mood was the somewhat less cheerful predicament of our competitors. Having won a landslide akin to John Diefenbaker's historic 1958 sweep only a few years earlier, Brian Mulroney's Conservative Party had been beset by scandals and was sagging in the polls. Still dazed from the bruising defeat of 1984, meanwhile, the Liberals now had a caucus barely greater in number than our own, and John Turner's leadership looked less than secure.

As is invariably the case in politics, the electoral picture was actually far more complicated than a simple survey of the polls might have suggested. Optimistic though I was — and still very much hoping for the breakthrough I had been seeking since becoming NDP leader — my personal hunch going into the campaign was that we might plausibly finish in second and replace the Liberals as the Official Opposition to a weakened Tory government. From there, it seemed to me, we would be in a strong position to realign Canada's party system so that it reflected the left-right split common in European countries such as the United Kingdom and West Germany. Achieving that outcome would obviously require a strong campaign in every region of the country. It was impossible to imagine a viable path to a social democratic plurality or majority that did not run through the province of Quebec.

From the earliest days of parliamentary socialism in Canada, Quebec had always presented a unique challenge for the CCF and NDP. Before the Quiet Revolution, the conservatism emanating from powerful institutions like the Catholic Church had self-evidently been an obstacle to obtaining a political foothold. Over the course of my own leadership, the greatest impediment was paradoxically represented by a movement with whom the NDP had a good deal more in common: namely the Parti Québécois under René Lévesque. The NDP and the PQ shared a commitment to tax reform, universal child care, workers' rights and, more generally, the necessary role of the state in social and economic affairs. Since the 1960s, the formative divide between sovereigntists and federalists that had increasingly dominated Quebec's political scene had helped to thwart efforts by outstanding figures like Charles Taylor and Robert Cliche to secure a beachhead. The cleavage only widened when the PQ came to power in 1976, explicitly committed to building social democracy within the borders of what it soon hoped to make an independent state.

Though I did not share Pierre Trudeau's overwhelmingly hostile attitude toward Quebec nationalism, my own view was that the aspirations of sovereigntist Quebeckers could ultimately be realized from within a federal union that adequately respected the distinctiveness of their society — particularly when it came to cultural and language rights. We could, in effect, say yes to Quebec without saying no to Canada. As a social democrat who envisioned a constructive role for the state in the battle against inequality, however, I was also instinctively resistant to proposals concerning national unity that involved further decentralization, particularly when it came to the major levers of economic policy.

The solution, as I saw it, lay neither in a rigid federalism that demonized sovereigntists and exacerbated existing divisions or in a further weakening of the federal state that risked balkanizing the country and increasing inequality. The more desirable option, as I described it to a meeting of the NDP's national executive in the wake of the PQ's election victory, was to try to build "a social democracy unlike any other in which genuine equality prevails, wherein the harm done to native peoples will be redressed, and in which two great transplanted European cultures can flourish."[5]


The federal election of 1988 was in many ways the culmination of a debate about the Canadian economy that had been going on since the beginning of my political life. In another sense, however, what the campaign ultimately brought to the surface was a series of far older questions about the Canadian identity and the nature of our relationship with the economic and military superpower to the south. After Confederation, Sir John A. Macdonald had recognized the necessity of reining in the forces of the continental market so that Canada could develop an economy and culture separate from those of the United States. In an earlier era of their history, many of those in Canada's conservative tradition shared a version of this perspective — attuned, as they were, to the reality that when a smaller country completely integrates its economy with a larger one, it will inevitably begin to absorb its values, norms, and customs as well. "It might be that the lion and the lamb would lie down together," as Macdonald once said of the Canada-U.S. relationship, "but the lamb would be inside the lion."[6]

From the end of the 1970s, the idea of free trade with the United States had increasingly gained favour. Proponents wanted to open our borders to the free flow of capital and ensure American markets would remain open to Canadian goods and resources. As a wave of market zealotry swept through conservative parties in North America and Europe during the 1980s, it also became attractive to elements in Canada's economic and political elite — a fact confirmed when Prime Minister Mulroney announced his intention to negotiate a free trade agreement with Washington in October 1985. When the deal's contents were finally released in the autumn of 1987, it was immediately obvious that we faced a debate altogether more expansive and existential than one concerned purely with the specific terms of international commerce or the precise details of a treaty. As President Reagan himself put it, free trade represented nothing less than "a new economic constitution for North America."[7]

From the outset of negotiations, proponents of the deal were eager to defend it in purely economic terms. Increased competition through the removal of trade barriers, they argued, would create jobs, make industry more efficient, and stimulate investment. To that end, finance minister Michael Wilson confidently predicted employment growth and strengthened family incomes in the years following ratification. Critics, meanwhile, were variously charged with being anti-American, subscribing to an archaic protectionist philosophy and opposing the expansion of trade in any form.

None of these claims reflected reality. My view was that the deal was certain to worsen the problems already intrinsic to Canada's branch plant economy. Because of its sheer size, deeper integration with the United States inevitably meant harmonization with its reigning economic practices: a process that transparently endangered Canadian industry and incentivized a race to the bottom in terms of wages, regulations, and social policy. Fundamentally, however, I believed the debate came down to two radically opposed visions about the future of the country — and whether a more egalitarian set of institutions and values would prevail over the cold and uncaring logic of markets.

---

**Frances Abele:** The politics of Quebec clearly played a significant role in shaping national politics prior to the period we're discussing. But during the elections and constitutional debates of the 1980s, they were particularly central. Perhaps we might begin by talking about your own approach to Quebec as leader?

**Ed Broadbent:** Quebec is hugely important for obvious reasons. You can't, and really shouldn't want to, form a national government in Canada without significant representation there, so on the basis of both pragmatism and principle I was determined to make inroads. But Quebec also presented a major challenge because we had a limited presence on the ground and had never won a seat there. The extent of that challenge was evident right from my very first visit as party leader when we landed at an airstrip to attend a meeting in Témiscaming that ended up being a scene straight out of the Marx Brothers. For some reason, our chauffeur from the airport was driving a Cadillac. Then, when we arrived there were maybe five people present — two of whom thought they were at a Ralliement créditiste du Québec meeting and one who had just heard there was a gathering in town and had decided to go. Several reporters were on hand to capture this barnstorming entrée, so inevitably that became a story about my impending conquest of La Belle Province.

More seriously, I think the persistent quandary Quebec has presented for the CCF and NDP has, at least in one sense, a very straightforward explanation. The rise of the independence movement was coterminous with the rise of social democratic thinking. Lévesque's own trajectory is a good illustration of that because, before founding the Parti Québécois, he had served as minister for hydroelectric resources and public works in the Liberal government of Jean Lesage and had helped to oversee a wave of nationalization. The idea that Quebeckers could only realize their aspirations by way of a state over which they had control was initially the preserve of a relatively small elite group. Over time, it grew into a deep feeling that extended itself on a widespread basis throughout parts of civil society, state bureaucracies, the leaderships of trade unions, and so on until it aroused passionate support across different classes and occupations.

Because of how the Quiet Revolution unfolded, that process became deeply interwoven with what was essentially a social democratic conception of the state. While the Catholic Church had remained entrenched, I think many Quebeckers viewed the state as, at best, a necessary evil to be tolerated by private individuals who pursued wealth and salvation elsewhere. However, as a more modern, liberal, and democratic state was constructed, the creation of a good society came to be seen in increasingly secular terms. From then on, the state was the principal forum through which a majority of Quebeckers expressed their economic and cultural aspirations.

What that eventually produced, in the form of the PQ, was a movement that was simultaneously separatist and social democratic — which, to understate things, was a challenging dynamic for the federal NDP to navigate. We would frequently encounter people who shared much of our ideology and analysis but who would nonetheless respond to our attempts at outreach by saying that they would build social democracy in Quebec while we did so in the rest of Canada. No matter how strongly we would try to convince them that their core concerns could be addressed within a federal state, they simply didn't view it as an acceptable alternative. They wanted something more. Simply put, nationalist feelings trumped good social democratic policy.

There were certainly other developments at play that helped solidify Quebec nationalist sentiment in the 1970s.* There was the PQ's 1976 election victory, which was, in part, a backlash against the Robert Bourassa government for its conservative approach to economic issues — which is to say, Quebeckers may have been voting on the basis of sovereigntist feeling, but they were also voting for social democracy. From 1968 onwards, Trudeau's blanket hostility toward every aspect of Quebec nationalism certainly inflamed tensions as well. It may have been philosophically consistent with his individualist liberalism and rejection in principle of the whole idea of group rights. But the way he so aggressively branded all nationalist demands as a form of irrational tribalism was both unfair and counterproductive to national unity. Abused and insulted, many Quebeckers were unlikely to view Ottawa in a favourable light. The desire for independence had become firmly embedded in parts of Quebec society.

**Jonathan Sas:** Language was a hugely significant issue as well.

**EB:** Yes, I think language rights were ultimately a much more salient element in nationalist sentiment because there had been an Anglophone minority forcing the Francophone majority to speak and play by their rules. The Lévesque government's Charter of the French Language, Bill 101, required that the language of work (that of the majority) be French. This was entirely justified. While there were some provisions restricting the use of English I thought unnecessary, I ultimately thought it brought elementary justice to Francophone workers — who deserved the right to grow up speaking and working in their own language and to negotiate contracts with their bosses in French. There had

---

\* One of them being the imposition of the War Measures Act. See Chapter Three: The Balance of Power.

been deep cultural repression going on, and many people outside Quebec were insensitive to that reality.

In one of my campaigns against Michael Starr in Oshawa, for example, I remember him talking about how French was going to be forced down the throats of English Canadians, which was completely false. At a UAW meeting in Oshawa, I remember this coming up and I asked the Local 222 members to imagine what it would be like if they had to negotiate their contracts with General Motors in French. I even had data on hand about how frequent this dynamic was for workers in Quebec, who were so often compelled to conduct collective bargaining in English. Most Oshawa workers I spoke to were sympathetic when it was put to them in those terms, and the idea of language rights as a political issue never made much headway in Oshawa. Ironically perhaps, I think Bill 101 has actually resulted in more Quebeckers becoming comfortable with the federal state.

Regardless, throughout much of Quebec history, nationalism has been positive in its impact on the large majority of Quebeckers. The achievement of language rights and the social democratic program of the PQ during the Lévesque era are both illustrations of that.

**Luke Savage:** You met Lévesque in 1977, not long after he became premier. What can you tell us about that meeting?

**EB:** There were two important aspects as I recall. The first thing that struck me was how remarkably social democratic in orientation he was toward the economy, social policy, and the need to address inequality. After the PQ came to power, they legislated a number of positive measures like raising the minimum wage and banning strikebreakers,[8] so when it came to those kinds of things, I saw Lévesque as a comrade in arms. I respected him and admired the progressive component of his project. At the same time, there was the question of independence, which we both knew was the elephant in the room and didn't discuss during the meeting. Nonetheless, when I reported back, I did my best to make it clear to my colleagues in the NDP caucus and to the public that Lévesque was clearly quite serious in his drive for independence. Speaking to him first-hand convinced me that he was genuine in his convictions and, from the point of view of national unity, I knew there would be a formidable challenge in the years ahead to try to keep Quebec within Canada.

Having said that, I later went to Quebec to try to convince Robert Cliche to run for the NDP in a forthcoming byelection — and I had a very noteworthy second meeting with Lévesque during the same visit. Cliche had been leader of the Quebec NDP during the 1960s and had come very close to winning a seat in the 1968 federal election. He got nearly 44 percent of the vote in Duvernay, but the Liberals were determined to stop him because they correctly recognized that a popular and widely respected figure like Cliche winning as a New Democrat could completely alter the dynamic of Quebec politics. To that end, they got Eric Kierans — a sharp economist who (ironically enough) later wrote the introduction to David Lewis's book *Corporate Welfare Bums* and supported me for leader in 1975 — to run against Cliche. Kierans narrowly won. If Cliche had been elected, then I am certain he would have been a serious candidate for the NDP leadership when David Lewis stepped down. Along with many others in English Canada, I would have supported him. And I don't have the slightest doubt that, had he become leader, the political landscape in both Quebec and the rest of Canada would have been quite different.

In any case, I was in Quebec City to encourage Cliche to stand again in the upcoming byelection and Lévesque indicated to me very clearly that, if Cliche became the NDP candidate, he would put the electoral machinery of the PQ behind him. Mainly for health reasons, I think, Cliche decided not to run in the byelection. But it would have been a historic development for

René Lévesque and the PQ to support the election of someone belonging to a federalist party.

**LS:** What do you think it was about Cliche and his politics that were acceptable to Lévesque?

**EB:** Lévesque liked and respected Cliche. He had tried to get him to join his government as minister of justice. I also think it's possible the episode was a reflection of a tension in Lévesque's psyche itself. Notwithstanding what I said about the seriousness of his stated commitment to independence, people who knew him well expressed concerns that he wasn't truly committed to independence; that he seemed torn about whether Quebec needed to be totally sovereign or whether it could realize its goals for political and cultural emancipation within a federal state. His offer of support for Cliche's candidacy for the NDP may well have reflected his own ambivalence about independence.

**FA:** The idea that Quebec's aspirations could be realized from within a federal Canada was central to the NDP's message. As you've said, it's pretty difficult to form a government without winning seats there — which is among the reasons you and the NDP made a big push to win them in 1988. Can you talk about the role Quebec played during that campaign and how free trade factored in? Why do you think the much-hoped-for breakthrough never materialized?

**EB:** We had very high hopes in Quebec going into the 1988 campaign. There were some positive signs. Our vote there had doubled in 1984 and we had launched a major organizational drive the following year. As leader, I strongly advocated allocating more resources and money to our efforts in Quebec and it seemed to be paying off.[9] The polling looked much better than it had looked going into previous elections, and we had grown to about 20,000 Quebec members by 1988[10] (which was certainly a significant improvement on that first meeting in Témiscaming).

Another big boost was the full-throated backing of the Fédération des travailleurs du Québec. Unlike the other big union federations, the FTQ had generally been favourable to the NDP. Thanks to their longtime president Louis Laberge, they really got behind us in 1988, and having a trade union with 450,000 members endorse the NDP meant a great deal to me. Laberge was instrumental in organizing one of the largest rallies for any party during the campaign. There were about 2,000 exuberant people cheering on NDP speakers from across the region. It was a truly joyful night. The venue itself, the Paul Sauvé Arena, was significant because it had been the site of so many important political events, including Lévesque's 1976 victory rally.[11] It was one of the most extraordinary and moving evenings of my political life.

The issue of free trade that came to define the national campaign, however, had particular significance in Quebec because the deal simply did not inspire the same hostility there that it did in many parts of English Canada. Quebeckers just didn't have the same apprehension about American influence on the economy and weren't as anxious about deepening ties with the United States. Many English Canadians, including myself, were worried about the prospect of becoming subordinate to a larger and more populous country. But there wasn't an equivalent concern in Quebec.

Mulroney and his strategists definitely recognized this and were aware that it represented an electoral weakness for the NDP. We had assembled an exceptional group of candidates in Quebec, but they were constantly on the defensive over the issue. That became especially apparent in the campaign's final days, when the Conservatives used their much more sophisticated polling to zero in on the half dozen or so seats we expected to win. Right until near the end, I recall us having been ahead in these seats. When the results came in on election night, we did not win even one of them. It was at that moment I decided I would step down as leader before the next federal election. If we had won those seats, I would have stayed on. But the imperative of winning in Quebec was very close to my heart and our failure to make gains there was a huge personal disappointment.

**JS:** It's interesting to think about why the CCF and NDP struggled so much to break through in Quebec. The basic idea that a national project around equality could create a common purpose for people to rally around regardless of the language they spoke is an intuitively attractive one, and some were genuinely drawn to it. But it persistently failed to overcome the majority debate that was polarized between sovereigntists and federalists. What do you think explains that?

**EB:** I don't really know. What we do know is that our approach didn't work. On an abstract level, you could promote the idea that there might be a common progressive project for English and French Canadians to rally around. But the forces on the ground, the feelings in the hearts and minds of so many Quebeckers, just didn't go in that direction — and I still can't offer a good explanation of why that was the case. Certainly, the party made every effort to recognize the legitimate linguistic and cultural demands of Quebeckers, in part because of the party's social democratic commitment to social rights. Later, I went on to join with Robert Stanfield to support the 1987 Meech Lake Accord which would have recognized Quebec as a distinct society. Although the Accord had obtained the support of business leaders, union leaders, and the large majority of premiers, it was ultimately (and in my view tragically) defeated. Quebec, having been the first province to give its support to the Meech Lake Accord, was profoundly disappointed.

The approach did attract some real political support later on. I mean, I believe that Jack Layton's big breakthrough more than twenty years later would not have happened had there not been a social democratic constituency in Quebec that had built up over the years. A significant plurality of Quebeckers saw Jack and the NDP as being open to their aspirations — and those aspirations were social democratic, thanks to the efforts of so many Quebec NDPers over the years. Improbable as it may seem, as an English-speaking guy from Oshawa, I was, for a time, the most popular national leader in Quebec. And I'm quite convinced that was a reflection of the social democratic values shared across Canada's linguistic and cultural divides.

**LS:** To turn away from Quebec, perhaps we can discuss the issue of free trade in a bit more detail. It obviously became the most significant theme of the 1988 campaign and, as you said, it inspired a strong nationalist feeling outside of Quebec. That seems to have been central to your own opposition, from what I can tell. In Parliament, for example, you characterized the debate as one about whether "the Canadian way or the American way" would prevail.[12]

**EB:** The free trade debate was certainly about much more than a narrow question of economics or competing preferences about how exactly to organize specific commercial activities. When I used that phrase, the American way referred to the manner in which market values seem to penetrate every aspect of life in the United States, a phenomenon observed by Alexis de Tocqueville in the 1830s and by many commentators since. Canada has always had a market-based economy as well, but the extent to which market principles pervade virtually everything from culture to religion is much reduced in comparison.

Without deluding ourselves about the extent of inequality or injustice in Canada, there has historically been a more entrenched egalitarian tradition here. At its best, anyway, that tradition has embraced the idea that liberty and community are complementary, rather than opposed, propositions. Prior to the 1980s, successive generations of conservatives accepted and embraced this idea. On the other hand, with few exceptions (the New Deal being an obvious example), the idea that the state should intervene in, or interfere with, the so-called natural workings of the marketplace to promote greater opportunity and equality has not been embedded in the dominant ideological system of the United States. The long-standing American treatment of a basic need like healthcare as a commodity to be bought and sold rather than a universal social right is a good illustration of that.

The effect of the free trade deal was to increase the Americanization of Canadian society and impose market principles in a way that was going to threaten the strength of our industry, the integrity of our cultural institutions, and our capacity as a nation to democratically determine our own destiny. As a democratic socialist, I had always believed that our country needed to maintain that capacity to protect and extend the egalitarian values I believe a majority of Canadians share. The free trade agreement was essentially a neoliberal document backed most strongly by the business class. Its ultimate goal was to cede even more power to corporations and entrench their rights to be more and more free from regulation by the state. Its proponents favoured expanding the reach of the market — one that, in my view, would inevitably be dominated by the U.S.

Left nationalist arguments, going back long before the 1988 election, had often been dismissed as anti-American. However, their thrust has mostly been aimed at the existing political and economic structures in the United States — and not at all at individual

Americans. After all, there is a long-standing American radical tradition reflected in figures like Thomas Paine, Eugene Debs, and Martin Luther King. Throughout my own political life, its great stewards have been people like Barbara Ehrenreich, Michael Harrington, and of course Bernie Sanders. Regrettably, however, it remains today the vital tradition of only a dissident minority.

**JS:** You alluded to the difference between earlier generations within Canada's conservative tradition and the ideological transformation that occurred during the 1980s. How would you characterize the trajectory of the Canadian conservative tradition, particularly vis-à-vis Brian Mulroney's extremely zealous pursuit of free trade?

**EB:** Historically, I think that conservatism (both in Canada and elsewhere) has seen two different traditions competing for ascendence. What happened in the 1980s was that one of them finally triumphed over the other. Going back to the nineteenth century and the conservatism of someone like Benjamin Disraeli, there was an influential strain that emphasized the importance of community and a sense of continuity with shared values based in a common past. Those beliefs made it possible for earlier generations of conservatives to embrace aspects of the market without accepting the idea that everything, right up to the common good itself, should be subordinate to it. In Canada, during my time, that was the tradition of people like John Diefenbaker and Robert Stanfield. But, beginning in the 1970s, at home and abroad, there was a steady redefinition of the common good that ultimately seemed to recognize no difference between the imperatives of the marketplace and the interests of the community as whole. That notion — that it was both inevitable and desirable for markets to determine the course of social life — was very much at the heart of the free trade agreement.

**FA:** That sense of inevitability and of there being no alternative remains quite deep-seated today. For that reason, I think it might be good to lay out what the alternative to something like the free trade agreement actually was — because I take it you didn't simply view trade as a binary "yes or no" question?

**EB:** That's exactly right, and I think the distinction between so-called free trade and managed trade was easily lost in those debates. The *Globe and Mail*, for example, criticized me at the time for my opposition to the agreement and, in doing so, cited the Auto Pact (which had already existed for nearly two decades) as an example of free trade.[13] In fact, the Auto Pact was an example of a very different kind of industrial and trade policy — and the sort of arrangement an NDP government would have tried to extend to other parts of the economy.

Vincent Bladen, chair of the Political Economy Department at the University of Toronto, specifically rejected free trade and, in his report to the federal government, he provided the framework for the Auto Pact that came into effect in 1965. (I actually took Bladen's course when I was studying at U of T.) The most important pillar of the Auto Pact was that the big three automakers (GM, Ford, and Chrysler) had an obligation to meet a particular level of production in Canada that was related in dollar value to their domestic sales. If they produced, in dollar value, parts, cars, and trucks equivalent to their actual sales in Canada, they could be completely exempt from paying duty on imported cars, trucks, and parts from the U.S. It was, in essence, a positive industrial agreement undertaken to ensure that Canada received a fair share of investment in an industry that employed a huge number of Canadian workers despite its ownership overwhelmingly being on the other side of the border. That's just one example, but it's a good illustration of why the debate wasn't ultimately about whether trade occurred. Trade between our two countries is both necessary and important. The real issue is what Bladen understood: namely, what the terms are going to be and whether they are merely going to reflect the interests of large corporations.

It wasn't inevitable that Canada would become so deeply integrated with the United States, just as it wasn't at all inevitable that we would develop into such an unequal and highly marketized society. The culture of inevitability we've seen since the 1980s deliberately obscures the fact that these things are ultimately political choices. There is always an alternative.

**LS:** In hearing you talk about the Auto Pact, it occurs to me that what we see today is almost the exact opposite of the industrial strategy you advocated for — and of the principles of industrial democracy. Corporate power is now expansive and transnational, and different jurisdictions will compete with one another to attract big companies by offering them tax breaks and other forms of subsidy. Given that many of your proposals as leader represented a challenge to corporate power, I'm curious what your thinking was about the possibility of resistance from capital and corporate interests in the event that the NDP formed a government? I ask not to engage in some kind of speculative political fantasy football, but because the question seems relevant to the issues of political practice we've been discussing elsewhere. Were you worried about things like capital flight or resistance from parts of the business sector?

**EB:** I don't know if worried is the right word, but in the back of my mind and in the minds of other people I was working with, there was always the possibility of global markets responding in a hostile way (and, of course, American markets in particular because so much of our industry, especially in the manufacturing sector, was foreign-owned). Whether we were concerned to an adequate degree is another question. I tended to think that once we got into power and moved step-by-step, we would brace for a challenge, push the limits, and be prepared not to back down when we came up against resistance. It remains an open question how serious that challenge would have been. I think there was a fairly broad array of possible responses from the United States.

Without indulging in fantasy, I like to think that the structures of a hypothetical U.S. administration, as opposed to Wall Street and corporate America, would have at least initially refrained from hostility for geopolitical reasons because Canada is an ally and collaborative partner. On the other hand, some people would call that utopian thinking and imagine something more like the response the Americans have periodically undertaken in parts of Latin America instead. So, there was certainly some concern, but it was not at all sufficient to persuade us not to try to win and implement our program. I felt there was at least a reasonable chance that a lasting social democratic model could get established. The Americans have had to put up with radical governments at various times in places like Spain, Portugal, and Italy. If we had been successful, they might have just had to learn to live with it. Keep in mind, we are partners with them, not only in trade agreements but also in NATO and NORAD.

**JS:** Turning back to the campaign, and the strategic as opposed to the philosophical dimension of free trade, it's clear that the Liberals became the main beneficiaries of the anti–free trade vote (free trade ultimately being the issue the whole election swung around). While the Conservatives won another majority, Liberal fortunes began to improve after the televised debate in which Turner vigorously pressed Mulroney on the matter of free trade, and it was the Liberals who won the greater share of the anti–free trade vote. The NDP's strategy, meanwhile, was criticized for not placing sufficient emphasis on free trade. How do you view that aspect of the campaign in retrospect?

**EB:** While I'm obviously a self-interested party here, I don't share the view that we under-emphasized the importance of free trade in 1988. No section of the NDP was in favour of the agreement and we opposed it strongly from the beginning. Our approach to the issue during the campaign was informed by a mixture of philosophical and tactical concerns about it becoming the singular theme of the election. Strategically speaking, we knew the deal was popular in Quebec and that (among other things), because the Liberal government in Ontario was against it, an election fought exclusively around the issue was going to benefit the Liberals federally more than it was going to benefit us.

As a matter of principle, however, we also believed the campaign should be about a broader alternative vision for Canada — and that meant substantively addressing a wider range of issues even if the free trade agreement was undeniably important. Something else we wanted to highlight was our proposal for a $580 million investment in environmental infrastructure that we were partly looking to fund by way of a 0.12 percent surtax on business profits.[14] In any national election, there is usually more than one significant issue that deserves to be addressed — and I believed that was the case in 1988.

As you said, the approach we undertook drew a fair amount of criticism. Both Bob White, the founding president of the Canadian Auto Workers, and Leo Gerard of the United Steelworkers were openly critical of the federal campaign and felt strongly that we should have placed an exclusive emphasis on the issue of free trade. At the subsequent Ontario Federation of Labour convention, they voiced those criticisms on the floor, which was maybe the only moment in my political life in which there was ever such a serious political disagreement between me and senior leaders of the labour movement. I had worked closely with Bob and Leo for years and it was both unpleasant and abnormal to have a dispute like that come out in public. Leo called me the day after the convention to reiterate his disagreement but also to apologize for not having kept it within the family — which I deeply appreciated. It took years for the relationship between me and Bob to heal, but when I was heading up Rights and Democracy and he had become president of the CLC, we eventually worked together again on some international workers' rights projects. That was very satisfying.

To return to the campaign: you mentioned the moment in the debate where Turner got off those good lines against Mulroney, and I remember thinking at the time that this exchange was going to be picked up as the main headline. And sure enough, it was. It did a lot of damage to our position because, for the remainder of the campaign in much of the country, it was framed largely as a battle between Turner and Mulroney on the question of free trade, except in BC, where we went on to win two-thirds of the seats. Turner was quite literally fighting for his political life, and I think there was something almost existential going on related to his own identity and his role within the Liberal Party. His position as leader had been constantly under threat from the Chrétien wing of the Liberals, and he undeniably fought a vigorous campaign that revived things in the short run. Having said that, I regarded the Liberal opposition to free trade as a cynical move. For quite some time, they couldn't even make up their minds as to whether they were going to support the deal. Of course, after they won a majority government in the next election, they not only failed to repeal free trade but actively supported its expansion through NAFTA.


**FA:** You've spoken about how disappointed you were on election night, particularly when the results from Quebec came in. On the other hand, with forty-three seats, it was still the best national result for the NDP or CCF up to that point, so you must have taken some satisfaction from that. I'm curious how you view that moment in retrospect, because 1988 was your fourth and final campaign as leader, and your long-standing determination to form

Canada's first social democratic government had been thwarted. Did the result alter your view of the NDP's role as a party or about the possibility of it eventually winning a federal election?

**EB:** I did take some satisfaction in us winning a record-setting forty-three seats and, among other things, getting two-thirds of the seats in British Columbia. But at the time, my biggest emotion was obviously disappointment because the result fell well short of what many of us had been hoping for — particularly in the province of Quebec. Nonetheless, it did nothing to shake my core belief that the NDP has a responsibility to try to win government. In that context, I reject the idea that there's a necessary trade-off between principle and the pursuit of power.

The NDP should never settle for being "the conscience of Parliament." Whether we're talking about inequality, human rights, tax policy, industrial strategy, housing, or the environment, surveys of Canadians have repeatedly identified a majority that is strongly social democratic in its values. I still believe to this day that — if properly explained and aided with a bit of good fortune in our electoral system — a social democratic program can rally the support of that majority behind it.

## CHAPTER NINE

# Globalization and the Struggle for Equality

*"The world is becoming one in fact — within the framework of that famous 'long run' which Keynes said is a fit subject only for undergraduates — and will become one political fact. That unification could be totalitarian or authoritarian — or it could be democratic. Internationalism is, then, an inevitability, not a utopian dream, and all that is in doubt is the essential: whether it will be the means of liberation or enslavement, whether the people can actually take control of this destiny, which until now has been the creation of gigantic national bureaucracies and multinational corporations."*

— MICHAEL HARRINGTON, *The Long-Distance Runner*

*"Cultural historical differences must certainly be taken into account, but they never absolve us of the obligation to judge, decide, and act. When we talk about democracy, pluralism, religious freedom, tolerance, human rights, and self-determination, we are not giving voice to mere abstractions relevant only to a few nations; we are talking about human values and ideals that we believed desirable to all people, at all times, in all parts of the world."*

— ED BROADBENT, "Nicaragua, the United States and Social Change," June 1986

A few weeks after announcing my resignation as leader of the NDP, I heard the phone ring. "Hello Ed," said a voice in an unmistakable husky baritone. "This is Brian. I don't imagine you're going to go out and work for some corporation, so if you have any interest in a government appointment, just let me know. I have something in mind." Curious but unsure of this thinking, I called the prime minister back to follow up a few days later. What he had in mind, it turned out, was an appointment to lead the nascent International Centre for Human Rights and Democratic Development, more commonly known thereafter as Rights and Democracy. Created in Parliament's final act ahead of the 1988 election, the centre was the product of an uncommon all-party consensus on the Standing Committee on External Affairs and International Trade, which then included a number of prominent MPs who shared a broadly progressive outlook on international issues — among them future Liberal foreign affairs ministers Lloyd Axworthy and André Ouellet, our own distinguished MPs Bill Blaikie and Pauline Jewett, and Conservative MP Howard Crosby.

Just as notable was the unorthodox nature of the committee's recommendation: for the establishment of an organization created by, but operationally independent from, the Government of Canada with a broad mandate to champion the goals enshrined in the International Bill of Human Rights throughout the developing world. Those included not only the contents of the Universal Declaration of Human Rights itself, but also the two covenants concerned with political, civil, cultural, social, and economic rights. By design, Rights and Democracy thus represented a departure from what was then the prevailing Western framework for international development — particularly the Cold War–influenced kind dominant in the United States, which saw the promotion of democracy and the promotion of the American model as basically synonymous. The centre's remit, in contrast, would incorporate an altogether more universal conception of human rights: pertaining not just to pluralist liberal freedoms like the right to vote but also to social and economic rights like the right to housing or health.

In considering the prime minister's offer, my main reservation was the extent to which the organization's official independence would actually be borne out in practice (in a human rights organization, independence from the government would be something that all members of the board should want). With this in mind, I had an encouraging conversation with the late Gordon Fairweather, a retired Progressive Conservative MP from New Brunswick who Pierre Trudeau had appointed as the first head of the Canadian Human Rights Commission, about how independent the organization could be in practice. He said, based on his experience, operational independence was indeed possible. The other outstanding issue was how the centre would be governed and, in particular, whether its board would consist of people with whom I could work effectively. To Mulroney's credit, he agreed to consult with me before making the appointments and, accepting his offer, I subsequently proposed the removal of three names from the appointment list while adding three others. Mulroney accepted the changes. The board would ultimately consist not only of distinguished Canadians but also of international figures, including former Costa Rican president Óscar Arias and Asma Jahangir, one of Pakistan's leading human rights activists.*

In my new role as Rights and Democracy's founding president, I enjoyed great latitude in the promotion of human rights abroad. I travelled on a diplomatic passport and had the support of Canadian embassies — meaning that when I travelled to El Salvador, Guatemala, Kenya, or anywhere else, they would assist in setting up meetings with important officials and often heads of government. Since our office was located in Montreal, Lucille and I spent a large part of the 1990s living there in Habitat 67, the building wonderfully designed by architect Moshe Safdie, which I had first visited along with so many other Canadians in the splendid summer of 1967.** I worked predominantly

---

* The founding board included: Dr. Norma Walmsley, a political scientist from University of Manitoba; human rights activist Kay Nandlall; Marcel Massé, head of CIDA; lawyer and businessman Ron Ghitter; Julie Davis, VP of the Ontario Federation of Labour; David Daubney, former Conservative MP and criminal lawyer; Irving Brecher, a McGill economics professor; Del Anaquod, an Indigenous rights activist and professor at University of Regina.

** As housing critic for the NDP during my early years in Parliament, I subsequently had lunch with Mr. Safdie in the parliamentary restaurant. He went on to offer good advice about housing policy.

in my heavily accented French with young activists and staff who were majority Francophone, and whose enthusiasm was an inspiration to me.

To my knowledge, there was no comparable institution at that time anywhere in the developed world. Brian Mulroney's government was commendably supporting something unique. The all-party committee that had recommended the creation of Rights and Democracy emphasized its human rights focus and in particular the need in Central America, which was undergoing revolutionary change. An institution like Rights and Democracy would be helpful to democratic forces in Central America in building their own models of democracy. I believe these conditions were uppermost in the mind of Joe Clark as the secretary of state for external affairs.

The importance of the independence of the proposed new institution was impressed on me when Rights and Democracy's application for consultative status at the United Nations was greeted with some skepticism and resistance. Both the Cuban and Indian delegates raised questions about our eligibility, the crux of which hinged on whether we could act independently of the government that had created us. Because I knew President Castro and a few of his ministers, I politely invited the Cuban delegate to confer with his own leadership over lunch ahead of the vote. My hunch proved to be correct and he rather abruptly changed his mind a few hours later. The Indian representative, on the other hand, continued to argue vociferously that Rights and Democracy could not be meaningfully independent as a creation of the Government of Canada. "You have a Supreme Court in India, don't you?" I replied. "Are you telling me its decisions are not independent of the Government of India?" She didn't answer, but the point had been made, and the committee was persuaded to approve our application for consultative status. (I should add that the thoughtful Canadian diplomats who had facilitated my appearance before the committee were not overly delighted by my less-than-diplomatic responses to the Cuban and Indian representatives.)

From the outset, I was keenly aware of the challenge of building credibility and legitimacy as a human rights organization from the global north. We began with a cross-Canada tour, meeting with NGOs, academics, and human rights activists. The first meetings we undertook, in fact, were with the Assembly of First Nations. If we weren't living up to human rights commitments at home, I felt, what business did we have advancing them on the international scene? The siege of Mohawk territory, Kanesatake, east of Montreal, in what is now known as the Oka Crisis, would draw me back into domestic politics almost immediately. I had been disturbed when Sûreté police in riot gear blockaded the delivery of food, goods, and medical supplies to citizens of the Mohawk nation. With other members of my board including Gisèle Côté-Harper, I worked behind the scenes to reduce tensions and went behind the lines to talk directly to representatives of the Mohawks. To help defuse the situation, I subsequently proposed a process of binding arbitration under which the Mohawks would end their blockade of Montreal's Mercier Bridge. In return, Mohawk citizens would not face criminal charges during a one-month negotiation period, during which time the police and the army would stand down. Unfortunately, as with some other attempts to broker a compromise, this effort was not successful.*

If our mandate at Rights and Democracy was notable for its inclusion of economic and social rights, it also proved increasingly at odds with the ideological zeitgeist that was sweeping across the globe. Neoliberalism had made its loud and destructive entry into politics by way of conservative figures like Margaret Thatcher and Ronald Reagan during the 1980s. By the early 1990s, it was waging a full-blown counterrevolution against the egalitarian spirit of the postwar era. Much as the decades after 1945 had seen even many traditional conservative parties accept the Keynesian welfare state, a version of the same process was now underway in reverse: bringing the dogma of unfettered capitalism into the liberal mainstream and, unfortunately, into a number of self-described social democratic parties as well.

* The siege at Oka/Kanesatake lasted seventy-eight days. Conflict spread to Kahnawake and other communities who acted in solidarity with the Mohawks at Kanesatake. The SQ, the RCMP, and ultimately the Canadian Armed Forces were deployed. It was during this period that I called for a royal commission to address the many outstanding issues in Indigenous-Canada relations. In 1991, Prime Minister Mulroney appointed the Royal Commission on Aboriginal Peoples.

As David Frum, the Canadian-born conservative, would later remark, the conscious task of the conservative movement had been to reverse the postwar march toward social democracy.[1] By the time I assumed my job at Rights and Democracy, it was alarmingly evident that this project was well underway. From the outset, our work was thus an active struggle against the rising headwinds of an economic and political orthodoxy that conceived of markets less as instruments or means to an end than as ends in themselves. Domestically, those who championed this agenda began an all-out assault on the principles of regulation, social security, public investment, and progressive taxation. Joined by both the newly created Reform Party and the Progressive Conservatives, the Liberals under Jean Chrétien lead the charge in Canada for this narrow and market-driven brand of politics, notably through Paul Martin's lacerating 1995 federal budget. (To his credit, Warren Allmand — who succeeded me as president of Rights and Democracy — was the only Liberal MP to vote against that budget.)

On the global stage, following the collapse of the Soviet Union in 1989, George H.W. Bush had triumphantly declared a "new world order" and set to work building institutions and trade agreements designed to facilitate the spread of markets and the flow of private capital above all else. The promise to put equal weight on the spread of democracy fell by the wayside. The net result, as I frequently saw throughout my time at Rights and Democracy, was not only spiralling inequality but a new framework in international affairs that increasingly put corporate interests ahead of both democracy and human rights.

These developments were neither necessary nor inevitable. Instead, they were the result of a concerted and highly successful political offensive which seized upon various short-term crises — oil shocks, sluggish growth, demographic changes — as a pretext to roll back the social gains of the postwar era and remake the world. Whereas social democracy at its best had attempted to strike a balance between private self-interest and public cooperation, its vision was of an anemic social contract that stripped away any notion of a public good independent of market forces. When the two clashed, it was markets that prevailed.

Social and economic rights, which had together constituted the foundations of the postwar settlement in many democracies, were in turn attacked as an illegitimate burden on individual self-realization. In asserting, as she once did, that society itself is merely an artificial construct, Margaret Thatcher was thus not only justifying an aggressive rollback of the welfare state. She was also articulating a deeper view of politics in which the pursuit of private self-interest alone can be considered virtuous. In this, Thatcher was not only attacking the Labour Party and its social democratic legacy but also a major wing of her own party. (Former Conservative prime minister Harold MacMillan described her selling off of public utilities as selling the family silver.) For neoliberals, the very idea of collective altruism or community obligation outside participation in the marketplace was and is anathema. Much as totalitarianism had sought to eradicate the personal in favour of the collective, so neoliberalism has sought to eliminate the political pursuit of the public good in its triumphant promotion of the private self. Through my work at Rights and Democracy, I was able to see quite directly what this new and market-driven conception of human society ultimately meant.

**Luke Savage:** Let's begin with your appointment to lead Rights and Democracy. It seems surprising that the Mulroney government would both create an organization like this and opt for someone like you to lead it. How do you explain it?

**Ed Broadbent:** As minister for what was then External Affairs, Joe Clark was a key figure in getting the original legislation through cabinet. I was reliably told that senior officials within his department were opposed to the creation of an entity they thought could be a source of trouble for the government down the road. To some extent, they were right: that's what an independent human rights mandate means.

I think the creation of Rights and Democracy was an expression of Mulroney's wider personal outlook, which was in many ways an improvement over the Liberals. Mulroney and Clark, for example, took on Thatcher over apartheid and favoured sanctions against South Africa, which she had strongly opposed. Mulroney also negotiated a major environmental treaty on the Great Lakes with President Reagan and began to take international cooperation to combat climate change seriously. And, notwithstanding the trade deal and cuts Mulroney made to some programs, it was the Chrétien and Martin Liberals who ultimately moved the country more sharply to the economic right through the deep cuts in social spending found in the 1995 budget.

I believe Mulroney has an instinctive feeling for certain issues of racial injustice in particular. As prime minister, Pierre Trudeau had refused to even consider an apology for the abominable way thousands of Japanese Canadians had been treated during the Second World War (my first wife Yvonne Yamaoka's family was among those who had been interned). However, Mulroney did respond to appeals from me and others and brought in a significant measure in 1988, apologizing on behalf of the government. He also set up a human rights foundation and issued small cash payments to those still alive who had been affected. So, it would be a mistake to think the creation of Rights and Democracy was inconsistent with values held up by Mulroney.

**LS:** Given the global scope of Rights and Democracy's work, you no doubt spent a lot of time talking to civil society activists, trade union leaders, and the like when you travelled abroad. But you engaged with state officials as well, many of whom belonged to decidedly non–social democratic governments and some of whom were implicated in corruption and human rights abuses. How did you approach that kind of thing? Was there any value to those conversations, or were they more of an obligatory thing that you simply had to do?

**EB:** To varying degrees, they were intermittently obligatory and valuable. There had to be at least some real independence of civil society before we could or would work in a country. This independence meant I could always meet with people outside the government before speaking to officials. Most often we would be working in developing countries that were opening up thanks to internal pressure, so we were able to partner with democratically oriented groups even in places with corrupt or otherwise unsavoury administrations. In fact, our normal operating principle was that we only appeared in a country at the request of some democratic civil society organization.

Our approach was in contrast to the development aid dispensed by the World Bank and the International Monetary Fund, who encouraged the establishment of multiparty democracy but provided aid only on the condition that recipient countries carry out severe structural adjustment programs (these included privatization and cuts in public spending). This top-down and coercive approach had the effect of undermining the very promotion of democracy they claimed to be fostering. It was emulated by some European countries, but less so the social democratic Scandinavian countries. Sweden, in fact, investigated the Rights and Democracy approach and established a similar organization.

Because smaller countries tended to have more of a relationship with UN agencies through aid programs, and because the Canadian government under Mulroney put a certain emphasis on human rights in the countries they dealt with, I would meet with a wide swathe of governments who had varying degrees of commitment to any kind of reform. Some, of course, had none whatsoever, and the meetings often led to no action. We would explain to ministers their government's obligation under international human rights law, but in the end, it was up to them to act.

In some cases, the picture was quite complicated. I had one meeting, for example, with the minister of justice of a Central American country in which she actually began by asking her own chief of staff to leave the room. She told me, almost whispering, that she couldn't trust him because he'd been put into her office by the president, who was spying on everyone. We then had a discussion about human rights in her country, the level of corruption, and how one reform-minded minister after another seemed to get nowhere — either because they were corrupt themselves, or because they had been forced out in retaliation for their reform efforts. She was visibly apprehensive and fearful, almost regretting she had talked to me but also wanting to speak so she could communicate what was going on.

As a general rule, I didn't like to have meetings just for the sake of talking with either state officials or representatives from civil society without some hope they would help us further a human rights agenda. There were some occasions, however, in which I wasn't confident much progress would be made but it seemed worth trying anyway — one of which involved Óscar Arias, who was a member of the board of Rights and Democracy. Costa Rica, where Arias had been president, maintained a police force but no standing army. It was something he was understandably quite proud of and thought would be a good policy for the neighbouring countries to pursue. We helped him convene a secret meeting of defence ministers from Honduras, Guatemala, Nicaragua, and El Salvador — some of whom were military figures with terrible reputations on human rights — to discuss disarmament for the region and the possibility of eliminating national armies. Although this particular meeting lacked a positive outcome, Arias's work pursuing peace in the region ultimately led him to being awarded the Nobel Peace Prize.

**Jonathan Sas:** Did you have any meetings that generated controversy or created a bigger headache you ended up having to manage?

**EB:** Oh, yes. One of my most serious encounters was with the president of Kenya, Daniel Moi. He had headed the government for years and was a powerful figure with both a poor record on human rights and a reputation for corruption. I had finished meeting with him and, unbeknownst to me, a photographer appeared and Moi asked if we could take a picture together. I really should have said no, but taken by surprise, I agreed to be photographed and left later that day for a conference in neighbouring Tanzania without giving it a second thought. While I was there, a group from Nairobi happened to arrive with a few newspapers in hand. Sure enough, one had the picture of Moi and myself on its front page, accompanied with text in which he said it had been a great pleasure to entertain this Canadian human rights figure and claimed I had given his government a clean bill of health. He had, of course, set me up. But what he hadn't realized was that I was flying back to Canada by way of Nairobi the next day. So, when I got there, I held a press conference with a number of international news agencies and spoke in critical detail about Moi's deplorable human rights record. His duplicity had backfired.

**Frances Abele:** Did Rights and Democracy ever come into conflict with the Government of Canada over its work?

**EB:** In most cases, our embassies would be supportive because they were, in principle, supportive of the UN human rights provisions that grounded our work. Often, they would actually be quite happy about our criticisms of a particular government because it allowed those criticisms to be made without getting them directly involved and thus not threatening bilateral relationships. Neither Mulroney nor Chrétien interfered in the slightest with what Rights and Democracy was doing, nor did any of their foreign ministers. That all changed when Stephen Harper came along, which was some years after I had left.

That conflict was mainly about Harper's one-sided approach to Israeli-Palestinian relations. For example, he made a number of pro-Israel appointments to the board of Rights and Democracy.

They set about tearing up agreements it had entered into with human rights organizations in both Israel and the Occupied Territories, including with the well-regarded Israeli human rights organization B'Tselem. (CIDA, an agency of the Government of Canada, had also supported B'Tselem.) Rights and Democracy had built relationships with civil society in Palestine and Israel since 1992. That year, I visited the region and witnessed the toll of the Israeli response to the 1987 Intifada, which included land confiscation, house demolition, and deportations.

Subsequently, Harper went even further. He abolished Rights and Democracy. This action was universally condemned by Canadian NGOs and by their equivalents abroad. Needless to say, I was outraged by this undoing of an institution that had previously been strongly supported by Liberal and Conservative governments alike. This attack on civil society and dissent became a hallmark of his government, which went on to prohibit public servants and other experts from speaking out in their areas of responsibility. Harper did not want an organization connected to the Canadian government operating at arm's-length and contradicting his own messaging.

**FA:** In general, these were dark times. The United States was leading the charge for markets in what was then a newly unipolar world. To what extent did you find yourself at odds with its officials in the State Department and elsewhere?

**EB:** I don't believe they ever complained about our work through official diplomatic channels, but we were significantly at odds when it came to certain regions in particular. The impact our work could have was in proportion to the size of a country, which was one reason Central America became such a key area of focus. In places like El Salvador and Guatemala, we were supporting activists on the ground who were quite literally risking their lives by resisting military governments, juntas, or anti-Indigenous right-wing militia groups. These regimes often had the explicit backing of the United States. For that reason, U.S. representatives in the region were often hostile to the Catholic Church, the United Nations and any other human rights activism that sought to protect the rights of Indigenous peoples and others living in poverty.

In many ways, that was just a continuation of the awful policy they'd maintained throughout the Reagan era. While a vice president of the Socialist International in the 1980s, for example, I had visited the State Department on my way to Central America with the hope of hearing their thinking about the region before I talked to the various governments there — the idea being that I'd also visit on my way back to Canada to give a frank assessment of what I'd seen. The official I talked to upon my return was Thomas Enders, who was then the assistant secretary of state for inter-American affairs. I'd actually met with him before in his capacity as the American ambassador in Ottawa and had been quite impressed by his breadth of knowledge about Canada. On domestic issues, he described himself as a New Dealer. But he characterized his own outlook on foreign policy as hawkish; in the meeting, I saw quite directly how right-wing the American foreign policy establishment really was in relation to Central America.

I began my report by talking about Nicaragua and was saying that I didn't think the Americans should make the same mistake with the Sandinistas that they had made in the early days of the Castro government in Cuba — which I felt had only helped push Cuba in a communist direction. I tried to explain that the Sandinista government was a mixture of communists, social democrats, religious reformers, and assorted progressive people who had managed to get control. An official sitting beside Enders cut me off and, in a deep southern accent, interjected: "Mr. Broadbent, I want you to know that the mistake that we made with Fidel Castro was that we didn't hit him fast enough and hard enough. And we're not going to make that mistake with the Sandinistas." I thanked him and promptly said I didn't think there was much point in carrying on the meeting, which then came to an abrupt halt. In any case, this incident was illustrative of the wider American outlook toward the entire region.

Shortly after he was elected in 1992, we were able to get some cooperation from President Bill Clinton in relation to the major international project in Myanmar after Aung San Suu Kyi's house arrest. This project, demanding that her election be recognized, had the backing of Mikhail Gorbachev, Óscar Arias, Bishop Tutu, the Dalai Lama, and some other recipients of the Nobel Peace Prize. Bishop Tutu and I met with President Clinton and Vice President Al Gore at the White House and asked Clinton to issue a statement condemning China's sale of arms to Myanmar's military, who were refusing to recognize Aung San Suu Kyi's election. "The Chinese are already mad at me for something else," he replied. "So, I might as well." Obligingly, he then issued the requested press release.

**LS:** Let's turn to the wider context in which your work at Rights and Democracy was taking place. The 1990s represent a strange and complicated turn in human history. In one sense, the spirit was overwhelmingly one of optimism and the mood, among elites in the affluent West, was triumphant because liberal capitalism was seen as the only project left standing — even reformist alternatives to it were no longer considered viable. How did you view all of this?

**EB:** It was a complicated moment in history. I think, to para-phrase that possibly apocryphal remark of Zhou Enlai's about the meaning of the French Revolution, that it's still too soon to tell what it all ultimately meant. I expect historians will still be pon-dering that question twenty or thirty years from now. In any case, the coming apart of the Soviet Union in '89–'90, and the dissolu-tion of the various Eastern Bloc satellite regimes was something that I, like most social democrats, was pleased about. That created a lot of optimism, initially at least, about the possibility of a much broader shift toward liberal democracy around the world. It soon became obvious, however, that the market-oriented strains of liberalism were exerting a much greater influence than the democratic parts, and that a kind of market fanaticism was taking hold across several continents.

I remember, for example, doing a suppertime TV program with Thomas d'Aquino, head of the Canadian Council of Chief Executives. He was defending the principle that in Canadian law, we should not require that our corporations respect workers' human rights in their operations abroad. Rather, we should leave it up to market pressure to push them in that direction and thus allow them to respect workers' rights when they see it is in their advantage to do so. That kind of thinking was characteristic of the business elite at the time: that something as morally and ethically rudimentary as human rights should simply be left to market forces to determine. (It is corporate decision-makers, of course, not some law of the universe that are shaping the direction of market forces.) The TV program was focusing on a recent UN report which had documented significant abuse of workers in Africa by Canadian mining companies. I strongly differed with d'Aquino. Just as we now have a law that a Canadian who commits a child sex crime abroad can be prosecuted for such behaviour in Canadian courts, so too should we require our corporations to respect workers' rights abroad just as they have to respect those rights at home.

Another incident comes to mind here. After I left Rights and Democracy, I spent 1996–97 as a fellow at All Souls College, Oxford, where I had a conversation with an intelligent neoliberal economist from the University of Chicago who had been consulting in Moscow. Talking to her over lunch, I was distressed by what she said about the need to break up and deregulate all elements of the economy in Russia and to impose a radical move to pure markets. You didn't have to be a genius to understand what the sudden imposition of that model was going to do to the Russian people — and that it was quite clearly going to yield great suffering and discontent.

These two incidents illustrate a much wider market zealotry that was pervasive throughout the 1990s. It's possible to imagine a whole alternative history here. The fall of the Berlin Wall might have seen a very different Europe and a very different world emerge in its wake. What if, for example, Gorbachev's original hope for a social democratic Russian Federation had succeeded? Under Gerhard Schröder, Germany's SPD became one of the main vanguards of neoliberalism, as did New Labour under Tony Blair. What if those two parties, and others like them, had instead retained a classical social democratic identity and program, like the one that had been championed by Willy Brandt and the other leaders within the Socialist International right up to the 1980s?

Imagining historical counterfactuals can be useful in helping us see alternative moral prospects. Here, they are potentially useful in underscoring the extent to which the neoliberal transformation wasn't in any way inevitable — and that a very different kind of order could have emerged.

**FA:** To follow up on your Russian counterfactual, I believe you met Gorbachev in the 1980s?

**EB:** I met Gorbachev twice, and also knew the Soviet Ambassador Alexandr Yakovlev very well. He later became Gorbachev's principal advisor and played a major role in shaping the reform policies of glasnost and perestroika (translated as "openness" and "reconstruction" respectively). I first met Gorbachev when he visited Canada in May 1983 as secretary of agriculture in the Soviet government. He immediately impressed me with his candour. In conversation, the question of Canada accepting cruise missiles came up for discussion. The Americans wanted to test short-range missiles in the Canadian north, which the NDP and others opposed.

Gorbachev looked at me and said, "Why would you take this position? After all, we're testing them in the Soviet Union." The fact is, I — and I believe most other Canadians — did not know this. It was an extraordinary diplomatic statement on Gorbachev's part to speak with such openness about what his own government was up to. I had never encountered this before, with the single important exception of Alexandr Yakovlev, who over the years as ambassador had spoken with me in the frankest possible terms. It was characteristic of the reform-minded course both of them supported in the decades ahead.

The second time I saw Gorbachev was during his 1990 visit to Canada en route to his meeting with President Reagan. Again, there's an interesting story about this meeting that is indicative of his decency. I had not been scheduled as part of his official itinerary — in fact, I hadn't known he was coming until just a couple of days before his arrival. When I learned of the visit, I contacted Soviet and Canadian officials to request a meeting with him in full knowledge that the schedule for such a trip would have been worked out weeks before. Within twenty-four hours of my request, I learned that Gorbachev would indeed meet with me. I had the strongest feeling that this visit would be his last one to North America and so I was delighted to meet with this extraordinary man one more time. There was no political advantage for him in meeting with me. He simply did so in a spirit of decency and respect. Our conversation was brief, perhaps twenty minutes long, but it was warm and frank, and he lived up to his reputation as one of the twentieth century's most significant figures.

**JS:** You've referred a few times to the market ideology that was so ubiquitous during the 1990s. Apart from the obvious things like privatization and cuts to social programs — how exactly would you characterize the essence of that philosophy?

**EB:** Theoretically and philosophically, political and intellectual partisans for this shift were drawing on elements of the classical liberal economic tradition, though in important respects they were also deviating from it as well. Both John Locke and Adam Smith were deeply concerned about the threats associated with monopolies or concentrations of power and aware of the extent to which they would inevitably be abused. In the eighteenth century, Smith had advocated for competitive markets complemented by a strong and regulating government tasked with enforcing the rule of law and ensuring that a majority actually benefited from a capitalist economy — while being protected from the avaricious instincts of its business class. Locke, writing earlier, justified liberal institutions on the grounds that individual rights had to be protected — both from the church and what was still then a quasi-feudal state. Whatever roots neoliberalism claimed in that tradition, it really did represent a kind of corporate capitalism more concentrated and unaccountable than what Locke or Smith would have favoured. During this period, Lucille and I had lunch with Canadian-born progressive economist J.K. Galbraith at his home in Cambridge, Massachusetts. I had just purchased a copy of the new edition of Adam Smith's *Wealth of Nations* at the bookstore in Harvard Square. With his usual insight, Galbraith wrote on the inside cover that "there is more wisdom in this book than Ronald Reagan would understand."

Of course, liberal rights were pre-democratic. In some countries, these rights were used to get democratic rights of political participation and to achieve democracy. However, there is nothing inevitable about this process. Some countries democratize and some do not. While at Rights and Democracy, I gave a speech dealing with this issue. I pointed out that about half a dozen western leaders were making the claim that the fall of the Berlin Wall and the turn toward markets would inevitably result in the spread of democracy. I believe this is seriously wrong. If you want to distill the market ideology of the early 1990s to its purest form, it is that those leaders believed there was a direct linkage between the introduction of markets and the flourishing of the civil and political institutions that characterize democracy. At Rights and Democracy, we made the case as forcefully as we could that it is entirely possible to have markets without them resulting in human rights or democracy. We pointed to Germany in 1938 or Chile under Augusto Pinochet: both had market economies but also deeply brutal and authoritarian governments who actively suppressed democratic forces. The same is true today of Russia, China, and other authoritarian regimes.

There's simply never been a necessary causal connection between the extension of markets and the spreading of democracy, and what ultimately happened in the 1990s was that Western governments put too much exclusive emphasis on promoting the former. It's also important to emphasize that the market model they were trying to export was very much of the neoliberal variety: that is, one with only the most barebones social protections and with many of the major utilities and industries that had previously been managed by the state sold off to private investors. I don't think this is what many ordinary people around the world believed was going to happen or wanted to happen. And I certainly don't think most Canadians wanted their own government to pursue a foreign policy that treated human rights as secondary to the spreading of markets either. (When I co-chaired the 2000–02 Commission on Canadian Democracy and Corporate Accountability with Avie Bennett, for example, we cited a poll which, to my memory, found that a significant majority of Canadians wanted human rights to be a key component of our foreign policy.)

We've been speaking about this broader shift in mainly ideological terms, but its economic and material impact was both significant and immediate. When we talk about the era of globalization, what we're ultimately discussing isn't just the growing hegemony of the market in the realm of ideas but the stripping away of legally erected barriers to the free flow of capital. That led not only to the dramatic expansion of markets but also an explosion in the total number of multinational corporations, which grew from 35,000 to 65,000 between 1990 and 2002.[2] At the outset of the 1990s, a large majority of funds going from the global north to the global south came in the form of transfers from governments. But, by the end of the decade, more than 80 percent of that flow was coming to developing countries through unaccountable private corporations. In other words: the most important entity those countries now had to deal with in the global north was no longer elected governments, but multinationals. While that process was unfolding, the corporate tax rate in virtually every OECD (Organization for Economic Co-operation and Development) country went down.

When we talk about this period, the most striking thing is the huge increase in the wealth and power of private corporations accountable mainly to their shareholders. That has continued to this day. Democracy and human rights took a back seat to the promotion of markets in their most austere and underregulated form.

**FA:** Another significant change was the creation of supranational institutions to oversee all of these less restricted and more liberalized capital flows. It's difficult to think of anything more illustrative of this new era of corporate power than that.

**EB:** This is one area in which it's increasingly become clear that the spread of markets has not only failed to extend democracy, but in many cases has quite actively undermined it. One of the most noxious innovations of the so-called new world order was the granting of power to corporations which gave them the right to sue governments for doing things, such as regulating to protect the environment, that impinged on their profits. Central to this project was the World Trade Organization, which was created in 1995 with the explicit objective of spreading markets. NAFTA led the pack in establishing investor-state dispute settlement mechanisms that allowed capital to tame the state and restrict its ability to make democratic decisions in the public interest.[3]

The WTO, the IMF, and the World Bank have exerted considerable pressure on both wealthy and developing countries to strip down and cut their social spending and to meet certain other criteria in exchange for cooperation on major trade agreements or credit for urgently needed loans. The various agreements that bestowed these powers on multinationals were not balanced with countervailing provisions concerned with either human rights or the environment. In many places, a direct result was the undermining of independent civil society and the other elements necessary for democratic institutions to flourish — to say nothing of worsening inequality.

**LS:** Among the biggest and most important counterweights to the power of markets are labour rights and strong unions. Both Reagan and Thatcher quite deliberately sought out big fights with the labour movement — Reagan with the Air Traffic Controllers and Thatcher with the National Union of Mineworkers — and were successful in rolling them back so that markets could operate unchecked. That offensive began on a national level, but you must have seen the international version of it during your time at Rights and Democracy.

**EB:** The rolling back of labour rights in the 1980s and 1990s is pertinent here because the development of democracy has historically been closely associated with trade unions going right back to the industrial revolution. In Europe, in particular, workers' movements were instrumental in the extension of basic civil rights and played a critical role in the push for universal suffrage. By undermining labour rights, neoliberals were thus not only putting corporations before workers, they were actively ignoring the visible and causal connection between unions and democracy (while wrongly insisting the latter would come through markets).

From the outset, Rights and Democracy viewed the right to organize an independent union as fundamental. The new trade agreements had serious enforcement mechanisms to protect the owners of capital. There was nothing remotely equivalent available to enforce the rights of workers. We advocated, unsuccessfully, adding a clause to trade agreements that would have compelled states to enforce the International Labour Organization's rules for labour protections: notably, the right to form a union and the right to strike. In effect, those rights would be given equal weight in international trade so that countries found to be in violation could have action brought against them — just as they would for violating other WTO provisions. Instead, any obligations to implement the labour provisions are to this day largely voluntary. So, there was a wider attack on workers' rights underway: both throughout the West and in newly liberalizing countries that were embarking on their own market experiments. We tried to intervene wherever we could, but it was a decidedly uphill battle.

I once went to Indonesia, for example, to attend a secret meeting with some men who were trying to organize an independent union, and it had to be secret because the law said that any meeting of five people or more required government permission (and the last thing the Indonesian government was going to allow was a meeting concerned with forming a union). In China, we offered our support to a very courageous railway worker named Han Dongfang. He was sentenced after Tiananmen Square and spent twenty-two months in prison for trying to organize an independent trade union — appealing directly to the Chinese constitution. It was scarcely reported at the time, but nearly fifty workers were sentenced to death in trials that followed the massacre. Plenty of students and academics were also sentenced, but none received a penalty so harsh and tended to have lesser prison sentences. After Han's release, he was a key participant at a conference we convened in Bangkok and eventually went to Hong Kong, where he founded an organization to fight for independent unions.

I had another experience, in Thailand, that was deeply disturbing. I had arrived in the country not long after 188 workers, most of them young women, had burned to death in a factory that was making Cabbage Patch dolls. They might have escaped the fire, but they were locked in as soon as they got to work each day. The case actually got a fair amount of publicity, I suspect because the Cabbage Patch dolls were mostly being manufactured so that they could be sold to young girls all over the developed world. But there were similar incidents, including a number of cases in China, where workers also died from fires after being locked inside, and those received considerably less attention, perhaps because the products they were making were not as well-known as the Cabbage Patch dolls.

Again, it all comes back to the same basic question, which is why certain rights and privileges are extended to corporations while others are withheld from citizens as workers. In a law that was being written at the time, the Government of Canada was developing a framework that would make it possible to prosecute Canadian citizens who were involved in crimes associated with the international sex trade (like the trafficking of children in Thailand). At Rights and Democracy, we responded by drafting a proposal for a law that would have applied the Criminal Code to other violations of human rights by Canadians abroad — including those carried out by Canadian corporations who denied the right to organize and in some cases were actually violently attacking their workers who were struggling to get a union. What I argued at the time was that if we were going to assert the need to protect children in Saigon from Canadians under the same laws which exist to protect children in Toronto, then their parents also deserved to have their rights as workers when employed by a Canadian company. Despite widespread support for this measure, such a law has not been pursued by Canadian governments.

**FA:** You alluded to it earlier when we were talking about Russia, but there were also profound political implications to the neoliberal turn that came about as a direct result of the economic order it imposed — not just in the formerly communist countries.

**EB:** The simultaneous impact of new trade agreements and market-oriented domestic policies — tax cuts, the gutting of social protections, financial deregulation, etc. — was profound in many Western countries, and especially in the United States where there was a particularly massive outsourcing of manufacturing jobs. All of that led to significant popular discontent. I don't think it's the only cause, but the wrenching economic transformations of the 1990s are undoubtedly one of the major factors in the rise of right-wing populism over the last decade.

Beginning with the collapse of the Berlin Wall, the 1990s started out with great promise. People all over the world were excited about the prospect of greater freedom and democracy. Instead, however, there was a step-by-step expansion of markets and the power of corporations. In place of a vibrant global civil society and wider enrichment of democracy, the world witnessed a serious retrenchment of social and economic rights. In many ways, that retrenchment has formed the context for my political agenda and focus ever since.

## CHAPTER TEN

# The Grey Ideology

*"With too much confidence and too little reflection we put the twentieth century behind us and strode boldly into its successor swaddled in self-serving half-truths: the triumph of the West, the end of history, the unipolar American moment, the ineluctable march of globalization and the free market. In our Manichean enthusiasms we in the West made haste to dispense whenever possible with the economic, intellectual, and institutional baggage of the twentieth century and encouraged others to do likewise . . . Not only did we fail to learn very much from the past — this would hardly have been remarkable. But we have become stridently insistent — in our economic calculations, our political practices, our international strategies, even our educational priorities — that the past has nothing of interest to teach us."*

— TONY JUDT, *The World We Have Lost*


*"Something is wrong, very wrong, when a single person in good health, a person who in addition possesses a working car, can barely support herself by the sweat of her brow. You don't need a degree in economics to see that wages are too low and rents too high."*

— BARBARA EHRENREICH

I n one of my final acts as leader of the NDP, I rose in Parliament
to table a motion committing Canada's federal government to the
goal of eliminating child poverty by the year 2000.* Following its
unanimous passage by the House of Commons, I was optimistic. The
objective, supported in principle by members from all parties, was both
morally worthy and practically achievable with the necessary political
will behind it. Eleven years later, when the long twentieth century
finally came to an end, Canada's child poverty rate remained a national
disgrace — and, under both Liberal and Conservative prime ministers,
would be allowed to rise even higher in the first decade of the twenty-
first century.[1] (The child poverty rate has started to decline only
recently, due in part to a redistributive child benefit— a progressive
income transfer that anti-poverty advocates, social policy experts, and
the NDP had been demanding for decades and which the Trudeau
government finally introduced in 2015.)

Our country's failure to eliminate the scourge of child poverty is
certainly indicative of successive governments' refusal to act. But it also
reflects the grim reality that the post-1989 world has, in a broader sense,
failed to deliver on what at least momentarily looked to be its promise.
In their ferocious embrace of markets as a panacea, the proponents of
neoliberalism have successfully undermined not only the cooperative
institutions that defined the best of the postwar decades — social enti-
tlements, progressive taxation, the strict regulation of corporate activity
— but the very notion of democratic citizenship itself. Social and economic rights, the great equalizing innovation of the mid-twentieth
century, have been stripped down to their barest form. The democratic
state, which under labour, socialist, liberal, and Christian democratic
governments alike once played a constructive role in fostering equality,
has been increasingly subordinated to market principles. Trade unions,
the bulwark of economic power for ordinary people since the dawn
of the industrial age, have seen their legitimacy steadily eroded. Citizens
themselves, meanwhile, have increasingly been redefined as taxpayers
and consumers.

---

\* A full version of the speech introducing the motion is included in the Appendices.

Toward the end of his life, President Franklin Roosevelt worried that his country might one day revert to the chaotic injustice and simmering discontent of the 1920s. In effect, recent decades have seen his fears realized on a global scale. Amid the retrenchment of economic and social rights and increasing commercialization of everyday life, market economies are being transformed into market societies. The long march of democratic equality after 1945 has not only been halted but, in many areas, actively reversed.

Quite predictably, the result has been a dramatic increase in inequality to levels unseen since the nineteenth century. Contrary to the self-serving prognostications of market liberals and conservatives alike, the fruits of economic growth have also visibly failed to trickle down. Between 1998 and 2007, the average wage of full-time Canadian workers rose at less than the rate of inflation. Over the same period, the wealthiest 1 percent of Canadians increased their share of total wages and salaries by 100 percent, while the annual compensation of the highest-paid 100 CEOs tripled.[2] Since then, little has changed for the vast majority of Canadians while the very rich have continued to get richer. Recent data from Statistics Canada shows that the wealthiest 20 percent of households now hold more than two-thirds of all net worth in Canada, while the bottom 40 percent hold just 2.8 percent of wealth.[3] An overly financialized, boom-and-bust marketplace with an expanding GDP, it turns out, is no substitute for redistribution. Exacerbated by events like the 2008 economic crisis, a similar process — often yielding an even greater degree of inequality — has unfolded in liberal democracies across the globe.

Since retiring from Rights and Democracy in 1996, I must confess that the actual business of retirement has eluded me.

After completing my fellowship at All Souls, Oxford, I returned to Canada and agreed to chair the recently convened Panel on Accountability and Governance in the Voluntary Sector. Over the course of some fourteen months, the panel conducted a detailed study on the inner workings and regulation of civil society, ultimately issuing dozens of recommendations about how to expand and strengthen its role in national life.

Throughout the 1990s, I had enjoyed a welcome reprieve from partisan activity. This came to an end when I decided to publicly support Jack Layton's campaign for the NDP leadership in 2003 and, at his request, stand again for a seat in the House of Commons the following year. Elected in the riding of Ottawa Centre, I had the singular privilege of being the only MP able to walk to Parliament from home. Less advantageous was the arduous workload I inadvertently assumed when I volunteered for three House committees — more, it turned out, than any other MP. Whatever else I enjoyed about being a backbencher again for the first time in thirty years, I had clearly grown a bit too accustomed to having a research staff at my disposal. In the NDP shadow cabinet, the files I took on were concerned with three areas long close to my heart: democratic reform, corporate accountability, and child poverty.

The work was exhausting but enjoyable and, as a member of caucus, I was able to see Jack's energetic and collegial style of leadership up close. Back in the House, I struck up a close friendship with my seatmate Libby Davies, a delightful, rabble-rousing politician from Vancouver's Downtown Eastside — with whom I traded many jokes and whose commitment to representing her constituents in one of Canada's poorest neighbourhoods I deeply respected. Libby and I remain good friends and have stayed in regular touch since leaving the House of Commons.

Soon after I reentered Parliament, Lucille became ill with cancer. She had been the love of my life, my constant companion throughout most of my time in politics, a wonderful partner to me and a loving mother to our two children. My task would now be to do all that I could to make her remaining days bearable, and I announced this would be my final term as an MP.

It would not be long before Jack Layton called on me again. In the fall of 2008, as the global economy teetered on the brink, Canada elected its third minority Parliament in four years. Well before he had ever become prime minister, there had seemed to be a vindictive and ideological streak in Stephen Harper — an impression that was confirmed when his government tabled a brazenly right-wing fiscal statement within mere weeks of returning to power. Pledging billions in spending cuts as countries around the world prepared to stimulate their economies, the Conservatives also sought to gut public funding for political parties, undermine pay equity, and suspend the right of public servants to strike.

Jack and his staff had been working on a proposal for a coalition government. At Jack's request, I met with Jean Chrétien to discuss a distinctly peculiar possibility motivated by these exceptional circumstances: the formation of Canada's first coalition government since the First World War. The coalition was thwarted by Harper's opportunistic (and highly questionable) prorogaiton of Parliament. The sudden threat of defeat nevertheless compelled the Conservatives to change course when the House reconvened two months later.

Harper led his party into another election in May 2011. If my initial instincts about Jack had been vindicated by my experience working with him in caucus, they were affirmed many times over by the results of that election. Electing 103 MPs, the NDP under Jack's leadership accomplished two significant objectives that had always eluded it during mine: surpassing the Liberals and achieving a breakthrough in Quebec. For the first time in Canadian history, the NDP formed the Official Opposition.

Just before Jack's tragic death only a few months later, I founded the Broadbent Institute with the aim of giving social democracy a greater presence in Canadian civil society and challenging the intellectual influence of the neoliberal right. The Institute has since gone on to publish research, train activists, and engage in social media debates fuelled by the investigative reporting of the young staff at PressProgress, an initiative of the Institute. It also holds national and regional policy conferences that attract hundreds of participants from Canada and abroad.

For six years before her passing in 2016, I lived and travelled the world with my wife, Ellen Meiksins Wood, an old friend whom I first met while teaching at York University in the 1960s. We both loved Bach, the Blue Jays, and long walks in London's Primrose Hill Park. As one of the foremost democratic Marxist scholars of her generation, Ellen was a formidable interlocutor in a series of friendly debates we had in front of audiences in Germany, Turkey, and Cuba.

In one way or another, I have spent the last twenty-five years continuing to advocate what the great Swedish filmmaker Ingmar Bergman once called the "grey ideology" of social democracy. Willy Brandt, Tommy Douglas, and Michael Harrington would all have understood what Bergman meant. These people, alongside countless others I have known, passionately believed this greyness, this acceptance of imperfection, was worth struggling for. The violent, tragic, and revolutionary twentieth century showed us that no form of politics can transcend or overcome every source of human sadness. In the twenty-first century, however, social democracy remains the form with the greatest potential, no more, no less, for liberating the creative, cooperative, and compassionate possibilities of humanity, and offering dignity to all.

**Frances Abele:** You took a step away from partisan politics after you left Parliament in 1989. What made you return to support Jack Layton's campaign for the NDP leadership in 2003?

**Ed Broadbent:** During the 1990s, I was out of the federal scene — blissfully enjoying my international work at Rights and Democracy in Montreal, and feeling very happy about having a break from joyous experiences like the Constitution and free trade. You have so little time as a national party leader, and I will admit it was a relief not to follow domestic politics much. The reason I got back involved was that I had become concerned about the survival of the NDP. We have no divine right to exist in Canada and we were in a precarious moment in the early 2000s.

In contrast to what happened in many social democratic parties both Audrey McLaughlin and Alexa McDonough kept the federal NDP from moving in a neoliberal direction. I supported Audrey's campaign to succeed me as leader and thought Alexa had both bountiful energy and a deep commitment to the cause of social democracy. But politics can be cruel and the 1990s, being the heyday of neoliberalism, were a very difficult period for social democrats around the world. For a number of reasons — including the rightward shift of global politics and the rise of the Reform Party in the West — the NDP's support ended up dipping lower than at any other point in its history.

That, and the fact that market dogma had become so dominant, only reaffirmed my long-standing belief that Canada needed a strong and credible social democratic alternative — and Jack seemed like the kind of leader who could excite people and inject a renewed idea of the public good back into the national debate. I did not know him personally before he ran, and my good friend Bill Blaikie had more support in caucus. But I ultimately decided to support Jack, who came highly recommended by a number of good friends in Toronto who had observed his exceptional work as a councillor.

**Jonathan Sas:** The party subsequently enjoyed its biggest electoral success under Layton. But in many ways, I wouldn't call him a left-wing firebrand. How would you characterize his politics yourself?

**EB:** One of the principal reasons I supported him was his record as a progressive municipal politician. He had been effective in getting things done and working well with others. He was also instrumental in bringing environmental concerns to Toronto City Council. In federal politics, Jack was instinctively progressive. He demonstrated this time after time, whether it was on housing and homelessness, the environment, or LGBTQ rights. His instincts were always the right ones. And they were precisely those that I believed that the party needed at this time.

**Luke Savage:** Perhaps we can talk about the short-lived 2008 coalition agreement between the NDP and Liberals you helped negotiate? I was in my first year of university at the time and remember being incredibly excited by all of that because it suddenly felt like federal politics had real stakes. There was a right-wing government elected by fewer than 40 percent of Canadians and we were going to replace it with a kind of progressive popular front — or that's what my younger self was thinking while at the rallies. I wouldn't say my own idea of things is quite as uncomplicated anymore — and not only because the whole thing ultimately fell apart. How do you view those events in retrospect?

**EB:** I'd like to preface my reply by noting that the events of 2008 would have unfolded completely differently if Canada had an electoral system that wasn't stuck in the nineteenth century. After the election that October, we ended up with a Conservative minority government elected by fewer than four in ten voters and without a single MP from Toronto, Montreal, or Vancouver. Federalist parties together accounted for more than 60 percent of the vote in Quebec, but the Bloc Québécois won two-thirds of the seats. Nearly a million people cast a ballot for the Green Party and they didn't even get one MP. An electoral system resembling those used in places like New Zealand, Scotland, or Germany — perhaps combining direct proportionality and the election of MPs in individual constituencies as mixed-member proportional does — would have almost certainly resulted in a multiparty, centre-left coalition of some sort, and there never would have been any parliamentary dispute to begin with.[4] The first-past-the-post model of electing parliaments really is an anachronism, and that came out both through the disproportionate results of that election (to say nothing of so many others) and also in the climate of generalized bewilderment about the nature of coalition government we saw after. So, among other things, the whole episode really was just further proof that Canada badly needs electoral reform (something that I advocated very strongly when I was back in Parliament).

Having said all of that, I have since come to think that the coalition agreement was a mistake. There was a serious level of groupthink going on between me, Jack, and others like Brian Topp and Allan Blakeney. We saw an opening to oust Stephen Harper and bring in a progressive agenda in response to the economic situation, which in principle seemed like a good idea. Momentum built quickly and negotiating with Chrétien proved fairly agreeable. As I recall, the only thing I really had to push on was the number of cabinet seats the NDP would get — I believe he ultimately yielded one more than what they had initially proposed — and there was some further wrangling that went on over details like the distribution of different portfolios. In terms of the policy proposals, we found ourselves in a position to dictate the agenda. They really had nothing concrete to say upfront in terms of a shared legislative program.

But we got it wrong in 2008. Because, even if the plan had succeeded in the short term, it was not in retrospect a very good idea. For one thing, the Liberals had, in Stephane Dion, an incredibly precarious leader with very little legitimacy. There was already a push underway within the Liberal caucus to anoint Michael Ignatieff while we were negotiating. We also failed to predict Harper's wicked and misleading attack on the agreement as some kind of illegitimate seizure of power. Knowing Harper, we should really have thought more carefully about the kinds of things he was likely to do in that situation and been better prepared for them.

Incidentally, after he got his majority a few years later, I had an opportunity to raise the issue of proportional representation with Harper in a one-on-one discussion. After all, he'd once written an article with Tom Flanagan that had indicated a preference on his part for some form of proportional system. I asked him, Why not bring one in now? He admitted that his colleagues, having just won an election under one system, would be in no mood to change to another.

**LS:** After Jack Layton's tragic death in 2011, the NDP had a leadership race and ultimately chose Thomas Mulcair to succeed him. You came out early and publicly for Brian Topp, who ended up finishing in second. Perhaps you can talk about that contest a bit — and your general assessment of Mulcair's leadership?

**EB:** My reasons for endorsing Brian were fairly straightforward: I knew him, had worked with him, and held him in high regard. He's also a Montrealer who is fluently bilingual, and I thought he would be well-suited to take on the Liberals and Conservatives in debates. Practically speaking I thought that, by announcing our support for Brian early, some of us could maybe persuade Thomas Mulcair not to run. If anything, it probably had the opposite effect and encouraged him instead. There was a concern many had, which I certainly shared, that Mulcair was quite conservative in his economic outlook.

When he was a Liberal minister in Quebec's National Assembly, as I learned too late, he was seen as being solidly on the right of cabinet when it came to most major economic decisions. However, he was also known for being quite progressive on the environment and had been kicked out of cabinet after refusing to approve condominium construction in a part of a public park the Jean Charest government had partially privatized.[5] Largely because of that, when he offered to switch to the NDP, I supported him and went to Montreal to campaign in the 2007 Outremont byelection he ended up winning. I knew nothing about his economic proclivities at the time and, given that he had left a cabinet position to join the NDP, he could hardly be accused of opportunism.

After he joined the party he was important in laying the groundwork for the successful election of 2011. As Leader of the Opposition in the House of Commons he was forceful and forensic in Parliament and was exceptionally skillful at grilling the government in question period. When the 2015 federal election arrived, however, his conservative economic views came out and he positioned the party against deficit spending while backing away from taxing the rich.

Those were the wrong positions for the NDP to take. Leaving the perception that the Liberals were on the left of the NDP was a disastrous strategy for the campaign. I don't think he was being duplicitous either. He was authentically a neoliberal on economics and had even at one point praised Margaret Thatcher. Ultimately, I think Mulcair's election as leader was not just a serious mistake, but a dangerous one for the NDP's identity as a social democratic party. I was glad to see NDP members correct that mistake after the campaign — and I think the 2017 convention vote was more a principled rejection of Mulcair's politics than anything else.

Since then, I have been pleased to note the commitment of Jagmeet Singh to traditional social democratic principles. He speaks with passion and conviction about inequality, the serious need for action on the environment, and issues of racial injustice. I consider him a friend and have enjoyed campaigning with him in Ottawa. He is a happy warrior, and I would love to see him become prime minister. He would bring not only a sense of competence to his obligations but also a joyfulness that would be an inspiration to younger Canadians in particular, right across the country.

**FA:** To shift the conversation away from partisan politics, something you've taken a strong interest in for the past several decades is civil society. I'm thinking of the panel you chaired in the 1990s and its report, but also of the founding of the Broadbent Institute itself. Historically, I think it might be fair to say that social democracy has been more closely associated, at least in many people's minds, with the state. Where does civil society fit in, for you?

**EB:** In a very real way I think this goes back to some of my earliest preoccupations, even prior to political life. Given the catastrophic way it's been redefined and restructured in recent decades, it's certainly imperative that we restore a progressive and interventionist model of the democratic state and reassert the primacy of democratic institutions over the market. Having said that, I think there's been a tendency among some people on the left, and not just in Canada, to pay too little attention to the voluntary sector (or civil society, as it now most often tends to be called). I don't see the two as being in opposition. On the contrary, organizations within civil society clearly have an important role to play, alongside political parties and other actors, in the wider project of revitalizing the democratic state and reviving the social democratic alternative to neoliberalism. There should be a healthy tension between civil society organizations and the government of the day because one of the functions of civil society is to produce constructive criticism of the government.

At the same time, I think the sector has a more permanent and less instrumental kind of importance. I've never myself envisioned the sort of society in which an all-powerful state is the only major player. That isn't what you want if you're a democratic socialist or social democrat, and at Rights and Democracy, I saw again and again how critical the existence of a vibrant civil society is to the overall health of democracy in general. I would argue that it is a precursor to a more democratic state because it's the foundation from which citizens are able to agitate for their rights and press their demands — both within the state and outside of it.

**FA:** It's been my experience that a lot of people get into politics through voluntary activities. Someone might, for example, be on a school board and then decide to run for city council. That's purely anecdotal, but I think that kind of trajectory is common, and to me, it's an indication of the importance of civil society in terms of establishing a culture with a democratic quality. Among other things, people often develop a sense of efficacy and an ability to work together in those kinds of settings.

**EB:** Yes, and it's integral to any serious conception of democratic citizenship. Democratic life, in the fullest sense, requires a diffusion or sharing of power between the state and other actors, including trade unions and groups in civil society. This is a theme that has defined my socialism going all the way back to my first serious engagements with John Stuart Mill in the 1960s: namely, that wherever power is allowed to exercise itself over people's lives, the people ought to have means to countervail and control it. That means democratizing the state but also having voluntary and participatory structures of various kinds outside of it.

Exactly the same principle applies to the private sector as well. A major recurring theme in so many of the speeches I gave as a politician was the problem of corporate power in our society, and that was inspired by an identical moral concern. Much as we shouldn't want an almighty state controlling everything, we also don't want the public interest to be subordinated to the whims of major corporations — or our destinies as individuals to be determined by market forces. As citizens, people should not have to lead lives in which everything around them is commodified and, as workers, they need to wield collective power for similar reasons. I spoke and wrote regularly about the challenge of corporate power throughout the 1960s, '70s, and '80s, but the problem has only grown more severe over the past thirty years. A vibrant and creative civil society along with strong, independent unions are all important means of reducing, containing, and checking that power. So is the democratic state.

People like Galbraith, and more recently Joseph Stiglitz, have laid out the case for vigorous regulation of the private sector, and that was something I engaged with directly throughout the Commission on

Canadian Democracy and Corporate Accountability I co-chaired with Avie Bennett in the early 2000s. All of the key recommendations were motivated by the basic idea that the behaviour of firms should be bound by a range of criteria beyond just the bottom line. For example, if a company is going to be publicly listed, it should be legally required to meet clearly specified standards of social responsibility, labour, environmental, and otherwise. Similarly, if it's going to do any business with, or receive any kind of contract from the government, it should have to conform to those requirements.

**LS:** To people of my generation, I think a phrase like "corporate social responsibility" has a rather bland and somewhat conservative connotation. At face value, it brings to mind corporate brands affixing themselves to pride parades, boasting about vaguely defined "sustainability" initiatives, and the like.

**EB:** Well, one of the problems is that both the corporate sector and neoliberals picked up on the language about corporate responsibility and sustainability. They realized that, because so many people are socially conscious, it was in their interest to align themselves with the idea of social responsibility. But, fundamentally, they want a voluntary version of it with no teeth. My own view is that Canadian firms, whether they are operating at home or abroad, should meet certain standards with respect to workers' rights and the environment. That's why the principle must be strict, mandatory, and underwritten by the state with strong enforcement mechanisms for companies operating at home and abroad.

**LS:** We've talked at length about your views on the state, and what you've called your Orwellian skepticism about a version of it that's too large or overpowering. Suppose I'm a right-wing newspaper columnist writing a review of this book, and I sarcastically reply that you've elsewhere argued for nationalization of the energy sector — or that you once campaigned on an industrial strategy that would have seen the state intervene quite actively in the overall direction of the economy. And suppose, just to ventriloquize the argument, I then argued that you actually do favour a big and overpowering government after all.

**EB:** For me, this is just the nature of a pluralistic state and society. I can simultaneously want an expansion of the state's democratic authority *and* to have its scope constrained and checked in various ways. When it comes to areas like healthcare, public utilities, or certain sectors of the economy, there's a clear need for the state to have significant and even exclusive responsibility. Some things shouldn't be commodified and, in the interest of equality and human freedom, should be removed from the market altogether. At the same time, the state can't and shouldn't be made all-powerful for the obvious reasons we've already discussed. I don't see any contradictions in wanting an activist state on the one hand and the promotion of other centres of power and activity on the other — either in the private sector or in civil society at large.

**JS:** The context for the paring back of the democratic state you've been talking about is really a wider rightward turn in politics. My impression is that you think there was a qualitative shift of some kind within conservative parties that was consolidated in the 1990s — and, in Canada at least, was manifested during the Harper years. A phrase you began using in the early 2000s was "the new barbarism" — which doesn't strike me as the sort of characterization you would make of people like Joe Clark or Brian Mulroney.

**EB:** I do think the Harper government was quite different from the preceding Liberal or Conservative governments. There was a high degree of intolerance in Harper that came out not only in his disagreements with political opponents, but also in his attitude toward public servants. When he was prime minister, there was a clamping down on the traditional freedoms of civil servants and a stifling of their right to speak freely about their work in a non-partisan way. The whole atmosphere he created within the federal government was one of control and repression. (This impulse to control information took on its most obvious form in the cancellation of the long-form census.)

However I might have disagreed with Chrétien, Mulroney, or any other recent prime minister, I would not have said that about them. In terms of policymaking, Mulroney was more ideologically flexible. Even though he did oversee some privatizations and make cuts to a number of public programs, Paul Martin's 1995 budget went significantly further. On a personal level, I think there was a kind of malice to Harper that I don't associate with previous Conservative leaders — for example in his administration's attacks on unions, public servants, and civil society groups.[6]

I think the conservative shift we've been discussing was fundamentally about a rabid embrace of the market that, for quite an extended period, reduced political debates to a series of dogmatic economic assumptions — none of which holds up under scrutiny. The first, and in a sense most significant, was the idea that a smaller state with lower taxes and public spending is necessary to increase productivity. In fact, a number of European countries maintained much higher levels of taxation and social expenditure throughout the 1990s and either matched or exceeded the increases in productivity in the United States and Canada. Another related assumption was that reducing state activity would organically result in greater citizen participation in voluntary activities. Yet volunteerism in Canada declined significantly toward the end of the 1990s in the wake of the Chrétien/Martin cuts. It remained stronger in Scandinavian countries that boasted the world's biggest equalizing social programs. Much of the mania for spending cuts was justified on the grounds that they would result in economic growth that would, in turn, reduce poverty and inequality. In Canada, and in plenty of other countries as well, high levels of growth have actually been accompanied by a widening gap between the rich and everyone else.

None of those assumptions has been borne out in the experience of the past two decades at all. The trickle-down philosophy has always been bad economics, but it also rests on the dubious ethical claim that people are not merely self-interested but also inherently selfish. That just isn't a credible or tenable view of human nature, and I do not believe it's one that most of us personally hold. People can be individualistic: they can have specific desires, appetites, and ambitions. But I have never seen that tendency as antithetical to cooperation. People are also social beings who find fulfilment through collaboration and community. That's obvious in so many areas of daily life. For related reasons, a clear majority in Canada continues to favour redistributive policies, cooperative programs like public healthcare, and the levels of progressive taxation necessary to finance them.[7]


**JS:** Throughout your political life and since, you've been willing to engage respectfully with the ideas of liberals and conservatives. But you've done the same, as it were, in the other direction as well — with Marxists and others on the left who have a critical orientation toward social democracy. You and your wife Ellen Wood, for example, participated in a series of friendly public debates held in different countries. Perhaps we can discuss your intellectual relationship with Ellen, and what emerged from those exchanges. How would you define her political analysis, particularly as compared to your own?

**EB:** The context of those debates was that Ellen had been invited to speak and had the temerity to suggest that this social democrat she was dragging around with her might add something to the discussion. She spoke first at each and my contribution always came after (which is the more advantageous position when you're debating someone, because you get to hear what they have to say!). However I already had a pretty good idea of what Ellen would have to say in her three different talks, and there were clear differences but also certain similarities in our two positions.

Ellen was, of course, a formidable critic of capitalism and the marketization of life. The two of us found a lot of common ground in this and in our objections to the neoliberal project. Tony Blair, Gerhard Schröder, Bill Clinton, and others, for example, all led governments that introduced privatization and expanded the role of markets in areas that had been previously carved out of the market in the political struggle for social rights. We shared a critique of that.

Where we differed was on the degree to which we thought a democratic socialist government could actually make a difference within our lifetimes. She saw the forces of global capitalism as being so strong that the social democratic pursuit of equality was excessively limited. I believed a left form of social democracy could be significantly better in terms of equality than any actually existing political model. We haven't reached the limits of what social democracy can achieve in any society. Sweden in the 1970s was great, but still left room for improvement. I also argued that the adoption of neoliberalism by some social democratic parties was by no means inevitable. Indeed, the federal NDP never moved in that direction. Political alternatives are always available.

It's certainly true that a socialist policy agenda faces strong headwinds in pushing against the market, and that it will almost always encounter ideological resistance. But it's also the case that a left party can continue to advocate for that agenda and mobilize support behind it in society at large. When you look at Canada and the countries of Northern Europe, they're surrounded by global capitalism and continue to have policies that push back in various ways against its pressures. One reason they're able to do that is the continued popularity of social democratic institutions originally won through struggles — struggles that faced strong headwinds. The fight for democracy within the workplace, within the state, and within societies is bound to be ongoing, and the more victories that take place in individual countries, the greater the possibility for international solidarity and cooperation.

However difficult it may be, I have always believed that it is possible to pursue and win reforms within a capitalist framework — and I don't believe it's helpful in this context to imagine either capitalism or socialism as discrete or pure categories. In the same sense that there are gradations in the development of democracy that allow us to say some societies are more or less democratic than others, there are also gradations in socialism that allow us to call some more or less socialist than others.

**FA:** Would it be fair to say that you're more inclined to accept the necessity of the market mechanism in some form as an efficient way to organize production? Your own approach is focused on immediate and practical steps toward equality in the near and medium term. That's in contrast with a more systemic or holistic Marxist view. However, it also differs from the approach favoured by liberals because the kinds of reforms you've advocated — decommodification, regulation, public ownership, economic democracy, and so on — are philosophically grounded in a social democratic idea of equality.

**EB:** Yes, I categorically reject the approach to politics which says you should just constantly identify the middle ground and pursue it. In so many of the important debates around policy and values, and indeed in so many areas of life, there is no real middle ground to seek out: you're either for something or you're against it; you either believe X or Y is a right, or you do not. Take the current situation in the United States regarding the right to have an abortion. There is no middle to be found there. You believe in the right to abortion, or you don't. Similarly, you support the right to a union or you don't. I think a similar logic applies to the policy debates about climate change: you can either support the kinds of measures necessary to preserve life on this planet, or you can resign yourself to catastrophe. The feminist and civil rights movements did not try to find some illusory middle ground and neither did Tommy Douglas, Willy Brandt, or Olof Palme. There have been others like Pierre Trudeau and René Lévesque with whom I profoundly disagreed, but who also rejected that approach and sought to break new ground instead. All of us are frankly better for it.

But you're right: I'm ultimately reform-minded in my outlook. If I cannot imagine something I cannot advocate for it either, so I favour working from within the framework of capitalism and taking individual steps in the direction of social democratic equality. In the future, perhaps a more profound kind of transformation will become possible to imagine. But you know what Keynes said about the long run.* I'd rather not wait until then.

---

* Keynes's 1923 book, *A Tract on Monetary Reform*, included the much-quoted sentence: "In the long run, we are all dead."

# The Good Society

Ed Broadbent

A s I write, the great challenges that were revealed throughout the twentieth century have reappeared and threaten to further erode the social and economic rights that serve as the bedrock of freedom.

As global inequality remains largely untouched by Western governments, its social consequences are becoming more violent. In our market-dominated society, severe inequality has increasingly come to be accepted as ineluctable and even necessary — and the resulting discontent is compounded by a sense that decision-makers are unable or unwilling to do anything about it.

Whether we look at Canada or abroad, the various sources of insecurity are similar: the rising cost of living for ordinary people and extreme concentration of wealth at the top; the breakneck pace of technological change and damage to the global environment on an industrial scale; racist attacks on the principle of multicultural pluralism and the related demonization of immigration as the source of societal ills.

In countries as radically different as the United States and Sweden, elements of the majority white population — spurred by far-right politicians and media — have come to see themselves as threatened by "minorities." Racism and nativism have consequently become a strong current in the politics of the U.S., UK, France, Poland, Brazil, India, and Hungary, among others. In Canada, the convoy of trucks that descended on and remained in Ottawa included people belonging to radical right-wing movements committed to violence. It also included many people simply fed up with what they perceived as the condescending arrogance of the government led by Justin Trudeau — one out of touch with their day-to-day struggles. Pierre Poilievre, the newly elected leader of the Conservative Party, explicitly endorsed the convoy and has played footsie with white nationalists. It is difficult to know how durable the rise of this largely white right-wing extremism will be in Canada, where official multiculturalism and the plain need to expand the labour force through immigration have historically moderated these impulses. But there are worrying signs — particularly given the power of social media to spread lies and hatred across borders — that this is a growing movement with the goal of securing political power.

The political right is gaining momentum by seizing upon the insecurity felt among many Canadians. They have fertile ground: citizens today feel their world undergoing destabilizing changes that they have neither created nor been able to situate themselves within. The great exception to this trend, at home and abroad, is the top 5 percent of the population. As in the 1920s, their wealth continues to grow and their lifestyle of conspicuous consumption is radically different from that of their fellow citizens. As was the case in the decade before my birth, many in this elite see their location as the simple result of innate talent and initiative rather than as a consequence of the sweeping economic changes that have accompanied the neoliberal model of capitalism.

The global pandemic laid bare the gaps in both our social supports and our social fabric and demonstrated yet again that the health and well-being of the individual is fundamentally connected to the health and well-being of all. Crucial innovations of the welfare state, alongside important public health measures, are giving way to fiscal restraint. Canada's healthcare system, care for the elderly, and its wider commitment to social and economic rights have been successively undermined by a starvation of resources and continued expansion of for-profit models and services.

Further, despite some progress in the relationship over the last generation, Indigenous peoples continue to fight the stubborn denial of their rights by Canadian governments. Recognized in Section 35 of the constitution, and enshrined in the UN Declaration on the Rights of

Indigenous Peoples, these rights must now be implemented without equivocation. Some hard choices lie ahead, as questions of institutional reform and Indigenous land rights must be resolved. These obligations intersect with the many consequences of the global climate crisis, which is driving the search for rare earth minerals on Indigenous lands and accelerating the destruction caused by fire, storms, droughts, and floods in Canada and abroad.

So, what is to be done? Are we going to sit back and watch conservative politicians capitalize on economic insecurity to erode the potential of the social democratic state and reimpose their new, hollow model of "freedom"? They see starving the state as the solution to our problems. Take away the power and money of the state, they claim, and humanity will be set free. I reject this blinkered vision. Generations of Canadians, notably after the Second World War, demonstrated that the opposite is the case. It was the establishment of social rights like healthcare, unemployment insurance, and national pensions that enabled millions of Canadians to feel free for the first time in their lives. Having been undermined by successive governments, the remarkable achievements of the democratic age are now at risk of full-blown collapse. Now more than ever, we require prompt and effective state action to respond to the new, destabilizing threats to people's livelihoods and preserve a sustainable life on this planet.

A key theme of this book has been that ordinary people themselves — through social movements, unions, political parties, and civil society — wield the tools to make our institutions more just and our collective life more abundant. By working within the social circumstances of their lives, ordinary people have always been able to find concrete answers to their problems. I see important flickers of this countermovement today: workers organizing unions in sectors dominated by multinational behemoths like Amazon and Starbucks; child care advocates in Canada seeing five decades of struggle culminate in the creation of an affordable, universal national child care program; climate activists on both sides of the border campaigning for a green industrial strategy.

There is no magic guidebook to consult, and there are no perfect solutions. Each generation must find answers to the challenges they face, although we may all learn from the past. In the wake of the Great Depression and two world wars, it became clear to people across the globe that the best instrument for countering the immense forces of global capitalism and achieving freedom was the social democratic state. In following their example, however, a new generation of Canadians will be able to achieve not the perfect society but the good society. Taking inspiration from the best of the social democratic tradition, I believe great things can still be done.

To be humane, societies must be democratic — and, to be democratic, every person must be afforded the economic and social rights necessary for their individual flourishing. On their own, political and civil freedoms are insufficient in the realization of that goal. I believed in 1968, and I believe today, that political democracy is not enough. In the twenty-first century, the rebuilding of social democracy must be our task. Social democracy alone offers the foundation upon which the lives of people everywhere can be made dignified, just, and exciting.

It is perhaps the appropriate moment to end this story with a reference to Willy Brandt. He, after all, illustrates the possibility of individual impact in history. His life, from fighting Nazism to bringing greater equality to West Germany and abroad, was one of political struggle. Like Brandt, activists today can overcome the impact of the right-wing forces of our time. We can build an alternative democratic agenda, creating more equality and decommodifying more of our lives. We don't need perfection as a goal. We require simply compassion and thoughtful engagement. There is no guarantee that social democracy will triumph. But it is by far our best alternative, very much worth our political energy.

# Notes

**Introduction**

1   Eda Kriseová quoted in the *New York Review of Books*, January 1993.

2   Michael Harrington, *The Long Distance Runner*, 216.

3   Ed Broadbent, *Socialist & Liberal Views on Man, Society, and Politics*, January 1969.

4   Ed Broadbent, *The Liberal Rip-Off* (1970), 21.

5   Alan Whitehorn, *Canadian Socialism: Essays on the CCF-NDP* (1992), 189.

**Chapter One**

1   Vivian Gornick, "What Endures of the Romance of American Communism," *New York Review of Books*, April 3, 2020, https://www.nybooks .com/online/2020/04/03/what-endures-of-the-romance-of-american -communism/.

**Chapter Two**

1   Anthony Westell and Geoffrey Stevens, "Seven and a Half Hours of Chaos, and an Enigma Chosen Next PM," *Globe and Mail*, April 8, 1968, A9.

**Chapter Three**

1   Joseph Levitt, *Fighting Back for Jobs and Justice: Ed Broadbent in Parliament* (LLA Publishing, 1996), 38.

2  Ibid., 38.

3  Judy Steed, *Ed Broadbent: The Pursuit of Power* (Markham, Ontario: Viking, 1988), 174.

4  Tommy Douglas, "Invoking of War Measures Act," House of Commons Debates, Canadian Parliament, October 16, 1970, Ottawa, Ontario, https://greatcanadianspeeches.ca/2020/10/14/tommy-douglas-october-crisis-1970/.

5  Jay Walz, "Commons Upholds Trudeau 190–16, on Wartime Law," *New York Times*, October 20, 1970, https://www.nytimes.com/1970/10/20/archives/commons-upholds-trudeau-19016-on-wartime-law-prime-minister.html.

6  Steed, 156.

7  Desmond Morton, *The New Democrats, 1961–1986: The Politics of Change* (Toronto: Copp Clark Pitman, 1986), 140; and Geoff Meggs and Rod Mickleburgh, *The Art of the Impossible: Dave Barrett and the NDP in Power 1972–1975* (Madeira Park, BC: Harbour Publishing, 2014).

8  Morton, 141.

9  Levitt, 47.

10  Morton, 165–68.

11  Ed Broadbent, "How to Help People Get Homes: Isolate Mortgages," *Globe and Mail*, September 14, 1973.

12  Ed Broadbent, "The White Paper on Tax Reform," speech, Halifax, NS. July 22, 1970.

13  Christo Aivalis, *The Constant Liberal: Pierre Trudeau, Organised Labour, and the Canadian Social Democratic Left* (Vancouver, BC: UBC Press, 2018), 70.

14  Ibid., 70.

15  Frank Jones, "Trudeau on Welfare: 'Enough Free Stuff,'" *Toronto Star*, April 5, 1965.

16  Pierre Trudeau, interview by Peter Desbarats, January 9, 1972, transcript, PET Fonds, 013, vol. 14, file 9.

17  Aivalis, 127.

18  Ed Broadbent, *The Liberal Rip-Off: Trudeauism vs. The Politics of Equality* (Toronto: New Press, 1970).

19  "Monetary Policy: Principles and Practice. What Are Its Goals? How Does It Work? Board of Governors of the Federal Reserve System," *Federal Reserve*, https://www.federalreserve.gov/monetarypolicy/monetary-policy -what-are-its-goals-how-does-it-work.htm.

20  "Trudeau Memoirs Version 3," YouTube, https://www.youtube.com /watch?v=WO89ARb-zyM&t=495s.

21  Thomas Axworthy, "The Price of Big Dreams: Liberal and NDP Cooperation in Minority Governments," *Policy Options*, 2022, https://www .policymagazine.ca/the-price-of-big-dreams-liberal-and-ndp-cooperation -in-minority-governments/?utm_source=rss&utm_medium=rss&utm _campaign=the-price-of-big-dreams-liberal-and-ndp-cooperation-in -minority-governments.

**Chapter Four**

1  This remarkable struggle is recounted in: Pamela Sugiman, "'That Wall's Comin' Down': Gendered Strategies of Worker Resistance in the UAW Canadian Region (1963–1970)," *The Canadian Journal of Sociology / Cahiers Canadiens de sociologie* 17, no. 1 (1992): 1–27, https://doi.org/10.2307/3340587.

2  Austin Clarke, "A Black Man Talks about Race Prejudice in White Canada," *Maclean's*, April 20, 1963, https://archive.macleans.ca/article/1963 /4/20/a-black-man-talks-about-race-prejudice-in-white-canada.

**Chapter Five**

1  "Cites Wish for more Time with Family: Won't Seek NDP Leadership, Broadbent Tells Party," *Globe and Mail*, January, 18, 1975.

2  Ed Broadbent, House of Commons Debates, 30th Parliament, 2nd

Session, March 8, 1977, Ottawa, ON, https://parl.canadiana.ca/view/oop
.debates_HOC3002_08/845.

3   Dave Gover, "A Note on Canadian Unemployment Since 1921," *Statistics
Canada*, https://www150.statcan.gc.ca/n1/en/pub/75-001-x/1992003/article
/87-eng.pdf?st=AaoeflyJ.

4   Levitt, 74.

5   Pierre Elliott Trudeau, House of Commons Debates, 30th Parliament,
2nd Session: Vol. 8. October 17, 1977, Ottawa, ON, https://www.google.com
/url?q=https://parl.canadiana.ca/view/oop.debates_HOC3002_08/845&sa
=D&source=docs&ust=1662868489216329&usg=AOvVaw3pWVsZTxixdh
YHN6ncQ5fY.

6   Levitt, 74.

7   "Saved by the NDP," editorial, *Globe and Mail*, February 20, 1982.

8   Lawrence LeDuc, John H. Pammett, and André Turcotte, *Dynasties
and Interludes: Past and Present in Canadian Electoral Politics* (Toronto:
Dundurn Press, 2016).

9   House of Commons Debates, CPAC, December 8, 1980, Ottawa, ON,
https://www.cpac.ca/episode?id=9e10f440-a74d-485b-8585-082a341483da.

10  Steed, 210.

11  Alan Whitehorn, *Canadian Socialism: Essays on the CCF-NDP* (London:
Oxford University Press, 1992).

12  Pat Orwen and Ken Ernhofer, "Clark's 'Hollow Laugh' Is Turn-Off for
Richler," *Montreal Gazette*, May 14, 1979.

13  "Dan Heap, a Reformist Clergyman and Toronto Alderman Shocked
Liberal Establishment," *UPI Archives*, August 17, 1981, https://www.upi.com
/Archives/1981/08/17/Dan-Heap-a-reformist-clergyman-and-Toronto
-alderman-shocked/2947366868800/.

14 Jim Coyle, "Don't Bet on Reform for Senate, Canada's House of 'Taskless Thanks,'" *Toronto Star*, January 29, 2014, https://www.thestar.com/news /canada/2014/01/24/dont_bet_on_reform_for_senate_canadas_house_of _taskless_thanks.html.

15 "The Choice for Canadians," editorial, *Toronto Star*, May 9, 1979.

16 "Broadbent Shows Leadership," editorial, *Toronto Star*, April 10, 1978.

17 C. McLaren, "Broadbent Says Rivals No Different," *Globe and Mail*, July 12, 1984.

18 "A New NDP Statement of Principles," Federal NDP Convention, July 1, 1983, Regina, SK. The full text of the Regina Manifesto can be found in Appendix Seven.

**Chapter Six**

1 "The Geneva Congress," *Socialist Affairs* 27, iss. 1 (January/February 1977): 5–6.

2 Ibid.

3 B. Vivekanandan, *Global Visions of Olof Palme, Bruno Kreisky and Willy Brandt: International Peace and Security, Co-operation, and Development* (New York: Springer International, 2018).

4 "Socialist International Congress 1978, Vancouver," *Socialist Affairs* (January/ February 1979).

**Chapter Seven**

1 Pierre Elliott Trudeau, *Federalism and the French Canadians* (Toronto: Macmillan, 1968).

**Chapter Eight**

1 Ed Broadbent, "Bizarre, Naive. What Manner of Political Universe Is This?" *Globe and Mail*, October 18, 1975.

2 Paul Gessel, "On the March," *Maclean's*, August 3, 1987, https://archive .macleans.ca/article/1987/8/3/on-the-march.

3 Whitehorn, 211–12.

4 Levitt, 264.

5 Ed Broadbent, "The Quebec Election and Its Aftermath," Report to the Executive, January 15, 1977.

6 Quoted in Ed Broadbent, "Canada-U.S. Free Trade Agreement," House of Commons Debates, August 30, 1988, Ottawa, ON.

7 Lamont Lansing, "A Singular U.S.-Canada Achievement," *New York Times*, January 19, 1988, https://www.nytimes.com/1988/01/19/opinion/a-singular -uscanada-achievement.html.

8 Levitt, 233.

9 Ibid., 263.

10 "Ed Broadbent's quest for Quebec," *CBC Archives*, 1988, https://www.cbc .ca/player/play/1774029468.

11 Daniel Drolet, "Quebec Rally Moves Broadbent," *Ottawa Citizen*, November 15, 1988.

12 Ed Broadbent, "Canada-United States Free Trade Agreement Implementation Act," House of Commons Government Orders, July 5, 1988.

13 Ed Broadbent, "Deal Threatens Canadian Values," *Globe and Mail*, July 16, 1988.

14 Jamie Bradburn, "'A crisis of unparalleled magnitude': How Environmental Concerns Did — and Didn't — Shape the 1988 Election," *TVO*, September 1, 2021, https://www.tvo.org/article/a-crisis-of-unparalleled-magnitude-how -environmental-concerns-did-and-didnt-shape-the-1988-election.

## Chapter Nine

1 George Packer, "The Fall of Conservatism — Have the Republicans Run Out of Ideas?" *The New Yorker*, May 19, 2008, https://www.newyorker.com /magazine/2008/05/26/the-fall-of-conservatism.

2   "FDI Policies for Development: National and International Perspectives,"
World Investment Report, *United Nations Conference on Trade and Development*,
2003, https://unctad.org/webflyer/world-investment-report-2003.

3   Stephen Clarkson, "Canada's Secret Constitution: NAFTA, WTO and the
End of Sovereignty?" *Canadian Centre for Policy Alternatives*, October 2002,
https://eweb.uqac.ca/bibliotheque/archives/18355540.pdf.

## Chapter Ten

1   Ed Broadbent, "Canada Has Failed to Create Equality of Opportunity,"
*Globe and Mail*, November 24, 2014.

2   Ed Broadbent, "Rise and Fall of Economic and Social Rights: What's
Next?" *Canadian Centre for Policy Alternatives*, May 2010.

3   "Distributions of Household Economic Accounts for Wealth of Canadian
Households, Third Quarter 2021," *Statistics Canada*, January 28, 2022, https://
www150.statcan.gc.ca/n1/daily-quotidien/220128/dq220128b-eng.htm.

4   Ed Broadbent, "21st-Century Canada, Home of 19th-Century Democracy,"
*Globe and Mail*, October 16, 2008.

5   Rhéal Séguin, "Charest Dodges Crisis in Caucus," *Globe and Mail*, April 6,
2006, https://www.theglobeandmail.com/news/national/charest-dodges
-crisis-in-caucus/article18159588/.

6   Janine Brodie, "Manufacture Ignorance: Harper, the Census and Social
Inequality," *Canada Watch*, Spring 2011, 30–2.

7   "The Wealth Gap: Perceptions and Misconceptions," *The Broadbent
Institute*, December 2014, https://www.broadbentinstitute.ca/wealth_gap.

# The Nature of Political Theory

A lecture given at York University, circa 1965–1967.

I would like in this lecture to say something about what we have been doing all year, ie., something about the nature of political theory or political philosophy. This enterprise might appear to you to be quite gratuitous. If we have been doing something for eight months, surely, it might be suggested, we need not spend time looking at what's been done. I would agree with this suggestion if all that was intended as an adequate approach to such a discussion was to offer précis of the works of the different theorists we have considered; this would be a redundant activity. However, what I have in mind is to make some observations about the general nature or common features of political theorising as such; to show how these features emerge in the work of the major modern theorists; and to distinguish political theory from the social sciences (including, of course, political science).

## Politics and the Vocabulary of Politics

The first thing worth noting is that political theorists are concerned about politics and about the institutions and concepts that have been associated with politics since Plato and Aristotle did the first systematic political theorising. Thus most have had something to say about the polis or the state, law, rulers and the ruled, justice and injustice, the economy, freedom, equality, duty and rights, community, and government. In doing this Mill, Marx, Friedman and Dahl form part of an intellectual tradition which includes Aquinas, Hobbes and Rousseau, as well as the classical Greeks. There is a common vocabulary which has been passed on to us. The reason it has been passed on is worth nothing. It is not that as each period in history there emerges a group of people who share common linguistic interest. Rather the reason is that Western man has continued to experience a common set of problems connected with the fact that he is a social being — or at least he lives in a social setting.

As I said the Greeks were the first to systematically reflect on this fact, and at a consequence we owe to them the conceptual framework within which almost all political theorising has gone on. The framework and vocabulary, however, would have long since disappeared (as has happened in other intellectual disciplines and may now be happening in theology) if there has not been the persistence of the related experienced problems; and if there had not been men concerned about them. I'll return to the notion of concern shortly.

How have theorists dealt with these problems? In spite of significant intellectual and social differences which separated those living in different epochs, I think it accurate to say that, to use contemporary vocabulary, each great theorist has combined in varying proportions empirical, normative, and imaginative elements in his work.

Like the social scientist the political theorist is concerned with establishing or at least using a body of what might be called public knowledge. He is concerned with "facts" or "empirical data", facts and data that anyone in command of his five senses would agree to when presented with sensory-testable evidence. Marx and Engels studied the conditions of the working class in England — at least indirectly by reading the carefully prepared studies undertaken by the British Parliament. Mill carefully observed the men about him; he studied revolutionary behaviour in France and parliamentary behaviour at home. The conceptual apparatus used by Schumpeter, Dahl and contemporary-behaviourally oriented theorists is more rigorously worked out but in principle it remained the same, ie., in contrast to religious and aesthetic "knowledge", it claims to require no particular subjective on intuitive insight for its attainment, but rather the use of the senses by an ordinary man.

Most political theorists have attempted not only to gather facts but also to develop general laws, principles or tendencies in political affairs, grounded or based on those facts. This is equally true of Machiavelli, Erich Fromm, and Karl Popper.

Unlike the social scientist, strictly defined, the political theorist has never restricted his activity to the development of empirical propositions. Rather, like the moral philosopher, he has always proceeded to recommend certain kinds of behaviour and institutions. (Many contemporary moral philosophers, it should be noted, simply analyse. Like the social scientist they refuse to prescribe.) The political theorist has always had some model of a preferred moral order which he wishes to commend to his readers. Normally, as in the case of Plato, Locke, Mill, Oakeshott, Schumpeter, and Niebuhr, the moral position is made explicit; it is consciously worked out and is grounded on some combination of purported facts and chosen ends. Other theorists have not deliberately worked out a moral position, but invariably — if they are political theorists as I am using the term — it can be found. Marx's criticism of the alienating effects of capitalism revealed his preferences for an alienation-free society. Similarly Dahl's description of the American hybrid of polyarchy moves at the conclusion of his work to the praise of polyarchy for its stability and order.

## Human Nature

At the centre of any political theorist's work is some model of existing human nature. Sometimes the political theorist, like the sociologist, has seen human nature at any given time to be chiefly a by-product of his socio-economic-political institutions. Plato, Marx, Mill, and Fromm would be among these. Other political theorists, like the psychologists, have seen the chief aspects of man's nature to be permanent throughout history: Aquinas, Hobbes, Bentham, James Mill, Hayek, Oakeshott, Niebuhr, and Freud are examples.

## Imagination

In addition to the directions of how man is, most political theorists have always had something important to say about how man could be. Imagination, therefore, is an important element in political theorising. Not only the actualities but also the possibilities of man are the theorist's concern. To a considerable degree these imaginatively conceived possibilities cannot be supported by evidence existing at the time the theorist writes. Like the creative artist or scientist, he had a vision of what might be; he has not certainty in this area. He goes beyond the bounds of the accepted orthodoxy of his time. Unlike the natural scientist however, the political theorist's imagination might in fact contribute to the actualization of what he imagines. In a very important sense the natural scientist, while he may reformulate scientific "laws", cannot remake the actual workings of the universe. In contrast the political theorist can contribute to the remaking of man and his political institutions. If his vision is believed in by many, or even by a few with power, then there is the possibility of what was once an ideal becoming real. The history of Marxism in the twentieth century in Asia is a good example of this. The political theorist then works imaginatively in a way that can lead to action.

This brings me to the final point I want to make about political theorizing. It is no mere coincidence that the political theorist, if believed in, may contribute to change in the political environment. It is no coincidence because the significant theorist has always been a committed man; he has been involved or concerned with this subject matter in a way that the social and physical scientist is not. Hobbes and Locke were reacting to civil war and the birth of commercial capitalism. They wanted to put an end to the former and make possible the latter; and their great contributions to our knowledge of the normative and factual importance of contract, sovereignty, the rule of law, representation, and right of civil disobedience were products of the imaginative concerned intellect. Rousseau, Marx, and Mill were profoundly disturbed about what was happening to man in an age of industrial capitalism. They saw that scientific and technological innovations were making it possible for the first time in history that the majority of men might be able to develop their capacities and talents in a way that previous theorists had seen to be a possibility for a minority only. At the same time they realized that there were certain built-in limitations of a technical possibility. Both insights were the product of concerned men.

In the twentieth-century representative works of the still prevailing nineteenth-century competitors, liberalism and socialism, still flourish because we have basically the same problems reflected upon by similarly committed theorists. Lenin, Kautsky, Rosa Luxemberg, R.H Tawney, Anthony Crosland, C.B. Macpherson, and Christian Bay are on one side; Oakeshott, Freud, Hayek and Friedman are on the other. In between we find Niebuhr, Camus, and probably Dahl. What is to be noted here is not the differences between these theorists but their shared concern. It is this concern with man's fate as a social being which links such otherwise disparate figures as Plato and Oakeshott and separates both from sociologists, psychologists, and political scientists.

The political theorist then is a concerned man who combines normative and empirical modes of argument into an imaginative model of the possibilities of human beings existing in communities. His vocabulary is the vocabulary of politics; he talks about law, rights, duties, government, liberty, equality, and justice. His concepts change infrequently because history moves slowly. There are no final solutions.

## APPENDIX TWO

# Speech to the House of Commons, September 20, 1968

Ed Broadbent's first speech in the House of Commons in the 1st Session of Canada's twenty-eighth Parliament.

**(5:10 p.m)**

**Mr. J. Edward Broadbent (Oshawa-Whitby):** Mr. Speaker, it is a great pleasure for me to rise and make my first speech in the House of Commons. I must say I am particularly pleased to see such a crowded house at 5:15pm on a Friday afternoon. Who would have thought that so many thousands would have turned out? Before I get to the main body of my speech I should like to say a few words about my predecessor. Michael Starr represented what is still the core of my new riding, Oshawa-Whitby, formerly the Ontario riding, from 1952 until this year's general election. There can be no doubt that in terms of his services to the personal needs of his constituents Mr. Starr performed an outstanding job as a member of Parliament.

**Some Hon. Members:** Hear, hear.

**Mr. Broadbent:** This is widely recognized by his constituents, whether they were his political supporters or not, and it is widely recognized, I am finding, among all parties in the House of Commons. I am also learning that among members of this house in all parties he is regarded as a man of great integrity possessing all the qualities of a genuine gentleman. I should like to add that I am not saying any of these things because it is, supposedly, the conventional thing to do; it is something I genuinely believe, because I heard it expressed on countless occasions since I arrived in Ottawa and, prior to that, in my riding. I have rarely agreed with the policies of the party which Mr. Starr represented for many years, but I unhesitatingly salute Mr. Starr the man.

**Some Hon. Members:** Hear, hear.

**Mr. Broadbent:** Now, in my short but, I hope, not completely irrelevant speech I wish to address myself to the two issues raised by the Prime Minister (Mr. Trudeau). In his speech on Monday of this week the right hon. gentleman suggested that in our discussions during the present debate we should concern ourselves with questions which relate to "the kind of country in which we want to be living and the directions in which we should be moving to build such a country."

Earlier this year the Prime Minister suggested, if I understood him correctly, that in Canada we had gone about as far as we could in our efforts to construct a welfare state. Once we have medicare established on a national basis, he implied, the structure would be almost complete.

As a member of the opposition, and more particularly perhaps, as a New Democrat, I am in the unfortunate position of having to agree with the Prime Minister on both issues. In short, it seems to me that the debate on when the social philosophical objectives of Canada should be discussed; and, second, it is true that we now have in Canada the basic structural components of a modern welfare state.

Mr. Speaker, I would like to begin my contribution by saying something about the second issue. The 100 years since confederation can be divided roughly into two socio-economic periods. Up to the 1930's Canadians were concerned with laying the foundations of a viable capitalist democracy in which our two principal cultural groups could at least co-exist peacefully within the framework of a liberal constitution. The central components of a liberal democratic society were firmly established throughout the land: universal franchise; freedoms of speech, religion, press and assembly; competing political parties, and a national banking system.

Since the 1930's we have experienced important modifications of the classical liberal structure. The more important of these include: (1) the right of trade unions to exist and to strike; (2) the gradual implementation of old age pensions; (3) some form of progressive taxation, (4) comprehensive medical and health programs and (5) an unemployment insurance scheme.

No sensible Canadian would deny that these measures have made a very significant change in the kind of life the majority of our people can now experience. They have provided the quantitative basis for a qualitatively enriched life for millions of adults and children. These five changes have provided the structural core of our modern welfare state.

I emphasize the point that we have the core. It would, however, be both false and irresponsible for me to suggest that we have the whole apple. Previous speakers in this debate have ably indicated serious deficiencies which still remain and about which the government gives almost no indication of seriously concerning itself. The most glaring of these are: (1) the abysmal lack of adequate housing, (2) severe economic inequality between both individuals and regions, (3) the absence of a guaranteed annual income, and (4) an outmoded and inequitable system of taxation — a shock to the western world, I might add.

Mr. Speaker, these four areas of concern should not in any way be dismissed as being of minor significance. They are the major evils of the day. They can be and should be remedied. Previous speakers from the New Democratic Party have indicated their existence and have suggested solutions in this house. Earlier in the year our leader — and soon to be returned to this house — and candidates across the land discussed them directly with the Canadian people. There is little need for me, at least in this debate, to add to what has already been said.

Instead, what I wish to stress is that every one of these evils can be substantially dealt with within the existing socio-economic structure. We do have the core of the welfare state. We need only the will to complete it. Houses can be built, taxation can be significantly modified. All this can be done without making any further significant changes in the distribution of power within Canadian society.

It is in this sense that the Prime Minister is almost right when he suggests that in terms of welfare we have gone about as far as we can go. It is also his implied suggestion, that it is as far as we should go, that makes me believe that the Prime Minister is a profoundly conservative man. His vision extends to the welfare state, but not one step beyond. His vision of the just society is what we almost have. To defend what we have and to refuse to go beyond is to cease to lead. And to cease to lead beyond the welfare state is to leave Canadians with a kind of society which is inherently inegalitarian, inherently acquisitive, and inherently unjust.

Having indicated substantial agreement with the Prime Minister on the nature of the welfare state I want now to proceed to suggest why we New Democrats, unlike the Prime Minister and the Liberal party, cannot accept it as being an adequate kind of society. Perhaps the major objection to the welfare state is that for all its advantages it rests on a grossly inadequate understanding of democracy. In Canada today children are taught in schools throughout the land that our country is democratic primarily because there is more than one political party and because citizens have both the right to criticize and the right to change their rulers every few years. This view of democracy, Mr. Speaker, is a distinctly modern phenomenon and is in marked contrast with the understanding of democracy of both the early Greeks and 19th century Europeans. Prior to our century democracy was seen by its defenders and critics alike as a kind of society in which all adults played an active, participatory role not only in the formal institutions of government but also in all the institutions which crucially affected their daily lives. Similarly a democratic society had been seen previously as one in which all its members had an equal opportunity to develop their capacities and talents; it was not seen as one in which citizens had an equal opportunity to earn more money or advance up the class ladder.

It is this old view of democracy that we must once again take up. We must use its standards and apply them to Canadian society. We must once again talk about equality. We must see justice and equality as going together. Of course, Mr. Speaker, if we do this we know we will find our society grossly inadequate and significantly unjust. Every sociological study done in European and North American welfare states in recent years has revealed their inherently inegalitarian nature. One of the most important of these, Professor John Porter's "The Vertical Mosaic" documents in chapter after chapter the inequalities of Canada's social system.

The recent report of the Economic Council of Canada provides additional concrete information on the existence of economic inequality.

It might well be granted that this is the case. But what, asks the defender of the status quo, can be done about it? The answer, Mr. Speaker, is a lot. We must begin by insisting that in a democratic society — in, if you would a just society — all adults should have equal rights in all those institutions which directly affect them. Where authority is delegated, then those to whom it is delegated must be responsible to those over whom they exercise their authority.

In concrete examples, Mr. Speaker, this means that in our factories, in our offices, and in our large commercial and financial institutions, legal power must shift from the few on the top to the many below. We can of course have no illusions about completely dispensing with authority. In a complex industrial society, this is impossible. But we can democratise authority in our non-political institutions just as we have in the political. Management can and must be made responsible to the workers, just as we are responsible to our constituents. More than this, however, is required. Not only must legal control pass from the few to the many, but also the many must be given the right to make more of the decisions themselves. Responsible university students around the world in recent months have initiated this process on their campuses.

I urge the Canadian government to promote this development, to lead the way, not only because such democratic institutions would be more just, but also because they would be infinitely more conducive to the development of responsible and creative men and women. Karl Marx and John Stuart Mill realised this one hundred years ago. Herbert Marcuse, Erich Fromm and many others have stressed the same truth in our own day. We as the political leaders of the country have a duty to initiate this battle for a truly democratic society. We have a duty, Mr. Speaker, not simply to praise our past and celebrate our present, but also to create the future. We must reject the sterile view of both the government and the official opposition. Both the Liberal and Conservative parties are bound not by bad intentions but by an outmoded and unjust ideology. They have their heads as well as their feet firmly embedded in the ideas and practices of the past.

No amount of parliamentary reform, social razmataz, or fiscal responsibility can lead to a just society. At the very most they can remove little pockets of inefficiency. The basic unjust and unequal structure will remain. What Canadians require is a leadership deeply dedicated to the democratisation of the whole of society and thoroughly committed to changing by means of law the existing power relations needed to bring this about. In recent decades we have built a welfare state. It is now time to go beyond it.

Mr. Speaker, in these brief remarks I have attempted to follow the Prime Minister's suggestion and discuss in a general way what I think the future of Canada should be. In so doing, I have also tried to indicate the inadequacies of the present. In addition, a serious approach to politics also requires proposals for specific legislation intended to bring about the desired future. In the past the Co-operative Commonwealth Federation and the New Democratic Party have accepted this important responsibility, and have led the way in providing ideas for the welfare state. In the days and months ahead we shall continue to provide programs intended to take us beyond the welfare state. Thank you, Mr. Speaker.

# Bill C-3
# An Act to amend the Criminal Code
# (Modernization of Law of Picketing).

Ed Broadbent's first bill as a member of Parliament.

Her Majesty, by and with the advice and consent of the Senate and House of Commons of Canada, enacts as follows:

Subsection (2) of section 366 of the *Criminal Code* is repealed and the following substituted therefor:

"(2) Persons do not watch or beset within the meaning of this section if, without violence or the threat of violence, and whether singly or in small or large numbers, they attend at or near or approach a dwelling house or place of business for the purpose of obtaining or communicating information or of persuading, or attempting to persuade, employees, customers, clients, or other persons to abstain from doing or to do something in order to promote the lawful interests of employees who, or on whose behalf such persons so attend at or near or approach the dwelling house or place of business."

### Explanatory Note

The amendment is intended to permit peaceful picketing by any number for the purpose not only of communication information but also of persuading other employees and people having business dealings with a struck company to support the cause of the picketers in the case, particularly, of a lawful strike.

Subsection (2) of section 366 at present reads as follows:

"(2) A person who attends at or near or approaches a dwelling house or place, for the purpose only of obtaining or communicating information, does not watch or beset within the meaning of this section."

# Industrial Democracy: A Proposal for Action

A speech or memorandum outlining the concept of industrial democracy and making the case for an alternative, socialist conception of rights. June 1969.

Since the emergence of industrialism there have been two other related developments: the birth of modern political democracy and the growth in numbers of a working class and their institution the trade union movement. There can be no doubt that the latter of these two gave rise to the former.

In Canada for a variety of reasons political or liberal democracy has become more firmly and broadly established than has the trade union movement. Even now only a minority of the non-agricultural workers are members of trade unions. Nonetheless, trade unions represent the single most important institution to workers. It is trade unions which have been most effective in obtaining and preserving those rights which currently exist for working men which are directly applicable to their function as workers. Trade unions through their strength have forced a degree of justice upon industrial capitalism. Because of their existence, workers' wages are higher, pensions are better, vacations are longer, jobs are more secure, and management is compelled to take on the façade of civilised behaviour.

So far in this century the Canadian trade unions movement has been the most important instrument in bringing to the worker that level of self-respect and independence which he possesses. Political liberties without the trade union movement would have left industrial man as a mere chattel. Political democracy without full industrial democracy in an economically advanced Canada will leave him in a state which is neither degraded nor emancipated; he will remain a semi-contented dependent, subject to the power of others. What is now needed is another step forward.

## Two Democratic Traditions: Liberal & Socialist

It is very important for New Democrats to keep in mind that as socialists our view of democracy differs in some crucial respects from that shared by our Liberal and Conservative opponents. For the old parties a society is democratic if three principal requirements are met: (1) all adults have the right to vote, (2) there are periodic elections in which those who wish to may compete for political office, and (3) there is the right of all to criticise the government.

For socialists this view of democracy is inadequate; it is inadequate because it is incomplete. We agree that any democratic society must have these three characteristics. However, we also believe that any society having only these qualities is not fully democratic. We insist that two further qualities are required. (1) A fully democratic society for us is one in which the opportunity for self-realisation is equally available to all. And self-realisation for us means the free development of our moral, intellectual, aesthetic, and sensual capacities. It does not mean, as it does for those Liberals and Conservatives who talk about equal opportunity, the ability to get ahead of and control others. (2) The second characteristic which a socialist believes a fully developed democracy requires is that the average citizen should possess direct or indirect control over all those decisions which have a serious effect on his day-to-day life.

From the middle of the last century, when our notion of democracy emerged, to the present, the goal of all socialists has been to create the kind of economy in which the equal opportunities for the development of the capacities and talents of people would be maximised and in which all those directly affected by economic decisions would have some effective power in the making of them. Analytically and historically, it has long been recognized that a capitalist economy based as it is on the private ownership of capital and the concentration of power in few hands, is inherently exploitative and thus inherently undemocratic. Thus to create a society based on the socialist democratic principle of the equal right to self-development and the equal right to self-management, we have attempted to help transform our economy from having a capitalist structure to one which is socialist in nature. Our central objective has been to replace an economy controlled by a private few, with one controlled by the public many.

Broadly speaking there have been two loci of attack: parliamentary and extra-parliamentary. At the governmental level the CCF-NDP has attempted to have laws passed which would check the economic power of those owning the economic system. At the nongovernmental level the trade union movement has fought the democratic battle in our factories and offices.

One by one the trade union movement has sought to overcome the so-called rights of ownership or management. What this has meant in the real life experience of people is that step by step the unjust barriers to equality have been broken down. Step by step working men have obtained more control over their day-to-day lives. Step by step they have achieved a higher level of democracy.

In Canada today, the worker who is a member of a trade union is in a much better position than the non-unionized worker of a few decades ago. He cannot be fired in response to a whim of his employer; his wages are proportionately higher; his vacation period is longer; and his sense of self-respect is greater. These differences between the present and the past are very important. They mean very much, therefore, to the lives of millions of Canadians.

This fact notwithstanding the unionised worker is in a position of extreme inequality when compared with his employer or the managers representing his employer. It is the employer or his agent who makes decisions about production, about the allocation of capital, about the nature and price of products and about the distribution of profits. Not only does the worker have no say in these matters, it is one of the central requirements or beliefs associated with a capitalist economy that he should not have a say. These are the remaining so-called prerogatives of management. And it is their existence that makes our present economic institutions inherently unequal and inherently un-democratic.

What is required? It is a truism to say that a socialist Canada would be a Canada in which workers of every kind and skill have significant decision-making power in every aspect of the economy. Socialist citizenship includes fundamental economic rights as well as political rights. Having said this, it is nonetheless important to indicate how this goal might be realised peacefully from within our present structure. Two simultaneous approaches suggest themselves.

(1) At the extra-Parliamentary level trade unionists must continue with their historical struggle against management's prerogatives. These so-called rights of ownership must yield one by one to be included in the class of items over which unions and management bargain. At present many unions in Canada are challenging management's traditional "right" to control technological changes. They rightly see that the chief significance of the Freedman Report (already three years old) is that Justice Freedman called into question our common law tradition which unjustly has bestowed so many "rights" of power on property ownership. Although the particular issue was technological change on the railways the broader principle raised by Justice Freedman was that workers have a fundamental interest and right in all the decisions which affect them in their place of work.

As early objectives trade unions should work for the immediate implementation of the Freedman Report and for the immediate establishment of joint administrative control of pension funds.

(2) At the political level, the New Democratic Party must vigorously support the trade union movement in its efforts to break down the traditional so-called rights of management. In particular, it must make clear that these "rights" of management have no more profound moral justification than the fact that they have always derived from the power-position of the property owner and have been sanctified by the title "rights" over many years of capitalist history.

We should make clear that our view that Canadian society as a whole and not just its political institutions needs to be democratised, entails a commitment to certain basic changes in law as it affects the rights of working people and trade unions.

Among the first steps to be taken is the removal of the legal obstacles to effective and speedy certification of bargaining units. It will also be necessary to remove any existing legal barriers to unions bargaining in the "non-negotiable rights" areas which our common law tradition has granted to management. The objective is to remove all rights of irresponsible control from the legal right of ownership.

To enable unions to bargain effectively in the new areas of responsibility legislation should be passed which will require employers to open their books containing information on manpower, profits, investments, product research etc. In short, there must be complete disclosure to both the union and the public of all information relevant to the running of an enterprise. For the same reason a means must be found for increasing the research funds for trade unionists. My own preference here is for the levying of a special corporation tax, whose revenue would automatically be turned over to the relevant union.

## Conclusion

Our goal is to help build a democratic socialist Canada. This requires a transformation of power relations in society; to hasten this the New Democratic Party must support the force in society which is most clearly moving in this direction. The trade unions are such a progressive force; their victories over the irresponsible concentration of power in our economic system belong to all Canadians. We must, therefore, support the trade unions, and together act with determination to turn a liberal democracy into an industrial democracy.

# Speech to the 1975 New Democratic Party Convention

Ed Broadbent's address to delegates ahead of the NDP leadership vote in Winnipeg. July 6, 1975.

The decision we must take at this convention is to accept the socialist challenge of the 1970's and beyond. That is our task.

Over the past years, the New Democratic Party, and the CCF before it, led the way in convincing Canadians of the need for crucial changes in social legislation. It was our movement and our party that fought the battle to get old age pensions. It was we who won unemployment insurance for Canadians. It was our concern for social justice that brought family allowances. We were the first to institute hospital insurance. And it was our government in Saskatchewan which won the great medicare victory.

Under the leadership of J. S. Woodsworth, M. J. Coldwell, Tommy Douglas, David Lewis, we have in forty years succeeded in quite literally transforming social legislation in Canada.

It is a proud record — a record that has benefitted every Canadian. But my generation cannot rest on the accomplishments of the past. If we are to continue with a contribution to Canadian life we must now move beyond social issues.

Our socialist challenge is to tackle what I have called the economic question. This fundamental question is about economic power, and who will wield it. It is about our national priorities, and who will decide them.

Ask yourself, why do we spend $40 million on a CN tower in downtown Toronto but ignore the desperate housing needs of thousands who live a few blocks from its base? Why do we spend millions every year studying new changes in toothpaste and TV sets, when we are virtually starved for research funds into crippling and killing industrial diseases?

Why are billions spent on new airports for jet-set travellers, when the serious transportation priority is a modern railway system to meet the real needs of those who live in our cities, of our farmers and of our industry? Why in short are so many of our economic and investment priorities so cruelly distorted?

The answer is, corporate power. It has been the corporations in Canada which have determined our past and who dictate our present. And if we let them, they will also shape our future. They are the ones who control investment and decide priorities. And their criterion is, what is good for them, not what is good for Canada.

Ce sont les grandes sociétés qui ont dominé notre pays au passé et qui veulent dicter notre avenir. Ce sont elles qui décident de l'investissement et qui déterminent nos priorités. Et ce quelles recherchent là-dedans c'est leur propre croissance. Ce que nous recherchons, c'est le bien du Canada.

Are we going to let the corporations continue in this way? Shell or Inco, or the Bank of Montreal to keep on deciding where our wealth should be invested? To keep on setting our economic priorities and our social values?

Or will we take courage and say: from now on, the people decide. From now on, Parliament and the Legislatures will make the final decisions. Corporate power must be broken. This is the socialist issue of our time.

Until this happens, economic decisions will continue to be narrow and selfish. Until we break corporate power, we will not succeed in redistributing income. We will not be able to end poverty and exploitation and disparity. We will not be able to achieve the noble human goal of equality.

That is why our generation must face this challenge squarely, and face it now.

I am optimistic that growing numbers of Canadians are in fact quite ready to question such power. They are no longer willing to accept that if it's good for Gulf or General Motors then it must be good for Canada.

They have been shaken by the damage to our environment when private decisions are taken regardless of the public consequences. Support for Tom Berger's Commission on the Mackenzie Valley pipeline is symbolic of their new concern.

It is up to our party to give political muscle to that concern. We have to extend it beyond the environment to the whole economy and society. It will be our job to insist that the public good always comes ahead of private interests. We must lead the challenge of corporate power.

Of course, it won't be easy. Even with growing public support, the fight will be tough. The corporations have money. Many are organised globally. They are strong in their faith in their international connections. And they play for keeps. But I say, let's take them on. Let us play for keeps too.

There is more at stake in this contest than our own domestic Canadian policy. There is a wider aspect to our fight.

Breaking corporate power will not only make it possible for us to order our own society according to higher and different values. It will also give us a real chance to share our wealth and resources with poorer peoples around the world.

Just as we want to redistribute wealth within Canada, we also want to do the same on a world basis. We want to respond to the moral obligation to combat the famine, the malnutrition, the poverty and hopelessness which now makes wretched the condition of so many millions.

But to do so we must have economic power. For corporate priorities have no room for global generosity, for giving without taking in return. Nor have countries governed by those corporate priorities been able to give without taking.

This is why it is doubly essential to transform the relations of power here in Canada. It frees us to meet our moral commitment at home and abroad.

In short, the struggle for equality is universal.

For some months, I have been talking about the need for our party to develop a new economic plan for Canada. I see this plan as the major step in our fight against corporate power. I see such a plan evolving over a two-year period, enlisting experts in our provincial governments, our universities, our labour organizations, and with the active participation of party members all across the country. I see it providing the principal focus for debate and improvement at our 1977 convention. And finally, I see us taking this plan outlining our goals for Canadians, our specific proposals for more equality and public power, to the Canadian people in the federal election of 1978.

Friends, I am certain such action will once again give us the initiative in federal politics. Our democratic socialist objectives will be outlined clearly and honestly. We will challenge the supremacy of corporate power and private decision-making. The other parties and the media will have to react to our proposals and our issues.

And Canadians, as never before, will respond to such serious and straightforward leadership.

In doing this we will be on our way to political power in Ottawa, and we will be able to look forward to victory, not in decades but soon!

It's in this context that I seek the leadership of our party. These are the reasons I first ran for Parliament in 1968. These are the directions in which all my experience since tells me we must go. These are the convictions that will guide me if you give me your support.

I am confident that, united together, we in the New Democratic Party can accomplish in the days ahead a record of economic change every bit as profound as the great transformation in social legislation that stands as the proud record of our party in the past.

We can build a nation with a sense of compassion, a sense of community and above all a sense of equality.

# Address to the Socialist International Congress

A speech welcoming delegates to the 1978 meeting of the Socialist International and outlining the democratic socialist alternative to both communism and market liberalism. Vancouver, November 3, 1978.

It is a great pleasure for me to welcome all of you to the first Congress which the Socialist International has ever held in Canada.

We are meeting in a province of Canada in which socialists have been elected to our provincial legislature since 1898 — in a province which my party governed from 1972 to 1975 — and confidently expects to govern again after next year's election. And just two weeks ago our national party made gains in federal byelections and the New Democratic Party of the province of Saskatchewan was re-elected with a resounding victory. There is, in short, a vibrant social democratic tradition on the northern half of this continent and we are proud to share it with you all.

As for my fellow Canadians, I ask simply that you look with care at this congress, at the parties and the governments represented here. You will find governments with highly successful economic records and the freest, most democratic institutions in the world. You will find parties and individuals who have fought dictatorships, of the right and the left, and have supported human rights throughout the world. You will hear leaders who have, with imagination, commitment and realism, confronted and reduced both national and international inequalities and injustices.

In particular, you will see the man who has done more for peace and justice than anyone else in our time, I refer, of course, to president Willy Brandt.

This congress will directly show many north Americans for the first time that many of the world's nations are not choosing either capitalist democracy or authoritarian communism — that more and more, people are moving toward the democratic socialism for which we stand — a distinct choice, with our own historic roots, our on priorities and our on approach to world problems.

For example, the focus of this congress is peace and world development, and those observing will learn how the notion of world development is approached by democratic socialists.

For the spokesmen of modern capitalism, both conservatives and liberals, development is fundamentally a process of accelerated economic growth in poorer parts of the world. The criterion of development that means most for them remains increases in average per capita income in the world, no matter how it is distributed or at what social cost.

For modern communist spokesmen, development is not all that different. The focus is on accelerating capital accumulation, by ruthless means if necessary, so as to raise economic growth rates,

Democratic socialists, however, have led the way in recent years toward a new notion of development. We ask not just what's happening to economic growth rates, but what's happening to income distribution, to employment levels, to absolute numbers of people in poverty, and to the right of people to participate freely in running their communities.

These differences in perspective come out dramatically when considering the institution on which I want to focus the rest of my remarks, and which is on our agenda, the multinational corporation.

For the spokesmen for economic conservatism, the multinational corporation is the key to world development. Well, democratic socialists know that reality is more complicated. More and more, multinationals do not necessarily mean more and better development, and if there is development by this route, it has its costs. Unfortunately, no country illustrated these problems better than Canada.

As of the latest year for which we have complete statistics, (1974), some 63 percent of Canadian industry was controlled by foreign corporations — including 57 percent of our manufacturing, 58 percent of our mining and smelting and 75 percent of our petroleum and natural gas. Foreign direct investment in Canada has been growing for decades, it isn't a passing phase. Foreign multinational ownership is the central reality of the Canadian economy.

The result has been increasing economic problems and a reduced capacity to respond to them. Perhaps for more than any other industrial nation in the world, economic decisions central to our future are made outside of our borders.

We presently have 3.5 percent of our workforce unemployed, manufacturing employment, indeed, has been falling in absolute terms, and we run a trade deficit in finished goods of eleven billion dollars a year.

Meanwhile, Canadian industry has the lowest rate of research and development expenditure in the western industrialised world. We are not generating new products, expanding new exports or building new manufacturing jobs. And the chief reason lies in foreign multinational control. As R&D is concentrated abroad, new product development builds home-base expansion abroad, and export restrictions stop Canadian subsidiaries from taking full advantage of world markets. Branch plant industry simply lacks dynamism.

For the nation state, these realities, of course, are not unique to Canada, many countries throughout the world have begun to see that multinational enterprises often do very little for national development and indeed can worsen development prospects through head office constraints, information dependence and built-in inequalities they can generate.

What also needs to be underlined for purposes of this international congress is that multinational corporations not only can create difficulties for the sovereignty and internal development patterns of a given country like Canada. Their growth and increased world role also makes international efforts at world development co-operation more difficult, let me outline why this is so.

Consider resource industries. What happens when a company like Canada's international nickel becomes the instrument by which nickel deposits throughout the world are opened up and exploited? The reality is that companies like Inco become the world centres of coordinating control, they make the decisions about where and when expansions and shut-downs will occur. And because of their coordinating world role, they exercise decisive bargaining advantages over national governments.

If Canada tries to increase its tax take and employment from nickel extraction, Inco simply threatens to expand elsewhere. Third world governments are even more vulnerable to these threats. The result is that a private company, by playing off country against country, can considerably increase its share of the overall benefits that should in fact belong to the people of the countries in which the resources are located.

The multinationals' power increasingly pushes one country into disputes with other countries, and workers and taxpayers into direct conflict with those in other countries. When the real issue should be the development of some mechanism in which nation states can exercise international control over the power of companies like Ford and Inco, it becomes instead a matter of workers in one country criticising workers in another for accepting lower wages. Or a matter of the citizens of two industrial countries coming into conflict because the government of one has bribed new investment from a corporation from the other.

The present dominant world role of multinational companies is therefore an impediment to international development and cooperation. Countries like mine, and workers such as those I represent, take on increasingly defensive positions, because the chief result of these changes as they perceive them is their own increased vulnerability and an expansion of the power of the multinational firm with whom they have to bargain.

Having stated these problems, I want to stress that as democratic socialists, we do not despair. We maintain a consistent optimism about the capacity of man through political action to plan and initiate policies which alter the direction of economic patterns for the common good. Certainly as social democrats in Canada, that is what we're doing.

We are fighting for political policies that will provide alternatives to the multinational enterprise within our economy — running all the way from the publicly-owned oil company, Petro-Canada, which we proposed and have supported in the energy field, to small-scale, high-technology Canadian industrial companies which we insist need much more government support than they are getting. We are also fighting for much tougher reviews and controls for foreign companies that are operating here. Most important of all, we've developed the goals and mechanisms that comprise a new industrial strategy that will give our

Canadian community much more economic dynamism and social direction in future investment decision-making.

We are committed to ending the overwhelming Canadian dependence on the foreign multinationals. Countries must shape their own destinies. They, not companies within them, must set their priorities, to this end, we are using every possible policy instrument at both provincial and federal levels.

This is also what this congress must aim to do at the international level. World peace, I believe, depends in good part on equitable international economic development. I am convinced that such development is simply not possible without breaking the increasing world economic dominance of the multinationals. One recent estimate is that multinational corporations, which controlled 25 percent of world marketable output in 1968, will control 33 percent by 1980, and if unchecked, more than 50 percent by the turn of the century. The allegedly sovereign state becomes weaker and weaker as the multinationals become stronger. This process must be reversed.

We must explore a number of possible responses at this congress. Can the nationally-owned companies in various countries be somehow linked together in international relationships that will challenge the obvious gains which world links have given the multinationals? Can the growth of the international trade union movement be such that industrial workers will be able to have direct and effective power in influencing the decisions of existing multinationals? Should we look at long-run international trade agreements in manufactured goods as an appropriate means by which to plan industrial adjustment in certain labour-intensive industries which would involve increasing the share of world production in third world countries?

I look to you all for creative answers to these sorts of questions in the next few days. Our debates will be both serious and exciting.

Once again, my warmest welcome. We have before us the continuing task of nation-building and of international development. We must demonstrate to the world that we have a human alternative not only to authoritarian communism but also to a world economy run by remote, undemocratic multinationals. For Canadians, such an alternative is essential.

For world development as a whole, this alternative is equally necessary. As modern socialists we accept with pride and determination our historic and continuing struggle for liberty and equality, not simply for ourselves but for all mankind.

# The 1983 Regina Manifesto

A Statement of Principles adopted at the twelfth Convention of the New Democratic Party of Canada. Regina, July 1983.

The New Democratic Party believes that the pursuit of peace and democratic socialism are the two imperatives of a more secure and just modern world.

We believe that as peace must prevail over war, so must co-operation and mutual responsibility prevail over private gain and competition as the guiding principles of social and economic life.

We seek a compassionate and caring society, servicing the needs of all.

The New Democratic Party is proud to be part of that great world-wide movement of democratic socialist parties which have always striven to replace oppression and privilege with democracy and equality.

## Our Ends

Socialists around the world share as their goal a society from which exploitation of one person by another, of one class by another, of one group or sex by another, will be eliminated. We believe in a society where each person will have the chance to develop his or her talents to the full. This ideal, a society based on equality, within a world of equally respected nations, is the major aim of democratic socialism.

Democracy and freedom are at the very heart of democratic socialism. We know that we must strive for those values which will uplift the human spirit. Our goal is a society in which the worth and dignity of every human being is recognized and respected, and in which differences of origin, of religion and of opinion will be not only tolerated but valued as desirable and necessary to the beauty and richness of the human mosaic.

But the human spirit cannot thrive when economic needs remain unsatisfied. And so we seek an end to material suffering, economic want and lack of opportunity.

We affirm our belief in the need for ecological priorities to guide technological and economic decisions so that valuable common resources are not depleted or polluted and global justice becomes possible.

We affirm our commitment to the preservation of the family farm, other family enterprises and small business.

We affirm our belief that aboriginal peoples have the right to shape their own future out of their own past and to possess the institutions necessary to survive and flourish.

The women's movement has challenged us to fulfil the socialist commitment to end sexual discrimination, unequal pay and opportunity and violence against women. The crisis of technological unemployment and changes in the family must be met by socialists so that women as a group are not victimised.

The right to participate in the trade union movement, including the right to organise, to engage in collective bargaining and the right of workers to withdraw their services if necessary are fundamental in a democratic society. Workers' rights in the workplace must be defended and indeed strengthened.

Our goals, then, are an egalitarian society guaranteeing human freedom and providing social and economic security in a world free of tyranny.

Socialists hold that together these goals form the moral basis for the political, economic and social order necessary for the future of humanity.

**Our Means**

We begin with democracy. The consent of the people, freely expressed, is at the heart of the socialist philosophy. We work to broaden and extend democracy into all aspects of human endeavour, and to create real opportunities for people to participate in making their decisions which affect their lives.

Socialists believe in planning. We reject the capitalist theory that the unregulated laws of supply and demand should control the destiny of society and its members. Society can control its own destiny by planning its future. And this planning must be an expression of the will of the people, not imposed on them from above.

Finally, socialists believe that social ownership is an essential means to achieve our goals. This means not simply the transfer of title of large enterprises to the state. We believe in decentralised ownership and control, including co-operatives and credit unions, greater public accountability, and progressive democratisation of the workplace.

## Our Historical Task

In the summer of 1933, delegates assembled in Regina for the first national convention of the Co-operative Commonwealth Federation, the predecessor to the NDP. The ravages of the great depression had brought them together to form one party, with a determination to realise the "Co-operative Commonwealth", and prepared to compromise their self-interest to forge a common agenda of reform: the Regina Manifesto.

Among these Canadians was an optimistic and defiant insistence that ordinary people — despite major differences of region, ethnic origin and social class — could act together, democratically and independently of powerful "vested interests" to realise the common good.

Much has been achieved since the passing of the Regina Manifesto.

We are entitled to say with pride that, because of the democratic socialist movement, Canada is a better place in which to live. The winning of the struggle to establish unemployment insurance and medicare has changed the lives of millions of Canadians for the better.

Much has changed since the Regina Manifesto. Stronger provincial and local governments capable of realising the important tasks of economic and social development have emerged. The public domain has been expanded on a scale unimaginable in the 1930s.

Much, however, remains to be done. Poverty, mass unemployment, and an unacceptable concentration of power and wealth persist as moral affronts to a society which values economic and social justice.

The environment has been damaged and the wastage will continue if not checked by strong measures. Many Canadians, having migrated in the millions from farm to city, now find themselves without a sense of community: living in large impersonal cities and working in alienating surroundings.

Finally, the technology of war has made ours the first generation which must confront the prospect of the annihilation of our species in a nuclear holocaust.

Now fifty years later we need to renew that convention's sense of urgency, of commitment to fundamental change, and of willingness to act beyond narrow self-interest.

## Commitment to Canada

In 1983 much still remains unsettled as to the nature of Canada.

The only basis for change in the Canadian federation can be respect for its regionalism, and for its duality.

We view the demand by Canadians to decentralise, where feasible, political authority as proof that Canadians want to participate more directly in the political decisions that affect their lives.

The desire to decentralise means more than provincial rights. Our cities must assume the imprint of their citizens. Credit unions and co-operatives can provide democratic alternatives to large financial and corporate institutions.

Canadians, however, also want a strong Canadian government, strong enough to guarantee our national independence and our ability to forge a strong Canadian economy in the face of world competition.

We want a federal government which will guarantee to each of us a share of our national prosperity regardless of the region in which we live.

Canadians face an enduring problem on the North American continent because of the extent of American corporate ownership of the Canadian economy. The Canadian government must serve as our collective instrument in pursuing the goal of a more independent Canadian economy in which the priorities are not set for us in a foreign head office.

The unique and enduring identity of the French Canadian people is a fundamental reality in Canada. Because few French Canadians attended the 1933 convention of our Party, the delegates were to underestimate the importance Quebecois attached, and would continue to attach, to the rights of their national assembly as the guardian of their culture, and as an instrument for the economic development of the only province in which French Canadians form a majority.

While we in the NDP assert the right of the Quebecois to determine freely their own future, we hope that in the exercise of their democratic rights they do not choose independence for we firmly believe that the aspirations of the Quebecois and all French Canadians are realisable within a new Canadian union.

Whatever our differences have been, it is long past due that we, in the NDP, join with those on the left in Quebec and French Canadians elsewhere, for the challenges which face us and the bonds which bind us are much greater than the differences, however profound, that have kept us apart.

In 1983, meeting again in convention in Regina, we rededicated ourselves in the struggle for a humane and democratic society.

The New Democratic Party will not rest content until we have achieved a democratic socialist Canada, and we are confident that only such a Canada can make its rightful contribution to the creation of a more just, democratic and peaceful world.

# A Tribute to David Lewis

A memorial address given for former NDP leader David Lewis
after his passing. June 26, 1981.

It is with profoundly mixed emotions that I stand before you tonight.
It is a pleasure for me to share with you some of my thoughts on that
extraordinary New Democrat, David Lewis, but it is with sadness that
the occasion should be to mark his passing from our midst.

My association with David spanned my entire adult life, from my
student days at the University of Toronto through to the last conversation we had by telephone shortly before his death. It was at the
University of Toronto in the late 1950s that I first encountered David's
unique combination of passion and intelligence. David was speaking at
a Hart House debate against William Buckley, Jr., editor of the right-
wing American publication, *The National Review*.

Those who were there looking for style in the sense of cuteness were
quite thoroughly impressed with Buckley. He managed to say nothing
of substance, but to do it in a disarming and titillating way that is so
appealing to a certain kind of undergraduate.

David in reply was not so cute, but much more profound in the depth
of his argument, both in terms of its application to contemporary North
American reality and his own understanding of history in comparison
with Buckley. And I remember leaving the debate with a number of
students, who thought that Buckley was ever so clever and, in their view,
had won.

But it was for me in the 1950s, which was a general apolitical period on
the campuses, a kind of turning point towards more activist orientation

in politics. Although I was already intellectually and morally committed to a socialist and political philosophy, David's argument and passion were so much deeper than Buckley's that I was in a sense scandalised at what I thought was the trivial reaction of many of my fellow undergraduates.

I saw in force a man of action, not just committed in some dilettantish way to chic ideas, but whose whole being was bound up in what he was doing. It was this demonstration of the fusion of intelligence and action that helped me change my political philosophy into political action.

When I finally arrived in Ottawa as a freshman MP in 1968, David was a constant source of encouragement and support. Indeed, he was the one who most strongly urged me to seek the leadership of the party in 1975.

The intervening years, when David was leader and I was caucus chairperson, were years of positive and progressive change in the party — change for which we must acknowledge an eternal debt to David.

It was from his eloquence and expertise in the area of economic policy, for instance, that we foraged a comprehensive industrial strategy that proved so successful in the 1979 campaign.

I think in particular of the two minority government years when David as leader negotiated toughly so that we obtained for the first time the indexation of very important redistributive income payments, such as pensions and family allowances.

But also of profound importance to the future of the country, we set the stage in that caucus for a socialist approach to energy. This we did in a crucial vote in pre-Christmas of 1973 by insisting that the government commit itself to establishing Petro-Canada.

Again, David's vision and commitment helped us move this country in a more progressive direction on an issue that turned out to be so vitally important in the latter part of the 70s.

Since I have been leader of this party, I have enjoyed the benefits of a much larger, more affluent party. I have travelled the country in two election campaigns, benefiting greatly from the party's much-expanded resources.

I often reflect on the campaigns of 1972 and 74. How gruelling it must have been — the interminable, all-night bus rides, the bumpy and noisy air flights. But David came through it all showing the same tough, indomitable spirit that characterised his every action.

One outstanding quality of David as a man is something in a sense that only a successor leader can really understand. That was his sensitivity to the demands of leadership. This became directly apparent to me after I became leader of the party and, from 1975 to the day of his death, David remained a tremendously important source of practical wisdom.

David Lewis led a life that was wholly committed to democratic socialism. When matters of the deepest kind affecting our party and our movement were involved, the mind and passion of this extraordinary New Democrat and human being, to the very end, were also involved.

# Nicaragua, the United States, and Social Change

Original draft of an article sent to the *Globe and Mail.* June, 1986.

The world of a politician is a world of light and shadow. Never merely pragmatic, it is always moral. For us in the international social democratic movement there has always been the difficulty of reconciling certain universal principles with their application in a variety of countries with widely divergent histories.

It is a problem, it is difficult — but it must be done. We apply the principles of equality, liberty and economic justice constantly within our own nations, of course; this is a difficulty we take for granted. But just as we must make critical judgments at home, so, too, must we when we look at other countries. Cultural and historical differences must certainly be taken into account, but they never absolve us of the obligation to judge, decide and act.

When we talk about democracy, pluralism, religious freedom, tolerance, human rights and self-determination, we are not giving voice to mere abstractions relevant only to a few nations; we are talking about human values and ideals that we believe desirable for all people, at all times, in all parts of our world. They are standards for judgement, imperfectly realised at home or abroad, now or in the future.

Having said this, let us consider Nicaragua.

We in the social democratic movement have watched, encouraged and supported the democratic overthrow of the Somoza regime and all it represented. Since 1978, we have assisted and defended Nicaragua's subsequent development towards democracy.

We have supported the Sandinista government's stated commitment to political pluralism, a mixed economy and non-alignment. Many social democratic party leaders and delegations have visited Nicaragua; we have kept informed on developments there and discussed the situation in depth as events have unfolded.

We admire the determined progress Nicaraguans have made in providing universal education, health care and other services. Immediately after the fall of Somoza, for example, there was a major campaign to establish universal literacy throughout Nicaragua; it was widely successful.

Great progress has been made in health care: infant mortality has been reduced to one-third of its level under Somoza, life expectancy has been raised from 48 years in 1978 to 57.6 years in 1984 and the incidence of disease, malnutrition and accidental death have been significantly lowered — polio, for instance, has not been reported in Nicaragua since 1981.

In spite of the severe demands of the war, the Sandinistas have also made important economic gains: a land reform and redistribution program has made steady progress. In 1979, 98 percent of the land was owned by 2 percent of landowners; since then 40 percent of the farmland has been distributed.

By 1984, 3,000 new, independent co-operatives were in business, providing income stability, credit on easy terms and better access to tools, materials and equipment for peasants who had been crudely exploited under the Somoza dictatorship.

It is worth noting that these worthy accomplishments are almost never mentioned in North American media coverage of Nicaragua; on the contrary, almost all reportage on Nicaragua is of the government's alleged violations of human rights.

In fact, there have been abuses of human rights. Sometimes inescapably the product of civil war, sometimes because of the presence in the governing body of Marxist Leninist elements who have no commitment to human rights as seen by social democrats. Willy Brandt's dictum "Socialism without human rights would be like Christianity without Christ" would have no meaning to some governing elements.

We are aware of discrimination against trade unions affiliated with the International Congress of Free Trade Unions; Amnesty International reports some departures from due process of law and the intimidation of the government's critics, along with other human rights breaches by both sides in the war.

In short, most social democrats see Nicaragua with open eyes and clear principles: we are under no illusions about circumstances in Nicaragua and their divergences from the principles of social democracy.

That said, however, we are also committed as a world-wide movement to the equally important, but quite different, principle of national self-determination. We assert that Nicaragua is as entitled as any other country on earth to this right. We hope they choose the social democratic path; but whether they do or not, it is their right to choose.

From a different perspective, the Reagan administration might want Nicaragua, Jamaica, Peru or Brazil to choose a conservative democratic capitalist path for development, ie., like that of Venezuela or Costa Rica following the second world war. But it is the right of these peoples not that of the U.S. government, to choose this destiny or some other. Similarly, in another corner of the world the Soviet Union has no right to impose its preferred regime on the people of Afghanistan.

We Canadians must make this very clear. Superpowers, domestically democratic or not, must keep their hands off other nations and their noses out of these countries' business. There cannot be two systems of international law, one for the weak and one for the strong. There is only one system and it must hold for all the nations of this world.

### The United States and Nicaragua

As a Canadian who regularly holidays in a small New England community and knows at first-hand Americans' deep commitment to democracy in their own country, I am constantly dismayed by their government's refusal to leave other countries in the hemisphere alone.

Reviewing this 20th century record of military harassment, economic sabotage and political upheaval, one can only shake one's head in sadness.

A partial but dismaying list of American actions against the Managua government and Nicaraguan people since the overthrow of Samoza includes:

- economic warfare: termination of all bilateral assistance to Nicaragua, reduction of U.S. imports of Nicaraguan goods, interference with and veto of loans from International bodies like the World Bank and Inter-American Development Bank and lobbying against investments by private American banks and companies;
- a full economic embargo against Nicaragua, announced at the Bonn Summit in 1985;
- "Big Pine" military manoeuvres in Honduras, assembling 1,400 U.S. and 4,000 Honduran troops on the Nicaraguan border in February 1983;
- CIA preparation of a terrorist handbook for the contras, "Psychological Operations & Guerilla Warfare", outlining means to frighten the populace into submission; engineering of an agreement with the former Argentinian military government to train contras and channel arms to them;
- extensive naval exercises off the Nicaraguan coast over six months in 1983, involving 19 U.S. ships and 4,000 American troops;
- small-scale air strikes against the Managua airport, civilian targets in the city and storage depots in Corinto in September 1983, carried out by aircraft belonging to a CIA front company;
- American-supervised mining of Nicaragua's harbours in January 1984;
- American contempt of an April 1984 UN Security Council resolution condemning outside military involvement in Nicaragua;
- refusal to be judged by the International Court of Justice's rulings on the harbour minings, culminating in June 1986, in refusal to abide by the Court's ruling against the United States.
- In August, the United States vetoed a UN Security Council resolution calling for "full compliance" with the International Court's decision.

How can this sustained American economic aggression and violation of international law against a struggling nation of 2.8 million people be explained?

Is it the security needs of the United States? Hardly! Nicaragua has a smaller population and is certainly poorer than the state of Massachusetts. No one could believe it could launch attacks or act effectively on behalf of the Soviet Union, even should it wish to. No, surely such sustained harassment must be seen as a refusal by the United States administration to accept as legitimate any newly emerging Central American state that does not comply with a model of development chosen by the United States.

The message is clear: either fall into a pattern acceptable to the Reagan administration or the U.S. will make life miserable or impossible.

The costs of this intractability are huge, not only for Nicaragua, but for the entire region. There has been a massive increase in the militarization of Central America, largely due to the shift in U.S. priorities from Development to "defence against communism". Thus while American public aid to Central America increased twenty-fold between 1978 and 1985, the share attributed to "security" grew from 26 percent in 1980 to 70 percent in 1985.

The United States has also clearly indicated its lack of faith in the Contadora Group's efforts to find a peaceful solution for Central America — notwithstanding the fact that virtually all of Latin America and Canada have supported Contadora. The Reagan administration refused to sign either the September 1983 agreement accepted by Nicaragua or any subsequent Contadora draft. It is now quite clear the U.S. is willing to facilitate or impose a military solution to the acute economic, social and political problems of Central America. Tragically, Members of the U.S. Senate and House of Representatives have now joined with Reagan in voting for military funding for the Contras in Nicaragua.

The effect of this undeclared war on Nicaragua has been devastating. As resources are increasingly diverted to war, the government's ability to improve the lot of its people is reduced. Already between October 1983 and October 1984, Nicaraguan workers lost 40 percent of their purchasing power and over 50 hospitals, 360 schools and 840 adult education centres were closed due to attacks or sabotage. Nicaragua is now spending half its annual budget on war.

By July 19, 1986, the seventh anniversary of the fall of Somoza, the war had claimed over 31,000 casualties among Sandinista and contra troops. The Sandinistas also claim 1,125 civilians have been killed.

In recent months the contras have stepped up their attacks on civilians, apparently singling out foreign aid workers as specific targets. This situation is unacceptable to Central Americans, South Americans and Canadians. Our government must stand united with Nicaragua today and other Latin American nations tomorrow in their insistence on shaping their own destinies.

It is clear that we must oppose the aggression of strong nations against their weaker neighbours even when those neighbours may be making decisions with which we disagree.

# Speech to the House of Commons, November 24, 1989

Ed Broadbent's last major address to the House of Commons as leader of the New Democratic Party, moving a motion for the elimination of child poverty.

**Edward Broadbent (Oshawa) moved:** *That this House express its concern for the more than one million Canadian children currently living in poverty and seek to achieve the goal of eliminating poverty among Canadian children by the year 2000.*

**Some Hon. Members:** Hear, hear.

**Mr. Broadbent:** Mr. Speaker, I want to thank my colleagues. One morning in the middle of June, lying in my bed, the alarm dock went off on my clock radio and I listened, as I usually do each morning, to the morning CBC news. On this particular day the news I heard was deeply distressing. The report on that particular morning was that we have in this country of ours 1,121,000 children living in poverty.

Normally I had been reasonably well aware, given my responsibility as the Leader of the New Democratic Party, of the general social policy oriented data, if I can put it in those very abstract terms, but I frankly say that on that particular morning I was totally surprised by how serious the problem of child poverty in Canada had become.

I went to my office that very morning, checked with members of our research staff and asked them to get me a copy of the report on child poverty which had just been produced and which formed the basis of the CBC news report.

It turned out that the figures used were true. There were well over a million poor kids in this Canada of ours in 1989, not 1939; in Canada, a developed industrial society, not a poor emerging nation in the Third World.

The situation is bad for our children. For the rest of us, no matter how we have been burdened by tax increases, no matter how hard done by we feel when we cannot buy an extra suit that we might have planned on, take our families out to another restaurant for a dinner on a given week, or have a more extended holiday, that is the reality for a majority of Canadians.

It is certainly our task as a party, our task as parliamentarians, to be trying to improve the well-being of the majority, but the well-being of the majority in recent years has been improving. While this has been going on in our country, the well-being of a significant number of our kids has been getting worse.

From 1980 to 1986, when the child population of Canada actually fell by some 4 percent, the number living in poverty in Canada at precisely the time the rest of us were doing better increased by 13.4 percent.

A few years after I was elected to the House of Commons a survey was taken in 1973. In 1973 it was found in this land of ours that 21 percent of our kids were poor. The most recent figure, according to the Canadian Council on Social Development, is that this percentage has increased from 21 percent to 25 percent, one child out of four from Newfoundland in the east to British Columbia in the west. Some provinces are obviously much worse than others, not necessarily because of the different political regimes but certainly because of the different capacities of the different regions to generate growth.

I repeat, while the overall sense of well-being for most Canadians has been getting better, that of our children has been getting worse. While the rest of us have been better clothed. There are more kids going without shoes. While the rest of us have improved housing, we have literally thousands of children who are homeless in Canada. While the majority now take their families out to a restaurant from time to time for a meal, we have thousands of kids, indeed 151,000 children, using food banks each month.

While we in Canada have witnessed in the statistics that Mercedes Benzes and Porsches and Cadillacs are selling in record numbers, one quarter of our children are wasting away. This is a national horror. This is a national shame. It is a horror and a shame that we should put an end to.

**Some Hon. Members:** Hear, hear!

**Mr. Broadbent:** Mr. Speaker, one of the major obligations of our democratic responsibilities — and I say this to all members on both sides of the House — is to improve the well-being of the majority. That is a fundamental requirement of a democratic society.

It is also a requirement to go back to an old-fashioned and for me fundamental notion of democracy which predates the view that you have a democracy simply if you have a competitive political system, legal institutions and the rule of law. The early 19th century and pre-19th century notion of democracy was that you had a society, not just governmental institutions as important as they are, so organized that all of its members had fully equal opportunities to develop their capacities and talents as human beings. It is to that notion of democracy that we in Canada should be committing ourselves.

When we apply this test we have to understand particularly here, now, in our generation, that we have the obligation of persuading a majority of Canadians to take on the task in the interests of a minority, in the interests of our poor, in the interests in particular of poor children.

In my maiden speech 21 years ago I noted in the euphoria of that time at the end of the 1960s that our task as a people was not simply to praise our past and celebrate our present. I said that our task was to create a future, a different future, to defend what we have, and that to refuse to go beyond was to refuse to lead. We have an obligation always in this chamber to lead.

For too long we have refused to go beyond into the future when it comes to our children. For too long we have ignored the appalling poverty in the midst of affluence. For years the United States and Canada had been regarded not only here in North America but around the world as the world's two most affluent nations and in many criteria well beyond average personal income, this remains true today. However, today also among industrial states, Canada has the second highest rate of children living in a condition of severe poverty. We are second only in this terrible indicator to the United States.

I want now to get beyond the abstractions of some of these statistics.

What is the face of poverty? It is dangerously underweight babies. It is infant deaths. The infant mortality rate of the poor is twice as high as that of the rich. Physicians in Quebec have stated that babies born in certain poor areas of the province run the risk of being as underweight as babies in developing countries.

Poverty means chronic illness, infection and viral diseases. The rate of poor children in poor health is 150 percent higher than the national average. This is appalling!

A recent study on poverty in Regina mentioned babies who were brought to the emergency ward with convulsions because mothers had diluted their milk to make it go further. We cannot allow this to happen!

An Ontario study found that being on welfare was one of the best and surest indicators of discovering a child with chronic health problems. Welfare payments are totally inadequate to deal with that problem.

Third, the face of poverty is malnutrition. It means going to school without breakfast and going to bed at night hungry. Again in the same recent study in Saskatchewan that I picked up and read when I was recently out there, it showed that a youngster from school during the summer vacation of two months lost 25 pounds. The weight was checked before school recessed and checked when the kids came back to school. Some 25 pounds in weight was lost by that child because the school lunches that that child was getting during the school year were not being provided at home during the summer in that it was a very poor family.

I repeat, this is happening in Canada 1989, not 1939.

Children dependent on welfare in British Columbia can meet daily nutritional requirements according to medical reports that have been done for only two and a half weeks per month. What are they going to do for the other one and a half weeks? Well, they suffer; that is what they do.

While the rest of us are well off, while the rest of us go to restaurants, while the rest of us have lots of pleasure, these kids are suffering. We should be suffering when we think about it so that we will move and put an end to it.

Being a poor kid means box lunches from food banks and soup from soup kitchens. Children make up 26 percent of the population, but they make up 40 percent of the users of food banks in Canada.

Around Thanksgiving I was speaking somewhere here in my home province. I picked up a copy of the *Toronto Star* and in that paper on Thanksgiving weekend, when most of us are with our families and enjoying our families and when most of us have lots to be thankful for, I saw a report that in Toronto, our richest city, there were 34,000 Canadians who could not feed themselves adequately. Over half that 34,000 were under five years of age. They have inadequate diets.

There are more food banks in Toronto than McDonald's hamburger outlets. Perhaps if we had neon signs in front of every food bank in the city of Toronto and in every city across Canada, when we drove around in this country of ours we would become as aware of poverty, and particularly poverty for young kids, as we are of McDonald's hamburgers.

Mr. Speaker, to be a poor kid means trying to read or write or think on an empty stomach.

A Harvard medical study has shown a direct link between poor nutrition and the ability to concentrate, so important in the learning process. A survey of 132 public schools in Calgary reported that in 46 schools, the number of children coming to school without breakfast was a serious problem.

It is not surprising that poor children are twice as likely to drop out of school as other children.

In Canada we know — and in every country where studies have been done they know it — that rich kids are not inherently better than poor kids, that they do not have a greater capacity to become musicians, poets, good hockey players or great skiers. The poor in our nation genetically have the same capacities overall, statistically, as the rich kids. But as every study shows if you are suffering from malnutrition and you are underhoused and you have all of the concomitant negative effects on your life that goes with that, you are not likely to do as well in the learning process, by a considerable proportion, as the rich or the average.

It is time we took our obligations seriously to ensure that every kid in this country has the right and the same right to develop his or her capacities and talents, that the child in Cape Breton Island ought to have the same opportunities to be what he or she can as the child in Rosedale in Toronto.

Mr. Speaker, to be poor means to be homeless and without hope. Three years ago, 30,000 children were looking for a place to sleep in shelters for the homeless. Others lived on the street or with poor families who skimped on food to pay the rent.

There is now in Canada and in the United States a vicious cycle involving the poor. Poor kids are undernourished, underhoused, more sickly, more poorly educated, get the second or third rate jobs, and when the lay-offs come, they get laid off first.

The same young people marry each other and then they produce children, statistically out of proportion, who go through the same cycle. We have a cycle of poor food, poor housing, poor clothing, poor education, poor jobs, poor spouses, more poor kids. This is a vicious cycle. It is a vicious cycle that can be broken and it is a vicious cycle that must be broken in this Canada of ours.

Our children, 25 percent of them, are imprisoned in poverty and we must get them out of that prison. There is a problem in this relatively well off democracy of ours in dealing with this. It is to get the problem recognized for what it is. It is to get people reasonably well off to care about the problem so that they will come to grips with it.

First and foremost, there has to be a change in attitude. Let me just cite some examples. I will not give names, but I will give positions here.

The Social Services Minister in the Province of Saskatchewan, when asked about poverty in that province, said — and I do not exaggerate — that poverty among children in Saskatchewan does not exist. Saskatchewan has the second highest level, in excess of 25 percent, of child poverty in Canada.

A premier in one of the western provinces said if poor kids go to school hungry, it is because their parents do not love them. That is outrageous. It shows a terrible insensitivity. Every member in this House has poor families in his or her constituency. Every member in this House knows them. Every member knows that poor parents care for their kids just as much as any other parents. It is terribly offensive to suggest that we have poor kids because their parents do not care for them.

In another province a cabinet minister said kids go to school hungry in her province because their parents spend their money on booze and cigarettes.

There is a psychological explanation for this. We have learned during the course of the 20th century about the psychological mechanism of denial. We all do it in varying degrees in our personal lives. People in political life do it too. That is to say, when there is a reality out there that you do not want to recognize, you do not recognize it. You pretend it does not exist, and at a certain profound level you believe it does not exist. This reaction, the psychological mechanism of denial, is going on at too many levels in our country.

If I may be personal again on this subject, when I discovered this in the middle of June and woke up to the reality myself from that newscast, I began to speak, and for five months, I spoke in every province of Canada on this subject. Every speech I have made since the middle of June, with the exception of two speeches which were exclusively devoted to the Constitution, I talked about child poverty. There is, to my knowledge, one and only one news report about that issue that has been made on a speech that I gave in five months of making speeches from coast to coast in Canada.

It would be interesting to understand why the news media in our country has ignored the question. Is there a kind of denial mechanism that is going on there as well? Is it because it is not conflict laden, not entangled in personality battles of some kind, or regional battles? Whatever the reason — I repeat, five months of speeches with the exception of two in every part of Canada — I have said almost word for word what I have said today, and the nation has little knowledge of it. There is a problem. The reality is there. The reality is abominable, and the reality is correctable. But many Canadians — I believe most Canadians — do not know about it.

A friend of mine many years ago, Michael Harrington, who is now dead, wrote a remarkable book on poverty in the United States, a book called *The Other America*. That was almost three decades ago.

As a result of that book and because it came to the attention of a president, a young man named John Kennedy, it did get attention. It was taken up in the centres of power, which is normally what happens in a society. I say to the minister, those who have power are in a position to do something. Something was done. There was going to be something done in that particular instance. President Kennedy was planning a 1964 campaign based on the issue of poverty in America. As the whole world knows, he was shot and it was not done.

It was written about the United States, and it happened to take off for reasons I know not exactly, but I know it became a political issue because a president took it up. I am convinced that this will become an issue in this country of ours when premiers from coast to coast and when the Prime Minister of Canada say, "We have to put an end to child poverty".

**Some Hon. Members:** Hear, hear!

**Mr. Broadbent:** I quoted some of the statements by ministers and governments who blame poverty of children on their parents. Many Canadians will believe that, and average Canadians will believe it as well. But I want to say that that is not the case. The study done recently for the city of Regina looking into hunger produced, as I understand it, a virtually unanimous report on the following points when it came to the causes of the poverty.

It was not due to waste. It was not due to laziness, mismanagement, bingo, booze or wilful neglect. It was due to the fact that the families were without money.

Poor kids are poor kids because they are poor kids. If we want to overcome poverty in this country, we have to do something about getting more money into the hands of poor people. That is where we have to start.

On Monday of this week the United Nations adopted the first-ever Convention on the Rights of Child. Canada co-sponsored that landmark agreement. Let us as a Parliament use that as a nation for a starting point. Article 14 of the Convention imposes on us to recognize, and I quote:

the right of every child to a standard of living adequate for the child's physical, mental, spiritual, moral and social development.

According to this Article we are now obligated to take:

appropriate measures to assist parents and others responsible for the child to implement this right and shall in case of need provide material assistance and support programs, particularly with regard to nutrition, health, clothing and housing.

We can, we must take up our obligations now.

The point that I want to make is that it can be done. In Sweden, Norway and West Germany there is a level of child poverty one-fifth as high as ours. Where over 25 percent of our children live in poverty, theirs are around 5 percent. Other societies that have cared, that have targeted the problem, have understood it is a problem, have done something about it.

In Canada, all parties — and I am not going to talk about the political genesis of it beyond that — in the late 1950s and early 1960s recognized that we had a serious problem with our elderly. We saw then that statistically speaking a much greater percentage of senior citizens were living in poverty than the percentage of children living in poverty today. The people of Canada did not sit back, and at one point people in all parties did not sit back. We all have parents. We know senior citizens. We know it is a human right that a man or woman, who spends his or her life working for the nation and with his contribution whatever it is in labour, ought to be able to retire with dignity, not just survive but retire with some dignity.

We began to move as a country. In the early 1960s we began the important struggle for elderly Canadians. In 1963, 41 percent of elderly Canadians were poor. The Canada Pension Plan came in. Old age security was significantly improved. Indexation of pensions and pension benefits took place. By 1966, the percentage of elderly couples living in poverty had dropped from 41 percent to 9.5 percent. We still have poor citizens. More has to be done, of course. But we made real progress for the elderly.

There is one person who is sitting here — I see him now — who sat here day in and day out, often in the front-benches of the New

Democratic Party rows, now before the Speaker, who in particular did a remarkable job for senior citizens, and that is Stanley Knowles.

**Some Hon. Members:** Hear, hear!

**Mr. Broadbent:** Mr. Speaker, I say to you if we want to succeed with our children we have to deal as specifically with their poverty as we did with senior citizens. We helped to bring dignity to the lives of the elderly. We must now do that for our children. We must show that for us human dignity is to be cherished as much in life's first pages as it is in the concluding chapters.

I say to the minister that the federal government must show leadership. The Prime Minister said this fall that our goal for social programs must be those that "bring us both peace of mind and pride in citizenship". I agree. All Canadians would agree. I simply say it is time to match the rhetoric with action.

**Some Hon. Members:** Hear, hear!

**Mr. Broadbent:** Basically, at the federal level the government must start by increasing the minimum federal wage which is now the lowest in the country and has not been increased in three years. It should be indexed to the cost of living, just as pensions were indexed several years ago. Second, the federal government must increase family allowances and the child tax credit and index them to the rate of inflation. This money goes directly to low and middle-income families to pay for food, housing and clothing. Third, the federal government must increase federal financing for low-cost housing.

Ten years ago, the government financed construction of 30,000 new low-cost housing units per year. Today, this number has dropped to 20,000.

We must also move to bring in child care legislation which has as its purpose and fundamental goal an increase in the number of spaces that will be available for children throughout Canada.

This in itself will help thousands of Canadian women who love their children, who want to care for them but who are now locked into welfare.

They cannot afford adequate child care and so are forced to stay home when they would prefer to be spending part of their time working in the economy out of the house and part of their time looking after children but they know that they cannot leave them if there are not adequate child care spaces available.

One recent survey showed that there were over 21,000 Canadian women who specifically said they would prefer to be off welfare, would prefer to be working out of the house if only this nation of ours had taken the proper steps some time ago to ensure adequate child care service is available. We must begin to make that child care spacing available for these women.

I would like to propose that the Prime Minister or the federal government before long convene a national conference on the elimination of child poverty, inviting first and foremost the provincial governments because much of the responsibility as we know in this federal constitution of ours to deal with this problem resides with the provinces. Also invited should be municipalities to send delegates, volunteer agencies, the trade union movement, chambers of commerce, service clubs and poor peoples' representatives themselves.

There should be a national effort to talk about and understand the gravity of the problem and to understand that things can be done. This conference should be called. In my view such a grand coalition that could be brought together should not be a one-shot deal, but it should obligate itself to meet on an annual basis to establish targets. I am aware we cannot do this overnight, as I am aware if we begin to spend money now and target spending to overcome the disgrace of national poverty for children certain other priorities would have to be set aside. No serious man or woman in political life can escape from that. I am aware that it cannot be done overnight and without some sacrifice in some other domain, but by God I am saying we should now organize our political community like we have never done before. This can be done by bringing in groups that have not been involved before, setting out a national target, and monitoring it on an annual basis until we eliminate child poverty in this country.

I want to conclude with these observations. Whatever their philosophical basis, whether Canadians are Conservatives, Liberals or New

Democrats, I know there is not the slightest bit of difference in terms of their commitment to the well-being of children. However else we may differ on other political matters, and the differences are real and serious on this issue. There is no difference on the commitment to overcome child poverty. I believe there would be no difference about that goal.

I think that if we speak to all of Canada and if all Parties took this on, we could get a response. I am convinced that a great attempt to mobilise the energy and effective imagination of Canadians would meet with a great response from the people of Canada. We have the resources. We have the ability. We have done it before on pensions. We have done it before on medicare. What we need now is to demonstrate the same will concerning the needs of our children.

For the sake of our children, let us find that same spirit of reform, of hope, of courage, of tenacious intelligence that has led this nation of ours to great accomplishments in the past. Let us affirm today in this Parliament that as a nation by the beginning of the 21st Century — only 11 years away — child poverty in this great Canada will be a relic of the past.

**Some Hon. Members:** Hear, hear!

# The Broadbent Principles for Canadian Social Democracy

Guiding principles for social democracy, adopted and published by the Broadbent Institute in 2021.

We believe in building a Canada that is just and equitable. In this, egalitarian social democratic values serve as our guide.

More specifically, we see social democracy as the sum of the values embedded in the United Nations system of human rights as found in the Covenant on Civil and Political Rights; Covenant on Cultural, Economic and Social Rights; and Declaration on the Rights of Indigenous Peoples. Canada is signatory to both of these Covenants and has adopted the Declaration, but the promise of all three remains unfulfilled.

All people have equal worth and equal rights — and all benefit from living in an increasingly equal society. To achieve this in a country with a market-based economy requires an ongoing process of decommodification, a process that sees important social and economic benefits taken out of the market and transformed into universal rights, such as in health services, education, social welfare and housing. This means an essential and robust role for governments at all levels in the provision of public goods.

To achieve economic stability, full employment and decent jobs, we support a mixed market economy, with private, public, co-operative and not-for-profit ownership. As evidenced by some of the most exciting economic advances of the last few decades, public sector investment is a key and critical foundation to entrepreneurialism and innovation.

A market-based economy must not be allowed to produce a market-determined society. When there are conflicts between the human rights of people and the property rights of corporations, those of citizens must prevail.

We believe the crises we face — whether unequal economic outcomes, racism and discrimination, climate change and environmental degradation, and declining democratic participation — require for their resolution an activist public sector and a strong civil society.

As such, Canadian social democracy should adhere to the following six principles for ongoing action:

1. **Furthering economic and social rights in addition to political rights.**
   Social democrats believe that people's rights are not confined to the traditional, though critically important, civil and political rights but also encompass being able to live a life of dignity, a life free from poverty and with access to essential services. It is for this reason that Canadian social democrats have always been at the forefront of expanding rights to include social and economic rights. We have led the struggle for comprehensive healthcare as a right, with the latest iteration of this multi-generation fight being the campaign for universal Pharmacare.

2. **Creating a green economy that leaves nobody behind.**
   Climate change is an existential crisis. As the world's economy decarbonizes over the next few decades social democrats must ensure that this process results in good new jobs, and that those in polluting industries receive a "just transition."

3. **Understanding the transformative potential of electing social democratic governments responsive to robust social movements.**
   Lasting societal change can only come about through harnessing the creativity and power of social movements and ensuring progressives are elected so that they can govern for the common good. Social democrats, therefore, work tirelessly for change in and outside of election periods.

4. **Strengthening workplace democracy including the right to a trade union and the fundamental role of the labour movement.**

The trade union movement is one of the few democratic forces with the heft to push back against the excesses of capital. As such, unions are good for our entire society not just for their members. As workplaces change it is more critical than ever that workers have access to basic necessities like paid sick days to make possible a life of dignity. Social democrats should also make room for other forms of economic democracy such as cooperatives.

5. **Dismantling structural systems of oppression.**

We need to actively dismantle historic and ongoing structural barriers — including but not limited to racism and sexism — that prevent people from having a life of dignity and realizing their full rights. The rise of right-wing populism, and its attendant bigotry, has made the moral case for stamping out white supremacy clearer than ever. The need to address the persistent wage gap and undervaluing of care work and other gendered work was emphasized by the pandemic.

6. **Fully implementing the rights and title of Indigenous peoples and supporting their goal of achieving self-governance.**

Canadian social democrats proudly stood in partnership with Indigenous leadership to insist on the inclusion of s. 35 in the Canadian Constitution Act, to recognize and affirm the inherent and comprehensive rights of First Nations, Inuit, and Métis people in this country, including Aboriginal rights, treaty rights, charter rights and human rights. With Canada and some provinces now moving to enshrine the UN Declaration on the Rights of Indigenous Peoples in law, this is the decade to resolve underfunding of essential services and to finally make good on repeated failed promises.

# Acknowledgements

$\mathbb{W}$ e would like to thank Jennifer Smith of ECW Press for her belief in this project from the very beginning and for her wise stewardship through each phase of the book's production. For their adept assistance, and for their belief in the value of this book, we are grateful to Anam Ahmed, Jessica Albert, Jen Albert, and Victoria Cozza, also of ECW. Hilary Little's digital skills and organizational acumen were invaluable as we assembled the photographs in this volume. Robin Sas transcribed many hours of interviews, accurately and quickly. We relied upon Library and Archives Canada and its helpful staff for access to the J. Edward Broadbent files, which contain a cornucopia of texts, photos, and other records. Thank you to Moira Duncan, Gilles Bertrand, Noah Reinoso, Marina Papadakis, David Pelc, Amanda Rodrigues, and Janelle Goertzen. We are particularly grateful to Michael MacDonald of the Private Archives and Published Heritage Branch. Svenn Haarman of the Friedrich-Ebert-Stiftung provided us with valuable access to the records of the Socialist International. Thanks also to Robin Sears for his early work in connection with the SI. We are all grateful to the Broadbent Institute and in particular to Executive Director Jen Hassum, whose enthusiastic support made this book possible; to Michael Valpy for his advice and counsel throughout the earliest stages of the project; to Bill Knight, George Nakitsas, and Andrew Jackson, for their thoughtful reviews of the manuscript; and to Judy Wasylycia-Leis for sharing her insights and memories on the importance of women's organizing within the NDP.

Frances is grateful to her colleagues in this project, and especially to Ed Broadbent for the opportunity to spend the better part of the last year learning and thinking about social democracy. Thank you too to her friends in the Rebuilding First Nations Governance project, whose work buoyed her spirit and provided some necessary time away.

Jonathan would like to thank his partner, Sheila Matthen, for her tremendous sacrifice during a whirlwind three years of becoming parents to Amalya and Riyan (during a global pandemic no less) without which his work on this book simply would not have been possible. He thanks his loving family; his mother Louise, and siblings Leora, Emily and Robin; as well as his best friends, Michael Tobin and Joseph Organ, and comrade Alejandra Bravo. He dedicates the book to his late-father George.

Luke would like to thank Tys Klumpenhouwer and University of Toronto Archives and Records Management Services for their timely help in retrieving valuable documents; Alex Ross for his assistance in accessing databases; Mitchell Thompson and Christo Aivalis for invaluable discussions on the CCF, NDP, and labour history; his colleagues at *Jacobin* magazine for their encouragement; and, most of all, his family, friends, and loving partner, Madeleine, for her unwavering support and advice throughout work on this book.

# Index

International Centre for Human Rights and Democratic Development (Rights and Democracy), 204; building credibility and legitimacy, 185–186; civil society, 217; and democracy, 183; Harper's approach, 192–193; independence from the government, 183–185, 188, 192; International Labour Organization, 203; mandate, 186; needed in Central America, 185; and non-social democratic governments, 189–191; relationship of markets and human rights, 200; rolling back of labour rights, 202–204

International Congress of Free Trade Unions, 275–276

International Democrat Union (IDU), 132

internationalism, 114, 115, 116, 182

international law, 276, 277

international trade agreements, 157, 264

Israel, 117, 192–193

Japan, 107, 119

Japanese Canadian internment in WWII, 74, 137, 140, 189

Jewett, Pauline, 72, 75, 92, 148, 183

Johnson, Beverly, 23

Judt, Tony, x, 206

Kanesatake Resistance (Oka Crisis), 186

Kennedy, John F., 287

Kenya, 191

Keynes, John Maynard, 182, 225

Keynesianism, xv, 106, 130n

Khrushchev, Nikita, 8–9, 11–12

King, Mackenzie, 43, 56–57

Kirby, Michael, 157

Knight, Bill, 88

Knowles, Stanley, 23, 94–95, 131, 140, 288–289

Kreisky, Bruno, 116, 130–131

Kriseová, Eda, xi–xii

labour movement. *See also* British Labour Party; Canadian Labour Congress

(CLC); industrial democracy; trade union movement: accusation of being communist, 99; addressed in Broadbent Principles, 294; attacked by Reagan and Thatcher, 202; in Britain, 136; co-option of labour by management, 32–34; International Labour Organization, 203; leaders' disagreement with Ed Broadbent, 179–180; means to become politically active, 26; relationship to patriation discussions, 150–151; relationship with NDP, 34–35; strides made by, 114; Wagner Act, 56

Lalonde, Mark, 59

Layton, Jack, 173, 209, 211–212, 214

Lenin, Vladimir, xii, 41, 125, 241

Lévesque, René, 88. *See also* Parti Québécois; Charter of Human Rights and Freedoms, 154; Charter of the French Language, 167; and Ed Broadbent, 168–170; finding middle ground, 225; as intellectual, xi; on invocation of War Measures Act, 44; Parti Québécois, 162; relationship to independence movement, 165–166; 1976 victory rally, 171

Levitt, Joseph, xvi, 12

Lewis, David: Broadbent's memorial address, 271–273; in CCF, 35–36; critical of United States policy, 128; debating Buckley Jr, 4, 36, 271–272; defeat in 1974, 47; desire to see Broadbent as successor, 87; federal election campaign 1972, 45; in NDP, 35–36; relationship to Pierre Trudeau's popularity, 65–66; relationship with Ed Broadbent, 36; resignation, 70; temperament, 57–58; view on embedded charter, 140

Lewis, Michael, 47

Lewis, Stephen, 88

liberal democratic society, central components, 244

liberal democratic society, modifications since 1930s, 48, 244–245